JENNIFER NOBLE

Chicago Blues Hall of Fame inductee (2014), Jennifer is a co-founder and the Director of Photography for *Chicago Blues Guide*. She has been photographing legendary blues artists for almost twenty-five years. Her photos have been published all over the world and recently featured in an exhibition about Women in the Blues in Chicago.

She has also been a DJ with her own radio show in the USA and has interviewed many blues artists over the years. She is now based in London and is a member of the UK Blues Federation, the Blues Foundation and the Windy City Blues Society.

When not out supporting live blues in London or at a festival somewhere in Europe or the US, she volunteers at the Eel Pie Museum in Twickenham, London, where her photos are on permanent display.

ZOË HOWE

Zoë Howe is a writer, musician and visual artist based in Essex. Her acclaimed music books include *Dayglo: The Poly Styrene Story*, *Lee Brilleaux – Rock 'n' Roll Gentleman*, the bestselling *Stevie Nicks – Visions, Dreams and Rumours*, *Barbed Wire Kisses – The Jesus and Mary Chain Story*, *Typical Girls? The Story of The Slits* and *Wilko Johnson – Looking Back at Me*. She was a contributing author to *The British Beat Explosion – Rock 'n' Roll Island* and was also *The Blues Magazine*'s "rock 'n' roll agony aunt". Zoë was a Royal Literary Fund Writing Fellow, taking up her position at Newnham College, University of Cambridge in Autumn 2020.

BACK COVER, LEFT TO RIGHT: *Liz Mandeville, Shirley King, Mz Peachez, The Countess Williams, Peaches Staten, Lynn Orman Weiss, Holle "Thee" Maxwell, Tracee Adams, Joan Gand and Destiny Pivonka.*

First published in the UK in 2019 by Supernova Books, an imprint of Aurora Metro Publications Ltd.

67 Grove Avenue, Twickenham, TW1 4HX

www.aurorametro.com   info@aurorametro.com

t: @aurorametro F: facebook.com/AuroraMetroBooks

50 Women in the Blues edited by Cheryl Robson copyright © 2019 Supernova Books/Aurora Metro Publications Ltd. Paperback edition first printed 2021.

Introduction copyright © 2019 Zoë Howe

'My Journey' copyright © 2019 Jennifer Noble

Interview with Barbara Carr © 2012 David Whiteis/*Living Blues Magazine*

Interview with Mary Lane © 2019 David Whiteis/*Living Blues Magazine*

Interview with Terrie Odabi © 2018 Heikki Suosalo/*Soul Express*

Interview with Chick Rodgers © 2015 Terry Mullins/*Blues Blast Magazine*

Interview with Susan Tedeschi © 2019 Iain Patience/*Blues Matters!*

Colour photographs copyright © 2019 Jennifer Noble, except:

p. 17 © 2019 Melanie Smith   p. 20 © 2019 Charlie Hussey

p. 24 © 2019 Lee Ann Flynn   p. 40 © 2019 Danny Day

p. 44 © 2019 Aigar Lapsa   p. 102 © 2019 Pierre Khan

p. 107 © 2019 Alain Hiot   pp. 168 & 237 © 2019 Laura Carbone

p. 185 © 2019 Walter Vanheuckelom   p. 188 © 2019 Joseph A. Rosen

Cover design: copyright © Supernova Books/2019 Aurora Metro Publications Ltd.

Editor: Cheryl Robson

Production Editor: Christian Müller

Aurora Metro Books would like to thank Taylor Gill, Maeve Burton, Georgia Kinahan, Marina Tuffier, Didem Uzum, Saskia Calliste, Ferroccio Viridiani

All rights are strictly reserved. For rights enquiries please contact the publisher: info@aurorametro.com

Printed by TJ International, UK

ISBNs:
978-1-913641-19-1 (print)
978-0-9932207-9-1 (ebook)

50 WOMEN
IN THE BLUES

SUPERNOVA BOOKS

CONTENTS

INTRODUCTION: THE BLUES IS A WOMAN

Zoë Howe

Ask someone to list their top five favourite blues artists, and it's likely that every name on that list will be male. However, you barely need to scratch the surface to reveal an abundance of not just female blues artists, but blues pioneers. Scratch a little more and you'll see there's a strong argument that rock 'n' roll itself was birthed by women.

This book aims to change the conversation, bring a little balance and spark further exploration. While it's not possible to include every single female blues artist, not least because so many names have faded into obscurity, the intention is to honour them and celebrate the incredible work they did, artistically and also spiritually: whether they realized it or not, their courage, strength, humour and in some cases radical individuality, often against unimaginable odds, continues to reverberate. These women might have been pushed down, shoved aside, forgotten or abused but they were – are – "stronger than dirt".[1]

I felt privileged and excited to be asked to write this, as well as feeling a great sense of responsibility. The more I delved into this thrilling and often emotional subject, the greater that responsibility felt: amid big names like Bessie, Janis and Sister Rosetta there are so many in danger of disappearing altogether – indeed many already have. At the same time, today's blues scene is thriving. Veteran artists such as Mavis Staples, Beverley "Guitar" Watkins (80 at the time of writing) and Bonnie Raitt are widely celebrated, while newer faces such as Susan Tedeschi, Shemekia Copeland and Samantha Fish take the music forward while still looking back to those who went before, and the deep, dark, real and often raunchy[2] roots of the blues.

There are many gentlemen of the genre whose music I love – Howlin' Wolf, Muddy Waters, Little Walter, John Lee Hooker, Lead Belly to name a few – but I knew instinctively that the blues really belonged to the women, although I initially had no idea to what extent this was true. I felt female artists would understand the blues on profound and myriad levels because of how the female journey personally, domestically, socially and politically has unfolded: living with persecution, restriction and prejudice under patriarchal, dualistic societies – something keenly understood by women of colour in particular.

As in many areas of the arts, female pioneers are often forgotten when the history books are written, so it is, perhaps, unsurprising that blueswomen are less spoken of, even though their contribution is so significant, and their understanding of what "the blues" really means may run deeper in many respects than that of some of the

---

1 *Stronger Than Dirt* was a 1969 Big Mama Thornton compilation featuring her immortal 'Hound Dog' (made famous by Elvis Presley) and 'Ball And Chain' (covered by Janis Joplin).

2 Look up "dirty blues" if you want to go down an extremely naughty rabbit hole – don't do it at work though.

male guitarists celebrated as trailblazers. As London's "black rose of the blues" Sister Cookie puts it, "If you look at the history of blues music, its early days are dominated by women – the notable male acts came along later."

Blues music evolved from a blend of African oral traditions, "call and response" work songs, vaudeville, Negro spirituals and the field hollers that could be heard amid the cotton fields and along the railroads during the dark days of the 1800s, before slavery was abolished. This music, visceral, simple and emotive, with repeated grooves (reminiscent of the fall and rise of tools and picks) and "blue" or "worried" minor notes, started with human feeling and human voice, not a guitar.

Blues Magazine editor Ed Mitchell: "We think of blues being three chords and a type of scale, but back then it was about subject matter. As far as [contemporary] music's concerned it's like, 'we'll go back this far but blues music started with the guitar...' No, it didn't. Before it was amplified in the 30s, the guitar had no significance, it was too quiet. Back then it was about how you put a song across and whether the audience believed you."

"Singing is the most natural form of self-expression," adds Sister Cookie. "The voice is one of the hardest instruments to master, [it's] working all the time. That's before we even get into the business of mastering vocal techniques [or] putting genuine feeling into a song. Most people can carry a tune, few can draw you in completely."

African American composer W.C. Handy famously heard the Delta blues in 1903 – although vocalist Ma Rainey recalled hearing the music in Missouri as early as 1902. In 1909, Handy was the first to publish a blues song as sheet music: it was called 'The Memphis Blues' (originally bearing the perhaps less inspiring but still memorable title 'Mr Crump Blues'). But it would be during the era of "classic blues", in the 1920s and 1930s, that the genre became dominated by female vocalists and songwriters, backed generally by male musicians including the likes of Louis Armstrong.

The first blues record was Mamie Smith's 'Crazy Blues', released in 1920. This surprise hit changed the landscape completely, selling a million copies in a year. Cue a record company scramble for quality female blues singers. They weren't too hard to find. Female artists had been performing this music for years in travelling shows, vaudeville troupes and minstrel shows, honing their personae, style and skill on the road and intuiting what worked. And what *really* worked was performing songs that reflected the audience's own experiences – marital problems, money problems, false friends and the understandable craving to kick back with a drink or reefer. Those themes are universal.

America during the early part of the twentieth century was a hard place to be for the working classes, particularly the women. It was harder still for black working-class women, and for those living in the Deep South, life could be a bitter daily struggle. The violence, poverty and pain, personal and collective, could be horrifying. The world was tough, but these artists were tougher. Despite everything, they also knew how to have a good time, which is inspiring in itself.

"My man done me wrong" and "My baby left me" aside, the cheeky defiance in many classic blues-era songs is dazzling, and the themes supremely empowering in that they encourage working-class women to be independent and free, sexually liberated and in control, eschewing conformism and embracing each moment as best you could, and to hell with anyone who disapproved. Life, after all, could be short. It was also cheap. The blues gave expression to a new emotional landscape in which anger, sadness and jealousy could be conveyed within a simple song. The music beckoned you to escape, party, reflect, and it also told you you had a friend. It might have been a friend you'd never met, but someone was reaching out to you across the club, the wax grooves, the radio waves, to assure you that you're in good company.

Sister Cookie: "You can say things through your music that you can't talk about in a conversation, and playing an instrument is an extra tool that allows me to tell a story. History books will tell you one thing about life as a black woman in early twentieth-century America, but you can listen to the music these women – and more – created and gain some extra perspective. That's what I have learnt from them and that's what inspires me to write the songs I do."

Blueswomen were tough, creative and often led defiantly unconventional lives, travelling from town to town, forming casual relationships with those they met in the bars and clubs along the way. They were operating outside the usual norms for women at that time, and rarely cared what others thought of them. Many also took advantage of the permissiveness of the blues scene to openly live a queer lifestyle at a time when this was still taboo for the rest of society. Lucille Bogan sang in 'B.D. [Bull Dyke] Women's Blues': 'Comin' a time, B.D. women ain't gonna need no men…' And with lines like, 'B.D. women, you know they work and make their dough…', we need look no further for an anthem of female empowerment that pre-dates Destiny's Child's 'Independent Women' by nearly seventy years.

"They say I do it, ain't nobody caught me…"

'Prove It on Me' – Ma Rainey

Songs like 'B.D. Women's Blues' and Ma Rainey's provocative 'Prove It on Me' (which talks casually of dragging up, talking to the gals "like any old man" and generally not being too keen on fellas), the lesbian relationships of artists such as Ethel Waters, Alberta Hunter, Big Mama Thornton, Bessie Smith, Billie Holiday and Sister Rosetta (and indeed the Sapphic antics common at aftershow parties) show that LGBTQ is nothing new. Bear in mind also that the queer women of the blues were expressing themselves in a time and environment where being gay or bisexual was considered "unnatural" and criminal, and being black meant you had to be on your guard at the best of times. Meet gender-bending singer, pianist and drag king Gladys Bentley, whose charisma and courage knew no bounds.

"Imagine what it was like being a black woman in the 1920s," begins *The Blues Magazine* editor Ed Mitchell. "Gladys walked around in a top hat and tails. She was openly gay and told everybody she could tell that she was married to a white woman. Even saying that in 1950s America would have got you into trouble! Some of these women were so strong they could do anything."

The hard-earned freedom and joy of cutting loose at the end of a day's work, hitting the juke joint and singing your guts out or dancing an intimate "slow drag" with a stranger could not be underestimated and, naturally, at this time, the women had the best tunes. "There's a whole sub-genre of raunchy female blues," explains Mitchell. "People think the blues is all about bad times, but there was a lot of stuff about sex and drugs and rock 'n' roll as it was in those days. Lucille Bogan was a bad girl – her song 'Shave 'Em Dry', she recorded two versions: a cleaned-up version and the out-and-out 'I can't believe she's saying that' version."

We'll leave you to look up the lyrics, but in the meantime, suffice to say that any man who assumes all women want "wining and dining" before being coaxed into bed just needs to hear 'Shave 'Em Dry' to know this is not true – Lucille at least represents the kind of woman who wants to get straight down to business, and she'll tell you so in quite extreme language too, making the "bump and grind" R & B stylings of the 1990s sound like the kind of thing you'd hear at Evensong.

'Shave 'Em Dry' is just one example of "dirty blues"; the slinky Dinah Washington's 'Big Long Sliding Thing' is another, although she at least pretended to suggest it *might* be about a trombone, rather than the trombonist. No double entendre with Lucille though. Another one to look up is Ruth Brown performing 'If I Can't Sell It, I'll Sit on It'. Suffice to say it's not about a settee.

Despite all this rampant naughtiness, the influence of the church was considerable, especially in the South. This would lead to, for some, a moral conflict, for others, an opportunity for quiet – and not so quiet – subversion, something women have always been rather good at. "There's an artist called Ida Goodson, her father was a deacon," says Ed Mitchell. "She and her sisters all played piano because their father wanted them to play in church, but whenever he went out, they'd play the blues, one of them standing at the window to look out for his car. If they saw him coming back they'd start playing gospel music again.

"There was a genuine fear of good versus bad. The Devil was not a fictional character. So you had 'good' people who went to church on a Sunday, and 'bad' people who listened to blues music. A lot of artists were genuinely frightened. You even found that in the 50s and 60s, Johnny Cash and Jerry Lee Lewis, they fought with themselves, you know, 'should I be singing these songs?' Every now and again they'd go back to gospel stuff to make their peace with God."

It's interesting to note, when you look into the personal stories of many seminal female blues artists in the twentieth century – Ida Cox and Victoria Spivey to name but two – that so many turned their backs on the blues and started playing in church, only returning to secular music in later life, usually when persuaded by someone else to step back into the limelight, allowing a hidden chapter of blues/black/female history to be briefly illuminated.

Perhaps life as a blueswoman had become unsustainable – certainly after the boom years of the 20s and 30s, once swing and rock 'n' roll had become more popular, and the craze for dancing in the post-war era led to big bands and even bigger venues, many legends of the genre found themselves scrabbling to find other work. Enter some unlikely heroes: a bunch of pasty youths in dreary post-war Britain.

Hungry to trace the American rock 'n' roll they loved back to its roots, British teenagers seized upon a compilation of Robert Johnson music – *King of The Delta Blues Singers*. They were also struck by Johnson's intriguing backstory, even if it had been invented by a smart record executive. Whether Johnson and the Devil made a deal at the crossroads or not was immaterial. This record helped spark a blues obsession amid the kids that were to become the Rolling Stones, the Who, the Bluesbreakers and many others, prompting a resurgence that changed British music beyond recognition and brought American blues artists back from the brink. They were confounded, thrilled and a little bemused, not least because, while America had turned its back on its own musical heritage, suddenly these stars of the blues were not only being required to play to enraptured crowds of British beatniks, they were having to dig out the old stuff again, which no one wanted to hear back home.

"African-Americans in the 50s wanted the music they listened to reflect their experiences *now*, not to remind them of a dirt-poor time working in the cotton fields," explains Ed Mitchell. "[Black] music is always moving forward – it goes from ragtime, jazz, blues, Delta blues, Chicago blues, soul, funk, R & B. It was only when white kids got interested in the 60s that blues artists put the anchors down, 'OK, you want to hear stuff we did in 1940?'

"Suddenly Muddy Waters, who pioneered electric blues, is playing folk festivals with an acoustic guitar playing stuff he played in the 30s. Sister Rosetta Tharpe couldn't believe people were queuing up to see her and asking for her autograph. They came over and were superstars again, and America rediscovered its own legacy through white British artists."

"Well, this is a story, a story that's never been told…"
'The Blues Had a Baby'– Muddy Waters

To quote the song, "the blues had a baby, and they named it rock 'n' roll". And that baby had many mothers: Big Mama Thornton's gritty howl inspired countless male imitators (Elvis Presley in particular), Sister Rosetta blew minds and saved souls with licks, chords and crackling distortion, the earthy growl and bluesy power of Etta James proved a bridge between the genres. Sister Rosetta is, in many people's eyes the original rock star, but before we discuss this coiffured queen of the axe, we must rewind a little first. When it comes to the use of "rock 'n' roll" as an adjective, blueswomen like Bessie Smith were living the life before Keith Richards was a twinkle in anyone's eye.

"With a mouth like a sailor, a penchant for whiskey and a taste for both men and women, Bessie Smith lived a life that would drop the jaws of even the baddest rock star," insists blues scholar C.C. Rider. She also could – and did – knock a man out cold if necessary. And Bessie was hardly the exception.

Hailed the "Empress of the Blues" for her singing prowess, Smith also taught herself to play the drums, as did Big Mama Thornton, while Beverley "Guitar" Watkins, guitarist with Piano Red and the Ink Spots amongst others, rocked hard with the best of them – *is* the best of them. The fact that a woman playing drums or guitar is still seen as unusual or "gimmicky" tells us that, while we might be some years on, we're slipping backwards, not only in how we are seen and treated (discrimination and harassment remains rife in the music industry) but how we see ourselves, and what we allow ourselves to expect or even imagine. "Female blues instrumentalists are so inspiring," says Sister Cookie, "because when you see and hear old recordings of incredible women like Victoria Spivey, Elizabeth Cotton, Odetta, Etta Baker, Algia Mae Hinton or Sister Rosetta Tharpe, you realize you're a part of something that goes way back and runs deep."

> *"Hoodoo lady, you can turn water to wine.*
> *I been wondering where have you been all this time..."*
> 'Hoodoo Lady' – Memphis Minnie

It is incredible that, to this day, so many people automatically assume any woman involved in making music must be a singer. That's not to say there's anything wrong with being a singer, rather there's something wrong with presuming a woman can't or won't pick up a guitar, a pair of drumsticks, a double bass, a trumpet.

We know that, from the late 40s onwards, Big Mama Thornton sang, drummed and, as Sister Cookie puts it, "played the shit out of the harmonica", and there's a raft of female blues pianists who could easily stride alongside the likes of Fats Waller. As for the guitar, it's high time we met the extraordinary Memphis Minnie.

Minnie headed North from Tennessee in the mid-30s with her husband Kansas Joe McCoy, as did many players, bringing the blues up-country to Chicago where a black person could at least breathe a little easier than they could in the South. Minnie and McCoy famously wrote the country blues classic 'When The Levee Breaks' about the Great Mississippi Flood of 1927, which they experienced. (The song was adapted by Led Zeppelin on *Led Zeppelin IV* in 1971.) Her talent was formidable, and so was she.

Dressed impeccably in elegant gowns and adorned with sparkling jewellery,[3] her hair perfect, she gave the impression she was every inch the lady – and she was. A fierce, tobacco-chewing, guitar-toting firebrand of a lady who'd pull a knife if you got fresh. That kind of lady.

---

3 "I once heard she used to wear jewellery made from silver dollars," says Sister Cookie. "That affords her instant heroine status in my eyes."

"Any men fool with her she'd go for them," recalled blues musician Johnny Shines in Garth Cartwright's book *More Miles Than Money*. "She didn't take no foolishness. Guitar, pocket knife, pistol, anything she get her hands on she'd use."

"They had guitar contests called 'cutting heads,'" says Ed Mitchell. "Somebody would play something fancy and then the other player had to make them look like an idiot. A woman with a guitar was weird enough in those days, but she went up against people like Big Bill Broonzy and Tampa Red and just destroyed them. It would have taken a lot to get noticed as a male artist, so a woman had to be exceptional. That's why we have that army of amazing female artists, because they had to go the extra mile."

Minnie, Kansas Joe and Big Bill Broonzy, Sister Rosetta, Koko Taylor and Muddy Waters – these were just a few of the many blues artists who'd moved up from the South over time, escaping the brutal Jim Crow laws to settle in Chicago, Illinois. This exodus was known as the "Great Migration" or the "Great Northern Drive".

The move from the rural Mississippi Delta to urban, industrial Chicago was a culture shock that injected new life into the music these artists brought with them. The blues had gone electric, the guitar turned up to the point of distortion and harmonica (or "harp") was added to an already heady mix. The sound of the Delta was evolving, and Chicago blues was crackling into life. Everything was changing. Arguably, the muscular, electrifying thrill of Chicago blues is the strand of the genre that would really make the world sit up and notice.

"Both of my grandfathers came from the Mississippi Delta and moved to Chicago, just like Chicago blues did," explains Chicago-born blues singer Deitra Farr. "Muddy Waters and Little Walter were the dominant voices that I heard. Motown was the soundtrack of my childhood, Chicago blues was always there as a companion sound for me. I feel this music is my heritage and in my DNA."

"Up above my head, I hear music in the air…"

Sister Rosetta Tharpe, hailed as a "singing and guitar-playing miracle" before she was ten, left Arkansas for Chicago in the mid-1920s after touring the South with a troupe with her mother, also a performer. Already well-versed with life on the road, Tharpe was still quite a different character to fellow guitarist Memphis Minnie. While each were talented, hard-working players, both presenting themselves with considerable style, Rosetta came from a deeply religious perspective and sought to bring spiritual "light" to the hedonistic murk of popular nightlife in the 30s and 40s. She did this at great volume with an electric guitar and a lot of heavy distortion. Praise be.

Sister Rosetta is the queen of electric blues, a pioneer of R & B, and is widely known as the "Godmother of rock 'n' roll". Why not go the whole hog and call her the "Mother" of rock 'n' roll"? As Ed Mitchell wryly notes, that was never going to happen.

"She was Johnny Cash's favourite singer, Elvis Presley idolized her, Jerry Lee Lewis thought she was the best. But she could never have been given the credit for kicking off rock 'n' roll. She was a wee gospel woman with a guitar, beautifully coiffured hair and a choir behind her. It just didn't fit. It had to be Ike Turner or one of these 'bad guys'. But listen to 'Strange Things Happening Every Day' – pure rock 'n' roll guitar-playing. It came out in 1944. Nobody had done that before. She's *the* rock 'n' roll pioneer, and she also helped kickstart the electric blues thing in the 60s with John Mayall's Bluesbreakers and Peter Green's Fleetwood Mac. Those guys would have considered her one of the gods."

And so this brings us back to that crucial time in the early 60s when everything turned around, specifically to the Blues and Gospel Tour of Europe, which was in its second year in 1964 when something quite out of the ordinary happened. One drizzly afternoon on the platform of a derelict railway station in South Manchester,[4] Muddy Waters and Sister Rosetta performed live. This was witnessed by a clutch of awestruck people on the opposite platform, and ten million people on their television sets. The performance was free – the experience of being there: priceless.

"Sister Rosetta turns up in a horse-drawn carriage with a white fur coat on," says Mitchell. "She was one of the first artists to use a Gibson SG guitar – it was white with gold fittings and she just looked like an angel. She starts singing 'Didn't It Rain?' and it starts raining! The kids are blown away. That was such an important appearance, because a lot of those kids who saw those tours went on to be the Stones, the Animals… basically any blues-influenced band, one of the members will have been at one of those gigs."

Knowing about this game-changing appearance, and seeing the footage thanks to YouTube, one feels empowered and relieved knowing that Sister Rosetta was there to change perceptions and smash assumptions about women and rock 'n' roll, if only for a little while – and I'm talking specifically about the assumptions that it's a rare woman who a) genuinely loves rock 'n' roll b) wants to play a rock 'n' roll instrument and c) is capable of reaching any level of accomplishment on that instrument if they do.

Considering that door Tharpe gracefully kicked open for music and for women, I also can't help but wonder, having seen this goddess with a guitar just rocking out and *owning*… I was going to say the stage, but I suppose I have to say "platform", why more women weren't inspired at the time to pick up a guitar themselves. Other than on the folk scene, women and guitars were rarely seen together, women and electric guitars even less so.

It would be another decade until groups like the Runaways plugged into an amp, and when they did, it was very much angled (literally) towards the male gaze. To simply be a good musician wasn't enough, it wasn't "feminine", it would have been emasculating for the men in the audience. It had to be geared, if it was to happen at all, towards titillation. Why so many women in the 60s and 70s just wanted to be *with* the band rather than *in* the band still confounds me. Screwing a rock star was seen as an

---

4   Specifically Whalley Range's Wilbrahim Road station, if you're planning a pilgrimage. It was mocked up
    for the performance as "Chorltonville" and made to look like an American railroad stop.

achievement in itself. I want to go back in time and say, "You know you can *be* a rock star, right?" Admittedly, there was a lot of conditioning to undo – there still is – but surely that heavenly vision of Sister Rosetta with her electric guitar bursting onto your television screen would have helped one see the light?

Making a name for herself as a teenager in the 50s with songs such as 'Roll with Me, Henry', Etta James was a blues singer who had incomparable range and feel. Bobby Murray, the guitarist who played with her for twenty-five years, credits her as a major inspiration: "I've always considered singers to be great musicians, and Etta's phrasing spoke to me more than any other musician." She was signed to Chess Records in the 1960s, where they marketed her as a pop ballad singer to white audiences. She had dozens of hits, including the classics 'All I Could Do Was Cry' and 'I'd Rather Go Blind'. In 1961, she released her signature song, 'At Last'. Despite all the success, she struggled with heroin addiction for many years before making a comeback in the 1980s after she sang 'When the Saints Go Marching In' at the opening ceremony of the 1984 Summer Olympics in Los Angeles. Bonnie Raitt wrote of her on Facebook: "Etta James stands as one of the greatest singers of all time – any genre, any era. Her perseverance, ferocity and vulnerability have been as inspirational to me as her monumental talent."

Emerging just a few years after Etta in the early 60s, Janis Joplin was another singer whose heart, soul and voice was drenched with all the pain and power of the blues, washed down with Southern Comfort. Joplin looked all the way back to the roots of classic blues for inspiration, not least because she identified with those characters, the flamboyant Bessie Smith in particular. Joplin was a woman whose fiery generosity and deep vulnerability were often exploited; she played the sexual predator just like many of the blueswomen before her, but beneath the tough veneer, she was intensely sensitive.

Joplin took solace in the blues and, as a terminal outsider with a heart all too easily broken, she related to the tribulations those women were singing about. Bad men, bad scenes, heavy living, comfort and distraction found in sense obliteration and sex with partners both male and female. Also in common with her early blues heroines was, of course, her voice and delivery – here we found not technical perfection or slickness but raw unbridled emotion and expression that swung from raging passion to quavering fragility.

Her deep respect for Bessie Smith was such that she helped pay[5] for her headstone after discovering her idol lay buried in an unmarked grave. Joplin herself would tragically die, famously at the age of twenty-seven, from a heroin overdose just months later. A very blues life, a very blues death.

During the 70s, an array of elderly blueswomen, such as the gloriously eccentric Alberta Hunter, returned to the stage and studio after years of obscurity, and the world caught a thrilling glimpse of another age before those artists passed over to the great juke joint in the sky. But there were many artists who straddled the eras, one being the redoubtable Koko Taylor, who recorded with the likes of Little Walter and Buddy Guy.

---

5   The headstone was paid for by Joplin and Juanita Green, who had done housework for Smith as a child.

Taylor came to fame in the 50s and 60s but, as Ed Mitchell puts it, "it was as if somebody had gone into a time machine and grabbed one of the 20s singers and taken her to Chicago in the 50s. She had the most incredible voice. She's another one like Sister Rosetta who was bridging that gap while it all went a bit testosterone-fuelled. She was there." She has been mentioned as major source of inspiration for many female blues artists, and this book has been dedicated to her.

One of Koko Taylor's near contemporaries who has achieved an equally legendary status, Mavis Staples, is still going strong, celebrating her eightieth birthday in 2019 with several star-studded concerts around the US. She is referred to as a major inspiration by Ruthie Foster, Peaches Staten and Teeny Tucker in these pages, and the current female blues scene would not be what it is without her as a role model, not to mention her influence on artists beyond the genre, such as the Rolling Stones and Prince. Her lifelong commitment to social activism since the days of the Civil Rights movement is another source of admiration.

Another female blues legend currently inspiring new generations of artists, while still performing regularly on tour, is Bonnie Raitt. The singer Kat Riggins enthuses: "Bonnie Raitt's voice is distinctive and legendary, but more than that, her activism is inspiring," while the blues guitarist Debbie Davies writes: "I was personally most inspired by Bonnie Raitt. I was watching and listening to a woman playing electric blues guitar, and performing the kind of music that was closest to my heart. Not to mention fronting her own band. Bonnie was doing everything I dreamed of doing, and at the highest level of quality and professionalism."

It takes a special kind of person to carry a beacon for the blues into the future, and while the scene today is healthy – as you will note from the sheer number of contemporary blues stars featured in this book – authenticity is as important as ever. "You can always spot a fake in blues," warns Mitchell, who explains that to be a true blues artist means, as ever, a great deal more than just being a virtuoso player.

Award-winning blues singer Deitra Farr: "What makes a blues artist authentic is being honest. Sing about what you know about. If you never picked any cotton, then you shouldn't sing about picking cotton. Tell your own story."

"Years ago I appeared on the same bill as some blues acts at an event in London," says Sister Cookie. "The other acts were white men twice my age with infinitely more experience, but I did my thing regardless. The audience must have dug my set because I was asked for more encores than the time schedule permitted. As I left the stage, a woman caught me by the arm and said to me, 'I'm sorry, but the blues is black and it's a woman.' Ever since then, I've tried to feel optimistic about the way women are seen within the genre."

Some things may have changed over the past century, but the fundamental stuff tends to stay the same, and the "blues life", as we know, involves "demons" – and we're not just talking about the so-called devil Robert Johnson negotiated with in a bid to play guitar the way he did. (That juju was all his own anyway.) We're talking anything from the trauma of toxic relationships, violence, an abusive childhood, underage sex work particularly in many of the cases of the early blues artists, substance abuse to dull pain and numb memories, illness, incarceration and, for many, an early death.

But, as Dr Feelgood singer and blues scholar Lee Brilleaux used to say, it's not about how many years you've got under your belt, it's about the miles on the clock, and these ladies went the distance. Years of oppression couldn't stop them. Violence couldn't cow them. Religion didn't suppress them and social conditioning couldn't inhibit them. One hundred years after the first blueswomen rocked a barrelhouse, we're still catching them up in so many ways.

What is the blues? What is a woman? A woman is primal and eternal, earth and water, blood and guts, heart and soul, a voice to be heard and a body to shake, dance, love and birth the new. A woman is deep power and magic as dark as the womb, pain and joy, rage and love. A woman is the blues and the blues is a woman.[6]

> *"You never get nothing by being an angel child.*
> *You better change your ways and get real wild."*
> 'Wild Women Don't Have the Blues' – Ida Cox

– With thanks to Deitra Farr, Ed Mitchell and Sister Cookie.

Photograph: Melanie Smith

---

6 'The Blues Is A Woman' is a T-Bone Walker song. It is also the name of a 1979 concert featuring Sippie Wallace and a cross-dressing Big Mama Thornton, who appeared in a man's three-piece suit and played the songs she wanted to play, rather than the programme.

Sisters in Blues Royalty, House of Blues, Chicago

Dedication to Koko Taylor

"Koko Taylor qualifies as the vintage of the blues, one who paved the path and opened doors for women blues singers like myself and many others. Ms Taylor lives on as the 'Queen of the Blues', who resided in the blues music land of Chicago, where she touched people around the world with her powerhouse vocals and commanding stage presence. She absolutely adored her fans and continued to entertain them full force even during her sickness. She will definitely go down in history as the best of all 'Wang Dang Doodle' of Blues music. I will forever appreciate our private discussions and her imparted knowledge and advice."

– Teeny Tucker

"As far as I'm concerned, Koko Taylor is the Queen of the Blues. But I am truly grateful that they feel I can carry this tradition on in my own way. And I feel blessed for that."

– Shemekia Copeland

"When I first tackled a Koko Taylor number, after listening to her so much, I found a different way to use my voice, which really set me free. There's nothing like the way she put herself directly into the music, no holding back – she just embodies the blues. She's the one who has inspired me most in terms of pushing my voice to places I wouldn't necessarily have dared to go before."

– Kyla Brox

"Koko Taylor was a true inspiration for me, she was very dear to me… I spent a lot of time with Koko and received the love of a mother from her in many ways. She will always be my queen."

– Nellie "Tiger" Travis

"She is the queen of the blues. She's the inspiration for all of us women blues singers out here. She lived hard, she endured and she conquered the blues world, and inspires me to keep on moving."

– Thornetta Davis

"Koko Taylor was the most honest, direct person I've ever known. There was nothing artificial, nothing slick, about her. Her music was just like her personality – proudly unvarnished, and straight from her soul to yours. Koko didn't know how to do anything less than 100%. She grew up in the country; she went to work after third grade, and she worked her whole life – in the fields, taking care of other people's children, as a laundress, as a housemaid/nanny and as a singer. She came up the hard way, and the blues helped her get through her hard life. So she knew what the blues could do for her, and knew what it could do for her listeners. She said, 'If I made someone's day better with my singing, then I've done my job.'"

– Bruce Iglauer, founder of Alligator Records

"Jennifer, I'm so grateful for all the beautiful tributes to my Mom. She is smiling I'm sure. It's an honor to have someone like you to still pay homage to my mother and recognize all the Blues/soulful singing women still carrying on. Thank you again & always."

– Cookie Taylor

Photograph: Charlie Hussey

MY JOURNEY

Jennifer Noble

I have spent a lifetime being passionate about the blues. I was lucky to grow up in Chicago where I was able to experience the greatest blues music in the world. As a teenager, I lived in the same town as the late, great Muddy Waters which was Westmont, Illinois. I used to go often to see him perform along with Willie Dixon, Junior Wells and so many other Chicago blues legends around then. I never thought to take one photo of those legends at that time. It's Muddy Waters I have to thank for showing up to our local music festival called Pow Wow Days back in the mid-1970s with an amplifier and his electric guitar (no band), which led to me falling in love with the blues right then and there. I have never looked back.

Fast forward to the mid-1990s. I couldn't believe that I did not have one photo of the many blues acts I had witnessed since the mid-70s, including my favourite, Muddy Waters. I decided to take up photography and so began my mission to capture as many legendary blues artists with my camera as I could, whether they lived in Chicago or were just passing through. For many years when I was out there taking photos in the Chicago clubs and at festivals, there were few other women blues photographers. The only one I can recall is Susan Greenberg, who by the time I started had stopped taking photos. I used to look at her photos on the wall at B.L.U.E.S. on Halsted Street and I wanted my photos to be on that wall. I found I loved taking photos of artists performing and tried to get out to the clubs two to three times a week.

We still have several important blues clubs in Chicago, providing stages where both new and established artists can perform. They welcome tourists, with music fans coming from all over the world just to listen to live blues music. Some of the clubs I frequented over the past three decades include the Harlem Avenue Lounge and Fitzgerald's Night Club both in Berwyn, Illinois, as well as Kingston Mines and B.L.U.E.S., which are across the street from each other on Halsted Street, making it easy for me to visit both in one evening. Other notable clubs are Buddy Guy's Legends, Rosa's and the House of Blues. Soon after I started taking photos, there was a restaurant very near where I lived in Downers Grove called Founder's Hill Brewing Company, and for about four years they brought in all the great blues acts from the city to perform there. It was an incredible opportunity for me to be able to photograph so many legendary artists there, only minutes from my house.

There were also countless outdoor music festivals in the vicinity of Chicago, and most of them featured a blues act or two. I could literally go out seven nights a week and always find exciting blues to photograph. I never took it for granted. I felt really lucky to live in the Chicago area and be able to capture incredible live performances with my camera. It was great to feel a part of the music scene that enlivens the city.

As a result of my passion, I've created a comprehensive collection of photographs over many years. It's taken me all over the world including to some fantastic blues festivals in Europe. My photographs have been published internationally in magazines, books, journals, in publicity and online and they have been featured on the covers of many CDs and some DVDs; I'm particularly proud of my collaboration with Chicago's Delmark Records. They bought my first photo for a CD cover. I am also a co-founder and Director of Photography of *Chicago Blues Guide*. Since its debut in 2008, my photos have been featured in the guide on a regular basis.

Eight years ago I moved to London, and now I attend music clubs in and around the capital to photograph the blues. I've also covered the blues at many festivals like the Ealing Blues Festival in London and on the continent the Blues Heaven Festival in Denmark, the Lucerne Blues Festival in Switzerland, the Beautiful Swamp Blues Festival in France and the Moulin Blues Festival in Denmark. I have also been fortunate enough to be on all the European Blues Cruises since they started in 2014. You can't beat sailing around the Mediterranean listening to great blues acts that hail mostly from the USA.

WOMEN IN THE BLUES

I have always supported women in blues because I felt there needed to be more women blues artists out there performing and being booked at festivals. Women could always use more representation in books and documentaries about the blues, and by capturing their live performances with my camera, I thought it might help them to promote themselves and keep on sharing their artistry. I would rarely pass up an opportunity to see a woman artist perform. Thankfully, there were many brilliantly talented female blues artists in the Chicago clubs giving tremendous performances. They were always exciting to photograph too.

From memory, Koko Taylor was the first woman blues artist that I ever saw perform and I went to see her frequently, along with Lonnie Brooks. They both seemed to be at a festival somewhere in Chicago almost every weekend in the summertime. That's why I am dedicating this book to her. She passed in 2009, but I am always looking for another woman artist who can sing her songs well. I really miss her.

During my time spent in the Chicago blues scene, some of the artists I was able to regularly see perform and photograph were, in no specific order: Nellie Travis, Zora Young, Deitra Farr, Chick Rodgers, Mavis Staples, Peaches Staten, Katherine Davis, Joanna Connor, Demetria Taylor, Holle Thee Maxwell, Delores Scott, Shemekia Copeland, Sharon Lewis, Mary Lane, Grana Louise, Lynne Jordan, Nora Jean Wallace, Sharon Lewis, Claudette Miller, Liz Mandeville, Shirley King and Ivy Ford, and, before they passed, Koko Taylor, Bonnie Lee, Patricia Scott and Big Time Sarah. I know there are more, but those are ones who come to mind while writing this.

HOW DID THIS BOOK COME ABOUT?

I came into contact with publisher Cheryl Robson of Aurora Metro Books/Supernova Books due to her involvement in promoting and preserving the musical heritage of Eel Pie Island in Twickenham, where her office is based. She noticed the photos of blues musicians which I posted on my Facebook account and invited me to her office. On seeing my portfolio, she suggested we might include my photos in a book and we discussed the kind of books that might work. I thought she was going to say, "Let's do a book on Chicago Blues", but when I mentioned to Cheryl an exhibition on women in the blues, organized by Lynn Orman Weiss, which had featured some of my photographs a few years previously in Chicago, she said, "What about a book about today's women in the blues?" We did a search online and found that there didn't seem to be any books out there on the subject. Although, there has been much written about the early blues artists like Mamie Smith, Bessie Smith, Ma Rainey, Victoria Spivey, Alberta Hunter and Memphis Minnie, there seemed to be very little about the amazing women who perform the blues all over the world today, with the exception of highly popular artists like Bonnie Raitt. So we decided to do a book about contemporary women in the blues, inviting them to contribute their own words too, while of course paying homage to the women blues pioneers who had inspired them.

HOW DID WE MAKE THE SELECTION?

Having spent most of my time photographing blues artists in Chicago, my book was undoubtedly going to feature more women artists from Chicago than anywhere else. However, I knew that in order for the book to be interesting, I would have to work very hard to get as much of a range of women in blues as I could, in terms of age, ethnicity and background. As I have been living in the UK since 2010, I had the opportunity to photograph women performing both in the UK and on the continent of Europe, to add to the many artists I had already photographed in the USA. I not only wanted to feature women who inspired me with their singing but also to include the many talented women musicians who played piano, guitar, saxophone, harmonica and drums along with the flute and frottoir.

Of course, I began my selection with the artists whom I had photographed many times in my home city. With such an extensive collection to choose from, it wasn't easy to narrow it down to only fifty women and I'm grateful to my editors for their help in selecting the interviews and photographs to feature in this book, but space, time and budget are all constraints within a book. If you'd like to see more of the blues artists in my portfolio, please check out the website at: www.womenintheblues.com.

ACKNOWLEDGEMENTS

A big thank you to my editors and to Zoë Howe for writing the introduction to the book and to all the contributors for their wonderful contributions, whether in the form of writing, interviews or images. Next I want to thank my colleague Linda Cain of *Chicago Blues Guide*. Our partnership has helped me gain access to the Chicago Blues Festival each year as well as to many European Blues Festivals. I'm also grateful to my husband Glenn Noble for being by my side and acting as my camera assistant, taking notes and doing write-ups. I would also like to thank my two children Kate and Brandon for putting up with a mother who was pretty much obsessed with the blues during their entire upbringing.

Linda Cain (Photograph: Lee Ann Flynn)

A shout out to Chuck Winans, who was an early mentor, and to Matthew Socey, who inspired me early on with his photographs. I want to thank the late Susan Greenberg, who was the only blues woman photographer I can remember when I started taking photos. I used to admire her prints on the wall at B.L.U.E.S. on Halsted.

A big thanks goes to the Fox Valley Blues Society which has evolved into the Aurora Blues Fest for being the first to publish my photos in their newsletter. Thank you *Big City Rhythm and Blues Magazine* for getting me started in magazines by printing my photo of Alberta Adams whom I photographed at the 2002 King Biscuit Blues Festival. I now contribute to magazines all over the world including *Blues Matters* in the UK. A big thank you to Delmark Records for buying my photo of Jimmy Burns. It was my first time having a photo published with a major record label. All of these firsts encouraged me to keep on taking photos.

I want to thank all the promoters who provided me with a photo pass, especially Lucerne Blues Festival in Swtizerland, Blues Heaven Festival in Denmark, the Moulin Blues Festival in Ospel, Netherlands, The Beautiful Swamp Blues Festival in Calais, France and of course my favourite in my hometown, the Chicago Blues Fest. Nor can I forget Lisa Panoyan and the Marseille Blues Society in France for starting the European Blues Cruise five years ago. I am grateful too to a few clubs in London such as the Blues Kitchens (all three), the Eel Pie Club in Twickenham, The Crawdaddy Club in Richmond, the 100 Club on Oxford St, the Bull's Head in Barnes, The Half Moon in Putney, Ain't Nothin But in Soho, and The Jazz Club in Camden for booking great blues on a regular basis.

Thank you to all the artists who have posed for photographs over three decades. As blues guitarist Dave Specter once told me, "I like the way you take photos because I don't know you are there most of the time."

I am also grateful for all the blues friends I have made over the years, especially Deb and Hazel for attending so many shows with me in London when I moved there and was not familiar with the blues music scene. I treasure all of you and look forward to catching more live blues with you in the future.

50 WOMEN
IN THE BLUES

BLUES LEGENDS
PAST AND PRESENT

All colour photographs in this volume are by Jennifer Noble,
unless credited otherwise.

MAMIE SMITH

Mamie Smith (1883–1946) was a vaudeville performer, born in Cincinnati, Ohio, who went on to become the first African-American to make blues vocal recordings. At the age of ten, she began touring with the white ensemble the Four Dancing Mitchells, and as a teenager she performed with Salem Tutt Whitney's Smart Set. Known for her spectacular performances, Smith's vaudeville training meant she entered the blues circuit with an engaging and well-rehearsed act. Her biggest hit was 'Crazy Blues', written by Perry Bradford and released in July 1920: it achieved phenomenal sales (said to exceed one million copies), bringing about the birth of the "race music" genre and opening the door of the recording industry to African-American musicians. Between 1921 and 1922, Okeh Records released 23 records by Mamie Smith. Smith's recording success led to what is now known as the classic female blues era, and she was dubbed "The Queen of the Blues". She frequently wore fabulous gowns and jewels on stage, setting the standards high for the next generation of performers. She eventually retired from performing in 1931 and appeared in a few films in the early 40s such as 'Jailhouse Blues' as well as singing with orchestras such as the Lucky Millinder Orchestra. She passed away in 1946, reportedly penniless, due to an ongoing illness.

MA RAINEY

Ma Rainey (1886-1939) was one of the first African-American professional blues singers. Born Gertrude Pridgett, she began performing as a teenager in black minstrel shows, where she met her husband, Will Rainey, and would go on to to perform in various acting troupes, including Fat Chappelle's Rabbit Foot Minstrels. Following her divorce, she continued to tour with her own band, Madame Gertrude Rainey and Her Georgia Smart Sets. In 1923 she was discovered by Paramount Records producer, J. Mayo Williams, who recorded her most famous track 'Bo-weevil Blues', along with 'Bad Luck Blues' and 'Moonshine Blues'. Over the next five years she recorded more that one hundred songs for Paramount, who marketed Rainey as the "Mother of the Blues", the "Songbird of the South", the "Gold-Neck Woman of the Blues" and the "Paramount Wildcat". She took part in a promotional tour in 1924, which led to the formation of her touring band The Wild Cats Jazz Band. With this band she would go on to tour the venues of the Theatre Owners Booking Association, the vaudeville circuit for African-American artists. Following the death of her mother and sister, she retired from music in 1935 and devoted her time to managing two entertainment venues up until her death on 22nd December 1939 of a heart attack. Ma Rainey was inducted to the Blues Foundation's Hall of Fame in 1990, as well as the Rock and Roll Hall of Fame. In 2004, her recording of 'See, See Rider' was inducted into the Grammy Hall of Fame.

BESSIE SMITH

Bessie Smith (1894–1937) was born in Chattanooga, Tennessee, on 15th April 1894. She had a passion for music from a young age and grew up performing on the streets with her brother before joining a travelling minstrel show, the Moss Stokes Company, where she was discovered by legendary blues vocalist Ma Rainey. She eventually signed with Columbia Records in 1923.

Her powerful, soulful voice quickly elevated her to become one of the highest-paid black singers of all time, with Columbia Records nicknaming her "Queen of the Blues", but the press quickly upgraded this to "the Empress of the Blues". 'Down-Hearted Blues', her most successful record, sold over two million copies. She famously collaborated with Louis Armstrong on the tracks 'Cold in Hand Blues' and 'St Louis Blues'. Her songs focused on themes of oppression, poverty, love and betrayal.

She has been described as a bold and extremely confident performer, often refusing a microphone. She died in a car accident en route to a show in Memphis, on 26th September 1937 at the age of 43. Bessie was awarded a Grammy Lifetime Achievement Award in 1989. She left behind an influential legacy of one hundred and sixty recordings.

MEMPHIS MINNIE

Memphis Minnie (1897–1973), born Lizzie Douglas, was a blues vocalist, songwriter and guitarist. Hailing from a family of sharecroppers in Mississippi, she learnt to play the guitar and the banjo as a teenager, and moved to Memphis, Tennessee, to busk on street corners. She married the blues singer and guitarist Joe McCoy, and in 1929 the pair were discovered by a scout for Columbia Records. In 1930, she recorded 'Bumble Bee' under the name Memphis Minnie, which would go on to be a smash hit and become her top-selling record.

Following her divorce from McCoy in 1935, Minnie started to play the electric guitar and experimented with her sound, adding a country twist to the blues. She toured extensively in the South, and recorded 'Me and My Chauffeur Blues' in 1941 for Okeh Records, her biggest solo hit. Despite her Southern roots, she reached the pinnacle of her career working the Chicago club scene. She retired from her musical career in the mid-1950s and returned home to Memphis with her second husband, the musician Ernest Lawlars, known as Little Son Joe. Her work of over two hundred recordings was influential in the development of blues guitar playing, and her song 'When the Levee Breaks' was adapted by Led Zeppelin in 1971. Bonnie Raitt paid for her headstone to be erected in 1996. She died of a stroke in 1973, aged 76.

SIPPIE WALLACE

Sippie Wallace (1898–1986), born Beulah Belle Thomas, was a singer-songwriter. Wallace began performing from the age of just seven, playing the piano and singing for the church. By night, she would sneak out with her siblings to watch performances at tent shows. In her teenage years, she began performing numerous acts such as acting, singing, and assisting the snake charmer at these tent shows.

She moved to New Orleans in 1915, where she met and married Matt Wallace. Later, she moved to Chicago with her brothers Hersel and George Thomas, and recorded her first songs with Okeh Records in 1923 in collaboration with them. Her first recordings were successful enough to make her a national blues star, with 'Shorty George' selling over 100,000 records. She toured throughout the United States and was known for shouting the blues without the use of a microphone.

After her husband Matt and her brother George both died in 1936, she joined the Leland Baptist Church in Detroit as an organist and vocalist. In 1966, however, she was coaxed out of retirement by Victoria Spivey and released the albums *Women Be Wise* and *Sings the Blues*, which inspired Bonnie Raitt. In 1983, Raitt helped Wallace to land a contract with Atlantic Records, for whom she recorded her Grammy-nominated album, *Sippie*. Three years later, following a severe stroke after a performance at the Burghausen Jazz Festival in Germany, Sippie Wallace died on her 88th birthday in a Detroit hospital.

VICTORIA SPIVEY

Victoria Spivey (1906–1976) was an American blues singer and songwriter born in Houston, Texas. Known throughout her career as "Queen Victoria", she came from a musical family: her father was a part-time musician, and both her sisters were professional singers. As a teen, she worked as a pianist in Lincoln Theatre in Dallas, and also appeared in local bars and nightclubs. In 1926, she signed with Okeh Records and moved to St Louis, Missouri. She recorded the songs 'Black Snake Blues' and 'Dirty Woman Blues', which became best-selling records. In 1929, she made her screen debut when she was cast as Missy Rose by King Vidor in the film *Hallelujah!* Through the 30s and 40s, Spivey found fame through films and stage shows, and frequently toured with Louis Armstrong's various bands.

A prolific songwriter, she launched Spivey Records in 1961, which produced musicians such as Sippie Wallace, Otis Spann and Buddy Tate, as well as various emerging artists. Her first release on her own label, 'Three Kings and the Queen' featured Bob Dylan playing harmonica and providing backing vocals. Unlike many from her generation, she continued to record well into the 1960s and 1970s up until her death. In 1970 she was awarded a BMI Commendation of Excellence for her outstanding contributions to the world of music. She passed away in 1976 due to an internal haemorrhage.

SISTER ROSETTA THARPE

Sister Rosetta Tharpe (1915–1973) was an American singer, most famous for popularizing gospel music in the 1930s and 40s. Her musical style combined powerful gospel vocals with a guitar and is considered one of the precursors for rock 'n' roll. She began singing in church where her mother was a preacher and performed in an evangelical troupe for many years, regularly performing religious concerts at the Church of God in Christ church on Chicago's 40th Street. She signed with Decca Records in 1938, moved to New York and recorded the song 'Rock Me'.

Tharpe's music combined gospel and folk, influenced by her religious upbringing and her skilled electric guitar playing. Her recording of 'Strange Things Happening Every Day' in 1945 was credited as the first gospel song to cross over to the "race records" charts, reaching Number 2. She was the first musician to use heavy distortion on her electric guitar and had a profound influence on the development of British blues, as well as inspiring the work of stars like Elvis Presley, Eric Clapton, Johnny Cash and Chuck Berry.

She toured Europe with Muddy Waters and Otis Spann, selling out arenas all the way into the 1950s. By the 1960s, she had moved to England, playing electric guitar to young blues fans in London and Liverpool. She died from a stroke in 1973, and in 2017 was inducted into the Rock and Roll Hall of Fame.

BIG MAMA THORNTON

Willie Mae Thornton (1926–1984) earned her name "Big Mama" for her big stage presence and even bigger voice. Born in Alabama, she spent her early years singing in church with her six siblings. She worked in a tavern until "Diamond Teeth" Mary McClain took her under her wing and put her on stage with Sammy Green's Hot Harlem Revue, where she performed for seven years and garnered a reputation for being a talented singer, songwriter, drummer and harmonica player.

She signed her first record deal with Peacock Records in 1952. It was here that she recorded the song 'Hound Dog', which shot to the top of the R & B charts, but was overshadowed in the public eye by Elvis Presley's 1956 version. She joined the Arhoolie label in the 1960s, and recorded many songs with them, including the title track of her album, *Ball and Chain*, which became Janis Joplin's breakthrough when she re-recorded it.

Being a bold and powerful woman who played with gender stereotypes caused the public to speculate about her sexuality. This, coupled with trying to thrive in at a time of racial segregation, is thought to be the reason she did not reach the heights that she should have done. Sadly, despite being the inspiration behind two of the generation's most iconic artists, Thornton died of a heart attack caused by years of alcohol abuse at age 57, alone and penniless. In 1984 she was inducted into the Blues Hall of Fame.

House of Blues, Chicago

ETTA JAMES

Etta James (1938–2012), born Jamesetta Hawkins in Los Angeles, was one of the most influential singers of this century. From the age of five, she learned how to sing. Her vocal coach subjected her to physical abuse to strengthen and deepen her vocals.

She formed a girl group and, at the age of 14, singer Johnny Otis helped them to sign to Modern Records under the name The Peaches. She recorded her first track, 'Roll with Me Henry' which topped the R & B charts, and stayed with Modern Records until 1958. In the 1960s, Etta James truly began to make her mark as a solo artist. Signed to Chess Records, thirty of her songs entered the R & B charts, including the iconic 'All I Could Do Was Cry' and 'I'd Rather Go Blind'. In 1961, she released her signature song, 'At Last'.

Despite her success, she battled an addiction to heroin and had several run-ins with the law. This did not stop her from releasing music, however, and she remained active throughout the following decades, recording with rapper Def Jef. She was inducted into the Rock and Roll Hall of Fame in 1993, the Blues Hall of Fame in 2001, and won six Grammys during her career. In 2008, Beyoncé portrayed James in the film Cadillac Records.

Her final years were plagued by illness, and in 2011 she was diagnosed with leukemia, passing away the next year.

Chicago Blues Festival

MAVIS STAPLES

Staples was born in Chicago in 1939. She began singing with her family, known as the Staple Singers, at churches and on local radio. Her father "Pops" was a friend of Martin Luther King, Jr., who wrote protest songs like 'Freedom Highway'. The family often performed in support of the civil rights movement in the 1960s. Staples was inducted into the Rock and Roll Hall of Fame in 1999 and in 2005, she and the Staple Singers were honoured with a Grammy Lifetime Achievement Award.

She has recorded over a dozen albums, often crossing genres, notably *Have a Little Faith*, which won Album of the Year at the Blues Music Awards in 2005. She received a 2006 National Heritage Fellowship, and 2011 saw Staples win her first Grammy Award for Best Americana Album for *You Are Not Alone*. She headlined the year after at Chicago's Annual Blues Festival in Grant Park. A documentary film titled *Mavis!* about Staples and the Staple Singers, directed by Jessica Edwards, was premiered at the SXSW Film Festival in 2015 and later broadcast on HBO. She was inducted into the Blues Hall of Fame in 2017 when she won the Blues Music Award for Soul Blues Female Artist.

To commemorate her 80th birthday in 2019, she performed a benefit concert at New York's Apollo Theater, where she had first performed in 1956 with the Staple Singers. She also returned that year to Glastonbury Festival and recorded an album at London's Union Chapel titled *Live in London*.

JANIS JOPLIN

Janis Joplin (1943–1970) was born in the oil town of Port Arthur, Texas and inspired by early blues artists such as Bessie Smith, she left school to try and become a singer. Moving to San Francisco in 1963 with friend Chet Helms, she sang in clubs and cafés, but her lack of success led to escalating drug use and after two years, she returned to Port Arthur, enrolled in college and tried to lead a more conventional life.

Big Brother and the Holding Company invited her to join in 1966. Her raucous rendition of Big Mama Thornton's 'Ball and Chain' recorded at Monterey Pop Festival in 1967, together with the hit album *Cheap Thrills* (1968), notable for the track 'Piece of My Heart', gained her the moniker "first lady of rock 'n' roll". But Joplin's rising fame caused friction and she soon left and formed the Kozmic Blues Band, playing a legendary set at Woodstock in 1969. A solo album *I Got Dem Ol' Kozmic Blues Again Mama!* including the now classic 'Try (Just a Little Bit Harder)' soon followed.

On 4th October 1970, she died of a heroin overdose. After her death, 'Me and Bobby McGee', was released as a single from her newly minted album *Pearl*, rising to number one in the charts. In recognition of her trail-blazing contribution, she was inducted into the Rock and Roll Hall of Fame in 1995, and honoured with a Recording Academy Lifetime Achievement Award at the Grammy Awards in 2005. In 2015, Amy Berg's documentary, *Janis: Little Girl Blue*, premiered at the Toronto Film Festival.

Grant Park Pavilion, Chicago

BONNIE RAITT

Singer, songwriter, activist and guitarist Bonnie Raitt was born into a musical family, and was given her first guitar at the age of eight, Raitt, kick-starting her musical journey. During her second year at college, Raitt moved to Philadelphia with a group of musicians and blues promoter Dick Waterman. From then on, she gained traction quickly within the blues circuit, opening for legends such as Sippie Wallace and Mississippi Fred McDowell. Soon she received a record deal from Warner Bros., who in 1971 released her self-titled debut album. At the time, there were few famous women guitarists in popular music, and her skills were widely praised by critics.

Despite early success and critical acclaim, her albums were not consistently commercially successful, and she was subsequently dropped by Warner Bros. in 1983. Even during her professional pitfalls and a struggle with alcohol and drug abuse, she was tenacious and carried on participating in political activism and touring her music.

Finally, in 1989, she was signed to Capitol. Her tenth and "first sober album", *Nick of Time*, was released that year and received great commercial success. It has since been listed one of *Rolling Stone*'s 500 Greatest Albums of All Time. Since then she has released seven more albums and won ten Grammys. She is still releasing music and touring to this day.

WOMEN IN THE BLUES
TODAY

BARBARA BLUE

Barbara Blue hails originally from Pittsburgh, Pennsylvania, but she first began performing in 1997 at Silky O'Sullivan's on Beale Street in Memphis. Continuing to perform there five nights a week for over twenty years, she has gained the moniker "Queen of Beale Street".

She has also competed in the International Blues Challenge and performed all over the world including on several of the Legendary Rhythm & Blues Cruises where she met the Phantom Blues Band. Since then she has collaborated on three albums with the band.

Nominated in 2007 as Contemporary Female Blues Artist of the Year, she has had the following recordings nominated for the Grammys in multiple categories: *Sell My Jewelry* (2002), *Memphis 3rd and Beale* (2004), *Love Money Can't Buy* (2006) and *Royal Blue* (2010).

Other releases include: *Jus' Blue* (2012), *Memphis Blue* (2014) and *Fish in Dirty H_2O* (2018).

HOW DID YOU START IN MUSIC?

I love this question. I was born with colic – nine months to be exact. My wonderful mother (Rose) and I make a huge joke: I came out singing… going down singing…

WHEN DID YOU START SINGING OR PLAYING AN INSTRUMENT?

I can't remember a time when I didn't sing: church, school, with my dad in the car to the radio or at his work bench (he was a carpenter), to records my dad would play – Ray Charles, Eddie Arnold, Petula Clark, Peggy Lee, Roger Miller, Frank Sinatra, Tony Bennett, Dean Martin, the Beatles… I played flute and piccolo in grade school to high school in the marching band, guitar – just chords – and some piano. I alway wanted to play drums, but the nuns said no! Flute or clarinet – so I picked flute after lots of tears and foot-stomping.

WHO WERE/ARE YOUR INFLUENCES?

All of the above, along with Billie Holliday, Sarah Vaughan, Nancy Wilson, Janis, Etta James, Koko Taylor, Big Mama Thornton, Nina Simone, Katie Webster, Willie Nelson, Johnny Cash, J.J. Cale, Tony Joe White, CCR, the 50s, 60s and 70s…

WHY CHOOSE THE BLUES?

Life… the blues chose me.

HOW WOULD YOU DESCRIBE YOUR APPROACH?

My approach is *real*, guttural, emotional…

DO YOU WRITE OR COMPOSE YOUR OWN MATERIAL?

Yes I would say it's about 60/40 now. My latest CD (*Fish in Dirty H₂O*, 2018) was eighty per cent my work. The most ever… it was an amazing project with a spectacular team of collaborators.

HOW DO YOU START MAKING MUSIC? WHAT IS YOUR PROCESS?

I write song hooks all day long… then when I have time I sit down and make some sense of it all. Recall the feeling, then the feel… then finish the lyrics and music.

WHICH DO YOU PREFER – PLAYING LIVE OR BEING IN A STUDIO? WHY?

I *love* both. The artistic element is my favourite… to collaborate with other awesome performers/musicians. It's a oneness that gives you amazing satisfaction.

HOW DO YOU FIND THE RIGHT MUSIC PRODUCER FOR A RECORD?

I've been very blessed. My very first CD was cut in my first hometown of Pittsburgh, Pennsylvania, at the Control Room. I was the producer. My engineer Robert Casper said I should hold seminars for artists and bands going into the studio, as I was so unbelievably organized! I just laughed. We cut that CD in three days – because that's all the money I had time for! It's a *great* CD – *Out of the Blue*. I have three CDs with Tony Braunagel (of the Phantom Blues Band) as producer. The *very best* part of that was that I got to go to Studio City, California, and record in Johnny Lee Shell's Ultra Tone Studio with the Phantom Blues Band. I am always co-producer or producer. Then there are three live CDs at Silky O'Sullivan's, 183 Beale Street. I was the producer and Dawn Hopkins was co-producer and engineer. Then three CDs with Lawrence "Boo" Mitchell as producer. His grandfather the legendary Willie "Pops" Mitchell had agreed to be my producer, then he fell and broke his ankle. He was a bad diabetic. He never recovered. So after about a year Boo said to me, "let's make that record…." and we made three. Then I approached the legendary Mr Jim Gaines (we were friendly, so I rang him up and we had a two-and-half-hour chat)… it was the *best* decision I have made to date. My award-nominated CD *Fish in Dirty H₂O* was produced in his studio… it was an awesome experience!! I pray we have more time to make a few more!!

ARE AUDIENCES DIFFERENT AROUND THE WORLD?

Yes… I love to travel. Europe is *always awesome*! They seem to *really* appreciate the artform… and don't take it at all for granted.

DO YOU HAVE A FAVOURITE VENUE? WHY?

No not really… most are more than gracious these days. For many years I was just learning, so I worked tons of good and bad venues… now mostly all good! Amen!

DESCRIBE YOUR JOURNEY AS AN ARTIST/MUSICIAN/SINGER.

I've been making music all of my life, over forty years. My journey has been one of joy, heartache, sorrow, wonder and fulfilment… Giving to others makes my day!

WHAT WERE THE HIGHLIGHTS?

So many… hundreds… I gotta write my own book. But I will share a few. On the Legendary Blues Cruise out of Kansas City I sang 'Wang Dang Doodle' with Koko Taylor's band… long story, but Koko had her daughter Cookie come and get me and bring me to her. She said, "Gurl… I thought… I was listening to da jukebox!" We were friendly from that day forward.

In Aspen, Colorado, I was hanging with Taj Mahal at the Blues & Brews Festival, and Ray Charles was there that year. We went to a quiet bar where some folks were jamming. I sang a song with the piano player, and then my friend Jana said to me, "Some guy just went to get his horn – he wants to do a song with you." That guy was Al Jackson, Ray Charles's band leader. We did 'Loverman', Ms Billie Holliday's song. I'll never forget us swapping licks… surreal. Finally, I was doing a festival in Canonsburg, Pennsylvania; Jeff Healey was the headliner. The organizer owned a bar down the street from the festival grounds, and my band was playing there after our slot on the main stage. It was packed beyond capacity. Jeff showed up and sang with me and played guitar… two or three songs… then he kissed me and a photographer caught the moment – I have a photo. That was the day I *really* fell in love with Jeff Healey.

WHAT WERE/ARE THE CHALLENGES?

Being a woman… I'm sure if I would have given in on the casting couch or had tons of money I'd have gained more recognition in my younger days… but I was raised with integrity and for that I am very grateful and I am *me*! No regrets! My biggest challenge is being away from my family and friends… I've been on Beale Street now for over twenty-two years, five nights a week if I'm not travelling. I talk to my mum three to five times a day… we kinda pretend I'm right next door.

IS THERE ONE SONG THAT IS CLOSEST TO YOUR HEART?

'Walk Away'.

IS THERE ONE ARTIST WHO HAS TRULY INSPIRED YOU?

Not one artist… maybe you could say the 60s.

HOW DO YOU PROMOTE YOUR IMAGE/YOUR BRAND?

I am the reigning Queen of Beale Street… Official emissary of Memphis music.

HOW DO YOU DEAL WITH OBSTACLES SUCH AS AGEISM, SEXISM AND RACISM?

One day at a time… It's mostly a man's world here in the blues, slowly but surely changing *but* … tits and ass sells. I'm not a ravishing 26-34-26, but I'm the real deal and can sing my ass off.

IS IT IMPORTANT TO UNDERSTAND THE BUSINESS SIDE OF THE INDUSTRY?

Yes, very very important.

ARE AWARDS HELPFUL?

Not sure. I haven't won one yet!

WHERE DO YOU SEE YOUR MUSIC GOING NEXT?

All good places! The blues is my first love, but I can do *all* types of music, so we shall see… I have many new songs written – definitely leaning towards the blues!

Photograph: Aigar Lapsa, Notodden Blues Festival, Norway

KYLA BROX

Kyla grew up in Manchester, England. She is the daughter of blues singer Victor Brox and actor/singer Annette Brox.

Kyla first sang with her father in Manchester in 1992, at the age of twelve. She joined his regular touring group known as the Victor Brox Blues Train in 1993. Other young members of the group included bassist Danny Blomeley and drummer Phil Considine.

Kyla went on tour with her father's band in 2000, playing in remote areas and mining towns in Australia. Kyla and Danny Blomeley formed a duo the next year, which became known as the Kyla Brox Band with Kyla Brox (vocals, flute), Marshall Gill (guitar), Tony Marshall (saxophone), Danny Blomeley (bass) and Phil Considine (drums). They played the northern club circuit and were invited to festivals such as the Colne Blues Festival in 2002. The band toured Australia in 2003 and 2004 and in 2007 they also ventured to the USA. In 2008, Kyla married Danny Blomeley and is now the mother of two children, Sadie and Sonny.

In 2016, the UK Blues Federation made Kyla an official Ambassador of UK Blues and in 2018 she was the winner of the 2018 UK Blues Challenge. In 2019, Kyla had the honour of representing the UK in Memphis at the 2019 International Blues Challenge, as well as the European event in the Azores. Her recordings include: *Window* (2003), *Beware* (2003), *Coming Home* (2004), *Live at Matt and Phred's* (2006), *Gone* (2007), *Grey Sky Blue* (2009), *LIVE... At Last* (2009), *Throw Away Your Blues* (2016) and *Pain & Glory* (2019).

HOW DID YOU START IN MUSIC?

I began singing in my dad's blues band when I was twelve years old. I started off just doing backing vocals and gradually moved to sharing the lead vocals with my dad. He's a singer and multi-instrumentalist, and he taught me so much! When I was 21 I formed my own band with Danny Blomeley, who is now my husband, and we have had a few different line-ups over the years, but the two of us are still going strong.

WHEN DID YOU START SINGING OR PLAYING AN INSTRUMENT?

I decided I wanted to be a singer when I was extremely young, having been immersed in the music that not only my parents, but also my siblings, created and listened to. I was always in the school choir. My Christmas wish when I was three years old was to have the clothes, hair and voice of Chaka Khan. I love her to this day! I discovered the flute when I was about six, and spent the next few years longing for my own. I finally got one and began lessons when I was nine, playing every day and doing all my exams until I put it down when I left school at seventeen. That was when I got my first guitar and began to really be

Ealing Blues Festival, London

IS IT IMPORTANT TO UNDERSTAND THE BUSINESS SIDE OF THE INDUSTRY?

Yes, although I leave most of the business side of things to Dan, I do understand what's going on. As we're completely independent and have never had a manager or a record deal (we have our own record label, Pigskin Records), we're always learning new things, new tricks to make things run more smoothly or reap more rewards. For us there's been a lot of trial and error, but being completely in control of our own schedule and finances works for our lives and family.

ARE AWARDS HELPFUL?

I was a finalist every single year that the now defunct British Blues Awards ran, in at least one category, usually two. I never won. However, I make a living from music and my career has grown year on year without those awards, so I've always felt I didn't absolutely need them. But winning the UK Blues Challenge and the European Blues Challenges definitely helped further my career, in terms of bringing my name and music to new audiences. I didn't win the International Blues Challenge in Memphis, but doing it has also elevated my status, so maybe sometimes it really is not just the winning but the taking part that matters.

WHERE DO YOU SEE YOUR MUSIC GOING NEXT?

I think the next thing I'll record will be a stripped-back acoustic duo album with Dan. I want to get right back to the roots of the Blues. I've also got a burning desire to record an album of Koko Taylor covers after I did a guest spot of exclusively Koko numbers earlier this year, at the Great British Rock & Blues Festival. I'd love to get the who's who of British blues to collaborate on it. Let's see…

Norwich Arts Centre

Blues Music Awards, Memphis, Tennessee

BARBARA CARR

Born Barbara Crosby in St Louis, Missouri, in 1941, she began singing gospel in church and formed a group with her two sisters. At age 16, she formed the Comets, and then sang in a band called The Petites, which were the opening act for Smokey Robinson. She became Barbara Carr following her marriage to Charles Carr, with whom she formed a record label. She was lead vocalist with saxophonist Oliver Sain's band for several years, which led to a recording contract with Chess Records in 1966.

After time out to raise her family, she returned to performing in and around St Louis in the 70s, and became known for her bawdy stage persona, winning a record deal with the Ecko label in 1996. Living Blues Readers Award named her twice as Female Blues Artist of the Year. Her album *Keep the Fire Burning* in 2012, climbed to the top ten on both the Living Blues Report and the Roots Music Report and was named by *Down Beat* magazine as one of the Best Albums of the Year. Carr was featured on the cover and in an article in *Living Blues* magazine in 2012. In 2013 and 2014, she was nominated for a Blues Music Award in the Soul Blues Female Artist category.

Her recordings include: *Good Woman Go Bad* (1989), *Street Woman* (1994), *Footprints on the Ceiling* (1997), *Bone Me Like You Own Me* (1998), *It's My Time* (2007), *Savvy Woman* (2009), *Southern Soul Blues Sisters* (with Uvee Hayes) (2009), *Keep the Fire Burning* (2012).

The following is an edited version of an interview by David Whiteis, which appeared in *Living Blues Magazine* **(Nov. 2012)**

Barbara Carr is singing to me over the telephone.

"The whole world is gonna know about me," she croons in a lilting warble that bears little resemblance to the grit-toughened rasp most of her listeners would probably recognize. She then breaks into a hearty chuckle and explains why she feels so optimistic. "I've never felt this good before, recording, in my life," she says, referring to *Keep the Fire Burning*, her 2012 release on Bob Trenchard's El Paso-based Catfood Records label.

In truth, a good part of "the whole world" already knows about Barbara Carr, even if her career trajectory hasn't always reflected her reputation. Through the years, she has recorded for labels ranging from Chess through her own Bar-Carr imprint to the southern soul powerhouse Ecko; she's worked with such fabled mentors and accompanists as St Louis sax legend Oliver Sain, and she's shared bills with the cream of the blues and soul-blues world. In 1997, after years of near-hits and near-misses, she came through with her version of Ruby Andrews's 1992 Goldwax release *Footprints on the Ceiling*, a jaunty celebration of erotic ecstasy that catapulted Carr into the southern soul limelight. If she never quite found a follow-up to sustain that success (double-entendre outings like 'If You Can't Cut the Mustard (I Don't Want You Lickin' 'Round the Jar)' and 'Bone Me Like You Own Me' kept her name alive in the southern soul world, but she never felt comfortable with that kind of fare, and in fact she has avoided including most of it in her performances), her subsequent output has still included such overlooked classics as 2001's sass-and-sandpaper throwdown 'The Best Woman Won' ("Get over it, girlfriend, and just congratulate me") and her 1999 cover of the old Gene Chandler hit 'Rainbow', a heart-ripping tour-de-force that stands as one of the all-time gems of southern soul-blues voicecraft.

* * * *

Growing up in rural Olivette on the western fringe of the St Louis metropolitan area, Barbara Crosby discovered early on that she had a flair for music. In fact, it ran in her family. "My father," she remembers, "he and his brothers – there were thirteen of them, [and] there were four of them that sang in a quartet. We had an old upright piano that we grew up with, and my mother and father both played. No one taught them; they were self-taught. I really did like to hear my mother and father have a sing."

These days, Carr is very protective of her personal life ("Some things I don't want to put in [the article] – my private family, you know?"), but she will say that her parents were both from Mississippi – her mother from Laurel, her father from the nearby hamlet of Soso – and that some of her fondest early memories are of singing with her sisters at Mt Zion Missionary Baptist Church in Elmwood Park, not far from where she grew up. She eventually formed a group called the Crosby Sisters, with two of them, Loretta and Gracie, and they made quite a splash around the local church community; unfazed by any potential criticism from church purists, Barbara also performed on a local television show called *St Louis Hop* with a youthful dance troupe called the Crumb Crushers.

But she had loftier ambitions than appearing with a bunch of poodle-skirted steppers on a cut-rate *American Bandstand* spin-off. "I loved Faye Adams," she remembers. "There used to be a radio show called 'Randy' [i.e. Gene Nobles's night-time R & B programme, sponsored by Randy's Record Shop, on WLAC in Nashville]; there was a certain part of the night that we could get that radio station. And my goodness, I used to love everything they played on that."

Despite her father's fears that his underaged daughter was growing up too fast, Barbara began singing with an ensemble called the Comets Combo in the late 50s. A standard guitar-bass-drums trio, the Comets "played everything that was popular then, everything from 'Stagger Lee' through everything [else]." They did some local club work, and they also appeared on shows promoted by St Louis deejay Dave Dixon; on one occasion, they opened for Junior Parker. But Barbara got married when she was 18, and by the early 60s she was the mother of four children. When her husband, Charles, joined the military and got stationed at Ft Carson in Colorado, she took a hiatus from music.

Upon returning to St Louis ("I still wasn't satisfied with not singing"), she re-entered the local circuit, and this time the results were more promising. Vocalist Charles Drain, former lead singer of the R & B/doo-wop group the Tabs, was working on furthering his solo career. His brother, Billy Drain, recruited Barbara and two other female singers, Pat and Dorothy (or possibly Dorothea) Ewing, to sing backup for him. Billed as the Petites, they accompanied Charles on a few recordings for the Top Track label, and they also recorded a handful of sides under their own name on Freeman Bosley's Teek imprint.

Once again, the premier local deejay was an important patron. "Dave Dixon put in a lot of time with us," Carr affirms. "He kept us exposed on all of the shows that would come in; anybody that would come in, we would open up that show. We did a show down at Masonic Hall in St Louis with the Miracles and Little Johnny Taylor. The Miracles at that point had a girl [Claudette Rogers]. After we had got done with this show, we found out, 'God! We performed with big stars!'" Things looked promising for a while, but after Dixon died in a car accident in 1964, the Petites found themselves foundering.

Not much later, vocalist Fontella Bass left the Oliver Sain Revue, St Louis's top R & B show band (Sain's closest competitor, Ike Turner, had moved to California a few years earlier). "There was a place called Gaslight Square in St Louis," Carr recollects. "That's where I met Oliver Sain. My brother-in-law was working at the club. He said, 'Barbara, this guy is looking for a female singer; Fontella Bass just left. Why don't you come down and audition?' 'Oh, I don't know...' 'He's been auditioning lots of people.' So I made up my mind to go down. I did 'There Is Something on Your Mind', and he liked it. Oliver was not only a nice, nice man, a beautiful person, inside and out – he taught me things. That's what made me want to be on my own, really."

Backed by sax virtuoso Sain and his skin-tight ensemble, Carr honed her chops and acclimated herself to the fast-paced life of the professional entertainer. But she still had to balance her aspirations with her personal responsibilities. It took a while, she says, for her husband Charles to fully come to terms with her career; she also had four children to take care of, and the bills still had to be paid: "I continued to perform locally, and I went from state to state, too, but I had a day job for twenty-five years, a full-time day job. Most of the times that I was entertaining, even going out of town, it was mainly a weekend thing. I would have my mother-in-law watch my children."

It was through Sain, who had a contract with Chess Records, that Carr garnered her first major recording opportunity. After signing with Chess in 1966, she cut a series of sides – some recorded at Sain's studio in St Louis, some at the label's famous headquarters at 2120 South Michigan in Chicago – that featured her disarmingly youthful-sounding vocals couched in the bouncy Chicago girl-group sound of the time. In retrospect, though, it's questionable how seriously the label took her; by most accounts, they didn't promote her very well, and during her six-year tenure there they released only four of her records. At least one of her sides, 1966's unissued *Somewhere Crying*, was given to Irma Thomas to remake in Muscle Shoals about a year after she recorded it.

For her part (although it's possible her memories have been soured by resentment), Carr says she was underwhelmed by Chess from the moment she first arrived there. "It looked like a big warehouse to me," she maintains, "and there was nothing appealing about it. We went in there and did what we had to do, and we left. We drove up and drove back down. So it really wasn't a big thing. Chess wasn't all that big of a deal to me. I don't really remember a lot of it, even though I was there."

Carr's swansong for Chess, recorded at Sain's studio in 1972, was 'Love Me Now' b/w 'I'm Gonna Make a Man Out of You', the latter a take-no-mess testifier that toughened her erstwhile teenybopper pep with a streetsy swagger. At about the same time, she officially parted ways with Oliver Sain and began trying to forge a career of her own. Over the next few years she worked with various ensembles, including Jerry and the Soulful Five (a band of ex-Sain sidemen led by drummer Jerry Fine) and an otherwise all-white group called the Apostles (she later fronted a mixed-race band waggishly dubbed One Shade Lighter). She even sang for a while with a jazz trio called the Stable Mates, working in "a lot of the white restaurants that they had, far out, you know what I mean, and a lot of private parties. I did a lot of Nancy Wilson; I did some things by Lena Horne; I did what I had to do where I was doing this act, where I was performing. People loved it." Probably their most prestigious booking was a long-term gig at St Louis's Playboy Club.

But despite her relatively full performing schedule, and even though "more people had heard of [the Chess recordings] than I knew – I sure got jobs from 'em", she found herself fighting off despair. "Sure, it was discouraging," she affirms, adding with a rare tinge of bitterness that "my whole life has been discouraging. I was so disgusted, I went into another bag. I wasn't too interested about anything."

That "other bag", incongruously enough, was country music. Although she says she had to be talked into it by a guitar-picking neighbour ("Oh, of course he was white – yeah, that's all I've ever lived around"), she proved herself to have a knack for it; a few of her brown-eyed hillbilly efforts (on Huron and MCR) even garnered some modest play on country stations. Soon, though, she was back to R & B with the crudely produced 'Love Me with Open End' b/w 'I Need Your Company', released on Yevoc in the late 70s to little fanfare. A session in Muscle Shoals with songwriter/producer Harrison Calloway resulted in a couple of more promising sides ('Physical Love Affair' and 'You've Been Doin' Wrong So Long'), but they sank into oblivion after being leased to Gateway in the early 80s. At this point, Carr and her husband decided it was time to take matters into their own hands.

"Charles and I were talking," she says. "We got tired of being bumped around, just being looked over. So finally, he said, 'Wife' – he always called me 'Wife' – 'let's start our own company.' I said, 'OK, let's do, Charles.' So we started that, and we came up with Bar-Car, just shortened my name.

"He worked his little hiney off," she adds. "Those instruments and things, and paying those guys, that cost a lot of money. Going back and forth to Muscle Shoals, Alabama, and doing this and doing that – it was costly."

Carr's output on Bar-Car over the next few years, mostly written by Calloway and/or George Jackson and recorded at Muscle Shoals' famed Wishbone Studios, was easily her most fully realized yet. Stylistically, she ranged from the deep soul-blues emotionalism of 1984's 'Good Woman Go Bad' to the chrome-plated disco sheen of 'I Want Your Body', and she also revealed herself to be a deft interpreter of others' hits: her version of 'Messin' with My Mind' transformed Clarence Carter's good-natured tale of infatuation into an eros-wracked plea, made even more effective by the unobtrusive, smooth-sheened pop-soul backing. Others began to take notice, as well: when the Pulsar label invited her to be a guest vocalist on pianist Johnnie Johnson's 1988 *Blue Hand Johnnie* solo debut album, she delivered an inspired reading of Lowell Fulson's 'Black Night' and did her best to pump some fresh energy into the all-too-clichéd (by then) 'Johnnie B. Goode'.

In 1989, Bar-Car issued the first full-length Barbara Carr LP, *Good Woman Go Bad* (it's since been reissued on Paula). A few years later, another album, *Street Woman*, appeared, first as a tape cassette and then as a CD. Although, like most of her Bar-Car output, these albums were well-written and strongly produced, the perennial small-label bugaboos of insufficient resources and lack of industry clout condemned them to semi-obscurity almost as soon as they were issued. "We didn't have the money to do what it took," Carr admits today, although she adds that her recordings during those years did a good job of keeping her working on a local and regional basis.

Unbeknownst to Carr, though, her music was being heard, and her reputation was expanding, in places she probably never imagined. In 1991, even as she was struggling to keep her label and her performing career afloat, she got what seemed like the opportunity of a lifetime – her first overseas tour. According to Carr's recollections, renowned blues photographer Bill Greensmith helped make the arrangements; even though "it wasn't paying making much money", she says, she leapt at the opportunity: "'Oh, I'll never get back over there again – I'm taking this trip!" She performed in Italy and Austria ("I went back and forth, I don't know how many times"), and like a lot of American soul and blues artists, she was almost overwhelmed by the adulation and knowledge of the European fans. "It was amazing," she enthuses. "A lot of stuff people told me over there, I said, 'What? You remember this?' It's been so far back in my mind I wasn't even thinking about that anymore! They come up with 45s for you to sign – I think it's amazing, I really do. I just love it."

Stateside, as well, the voice of Barbara Carr was finding its way into the awareness of an expanding circle of listeners – some of whom would eventually help break her more forcefully into the burgeoning southern soul-blues market. Back in 1985, she'd recorded a song on Bar-Car called 'Not a Word' that featured her breathy, behind-closed-doors murmur along with songwriter George Jackson's insinuating loverboy croon. In Memphis, it reached the ears of John Ward, who at the time was scuffling around town trying to insinuate himself into the local scene as a guitar player and songwriter. Although he wouldn't officially launch his Ecko label until almost ten years later, he never forgot the song, and he never lost his desire to find out more about the singer. "I just liked Barbara's voice," he says, "hearing her on that record with George. When I first heard the record, she sounded so good to me, I thought, 'This must be somebody that used to be big.'"

Eventually, Ward put two and two together. "I read a thing in *Living Blues*; it was a review of her CD [probably the CD version of *Street Woman*], and it said that some company needs to pick her up. So I told [Ecko promotions director] Larry Chambers, 'Man, let's see if we can get in touch with Barbara Carr. See if she's interested.' So we got her number, called her, and talked with her and her husband Charles, and they said, 'Yeah, we'll come on down.' And they were in St Louis. So they came on down, I think it was a Saturday, and we sat around for three or four hours, talking, and they went on back, but before they left we all decided that we were going to do an album. And Barbara turned out to be a good artist."

To Carr, still sceptical in the wake of the Chess and Gateway debacles, it sounded almost too good to be true. "I got a call from them," she remembers. "I said, 'I wonder what these people want? What does Ecko Records want with me?' And Charles said, 'Well, Wife, call 'em back; return the call, and see what they're about.' So I did, and we went to Memphis."

At that time, Ecko didn't have its own building – Ward was running the entire operation out of his house. But the woman who professes to have been turned off by the "warehouse"-like appearance of Chess Records in Chicago seems not to have been fazed by the low-rent ambience: "We went to talk with them and everything, and we agreed on a lot of things, and I think I signed up with them for some years. And with Ecko Records, I am just so pleased with them, because they are the ones that really put me out there nationally. And that was great. More shows down South, down through the South; I got some [more] shows overseas. They're the ones that made a way for me."

Although she would eventually come to dislike the modern soul-blues emphasis on double-entendre raunch, Carr eagerly embraced the jubilant naughtiness of 'Footprints on the Ceiling' (the title track of her 1997 debut Ecko CD) when Ward suggested it to her during her initial sessions with him. He had co-written it with Sidney Bailey some years earlier and pitched it to producer/label owner Quinton Claunch, a well-known Memphis music industry figure who had been an original partner in Hi Records and later, along with pharmacist/wheeler-dealer Rudolph "Doc" Russell, launched the Goldwax imprint, the label on which James Carr (no relation to Barbara) recorded his now legendary mid-/late-60s deep soul sides. Goldwax dissolved in about 1970, but in the mid-80s a Memphis businessman named Elliot Clark teamed up with Claunch to revitalize it. They began issuing new product in 1991, and Claunch eventually also initiated a new label called Soul Trax. Ward worked with him as a songwriter and co-producer on several of his projects, including Carr's 1994 comeback effort, *Soul Survivor*.

"'Footprints on the Ceiling,'" Ward says, "that was a song that I gave to Quinton Claunch and this other guy that was his partner at the time, a guy named Elliot Clark. The first time they came over to talk about recording James Carr, I gave 'em a bunch of songs to consider recording; 'Footprints on the Ceiling' was one. And Elliot Clark ended up taking that, and he recorded it on Ruby Andrews [for her 1992 Goldwax album, *Ruby*]. And that was it; I didn't know anything more about the song. I knew it got recorded, because somebody told me or something, but I never heard it; they didn't play it on any blues stations that I ever heard, they didn't really play it in the South – I never heard the song.

"Once we put it out on Barbara, it did well, especially in the Beach Music market. But in our normal blues market, 'If You Can't Cut the Mustard' and 'Bo Hawg Grind' were probably the main two from that CD. I thought she was a good artist; we did that first CD, and [it] really turned out good."

In many ways, Carr's newfound status as a soul-blues recording star felt like the fulfilment of a dream ("I really want to thank John Ward," she emphasizes. "I really thank Ecko for all they did for me"). But as she became more deeply involved in southern soul-blues, she discovered some things she didn't feel comfortable with – the well-raised woman from Olivette, Missouri, simply could not recast herself musically as a juke joint hoochie, regardless of what anyone around her might have wanted. "I didn't care for a lot of the songs," she admits. "Different songs, some of the songs that I didn't really want to do. I don't do them [in performance] at all. I have heard some say, 'That's what the people like; that sells.' And I'm going, 'Oh, man – but not with me.' I just didn't want any part of it. It isn't that way with me; not at all.

"But I went through that little hurdle; I'm not ashamed of anything I've ever done in my life. It was just a learning thing. I go in with my show, my songs that I have [prepared] for each set, I'll do them. Every now and then, [the audience] would scream out, 'Bone Me Like You Own Me [the title song of her 1998 sophomore CD on Ecko]!' And I said, 'Oh, God,' you know. We get offstage and… 'Barbara, you were fabulous, but what about 'Bone Me Like You Own Me'?' 'Oh, honey, the band don't even know it.' I'd just slide right through. They really don't ask for that any more; I think they know that's just not something that is in my repertoire."

It was most likely creative differences like these that prompted her to leave Ecko for a while after she released *The Best Woman* in 2001; over the next couple of years she recorded a CD for Bar-Car (*On My Own*) and one for Mardi Gras (*Talk to Me*, about which she says, "I didn't like none of that stuff – [the production] was very shaky"). But by 2006 she was back with Ecko, and she remained there for another year or two, holding on to her place in what might be called the second tier of the southern soul-blues pantheon – not quite a "star", perhaps, but more than just a name in a lineup. In 2009 she moved to CDS in California and recorded *Savvy Woman*, a disc she says could have been much better if she'd been given more time to prepare ("We were learning that stuff in the studio, and I got so frustrated").

But once again, just as her collegial relationship with Oliver Sain had led to that initial break at Chess, another longtime musical association was about to bear fruit. Carr and guitarist/vocalist Johnny Rawls had been acquaintances for years, "just in passing", as they both put it, sharing bills on various shows and encountering each other occasionally on the soul-blues highway. In the 2000s, they began to get to know each other a little better through their mutual association with North Carolina-based blues artist Roy Roberts. In 2004, Roberts and Rawls collaborated on *Partners and Friends*, issued on Roberts' Rock House label. Roberts co-produced Carr's *Savvy Woman* at CDS, and he has recorded several duets with her: two of them, 'How Long' and 'It's Only You', were included on *Savvy Woman*; they're anthologized along with another duet, 'Don't Let Our Love Slip Away', on CDS's *Southern Soul & Party Blues* series. 'Don't Let Our Love Slip Away' and a Carr/Roberts beach music party song called 'Shaggin' Down in Carolina' also appear on a Barbara Carr/Uvee Hayes compilation called *Southern Soul Blues Sisters* on Aviara. Through the years, Roberts and Carr have worked various festivals and shows together.

Rawls, who merged his own Deep South label with Bob Trenchard's Catfood operation some years back, came to believe that his and Trenchard's rootsy soul aesthetic was just the thing Barbara Carr and her long-time admirers were looking for. "Me and Roy were doing things together," he explains, "and we became friends through the years, and he was working with Barbara, doing a lot of shows with her. And I went to one of the shows, and we talked; [then] I met Barbara at the Blues Awards, must've been 2010, and I got to telling her about, 'Hey, you should come on and do something with us; I would like to do some different kind of music on you.' I just told her, 'Why don't you come on over there? I'll write you some songs and steer away from more of that graphic-type music [in favour of] a different type of sound and words.'"

It was as if Rawls had been reading her mind. "The songs that she did were great songs," he acknowledges (a bit more charitably, perhaps, than she might). "I like 'em, like 'If You Can't Cut the Mustard (I Don't Want You Lickin' 'Round the Jar)' – it's one of my favourite tunes. It was a good song, and I liked it a lot. But I think she has a lot more to offer the world than a song about lickin' the jar. She's a hell of a singer; I think she can deliver a much more constructive song than that."

The result, *Keep the Fire Burning*, is a CD that combines the best of what might be called an old-school R & B/soul aesthetic with a modernist lyric sensibility that, while it avoids cheap-thrills pandering, tackles mature themes with a bracing meld of bluntness and elegance. But will music like this, tailor-made for revivalist-minded aficionados ("We got the real instruments, man," boasts Rawls; "we don't use no synthetic nothing") still appeal to the predominantly African-American soul-blues listeners who've been Barbara Carr's mainstay at least since she broke through on Ecko in the 90s? She considers the question carefully before responding with the same ambivalence – enthusiasm tempered by resignation – that blues and soul artists have been expressing since they began "crossing over" to the white market decades ago. "I think it would be a different audience," she admits. "Big difference. Right now, I'm looking at it as, it's not a real good thing, but I don't really care who – I wish they [i.e., African American fans] would come, but really, this is the route I'm going. I really want to go this route. It's going to be good for me."

Rawls, who has spent most of his career bridging the black and white blues/soul-blues worlds, concurs. "If you're going to advance your music," he maintains, "you are going to have to play to more of a mixed audience, instead of just a predominantly chitlin' audience. You're going to have to move out if you're going to move forward. So that's really a good thing – college students, tractor drivers, just all people from all walks of life. You've got to move forward.

"Those [southern soul] labels, they've helped a lot of artists, but I like to take the music to where everybody can listen to it, everybody can dig on it, you know what I mean? Like a friend of mine in California who's been on the radio for twenty-five, thirty years, he loves Barbara Carr's singing, but he just hates electronic instruments and the topics that they sing about. He loves her, but he just doesn't play the music because of that; but now he's going to be excited about it."

Right now, though, it's hard to believe that he or anyone else is going to be any more excited than Barbara Carr herself. Talking about her still-nascent relationship with Catfood, she can barely contain her enthusiasm. "Everything [there] is very new to me," she exults. "It hasn't been done before; the recording with the other people hasn't been done the way this is. This is laid out completely different, and everything is like – oh, man, I have beautiful people that I'm working with; I have Johnny Rawls and Bob Trenchard – it feels great. It feels wonderful. Because I say, this has never been done this way before. I even dreamed, I actually dreamed these words: 'Maybe I didn't make it before, but this is the beginning of a lot to come.'

"I've been trying to climb to the top for a long time, and I'll never stop. Ain't no stoppin' me now."

Lucerne Blues Festival, Switzerland (pictured with Marquise Knox)

Chicago Blues Festival

JOANNA CONNOR

Joanna Connor was born in Brooklyn, New York, in 1962, and grew up in Worcester, Massachusetts, with her mother, who owned a large collection of blues and jazz records. She received her first guitar when she was seven, and started played and singing in local bands from the age of 16, before moving to Chicago in 1984, where she connected with the local blues scene and performed with the likes of James Cotton, Junior Wells, Buddy Guy, A.C. Reed and Dion Payton.

In 1987, she played the Chicago Blues Festival, formed her own band, and later released her debut album *Believe It!* through the Blind Pig label. This album was followed by *Fight* (1992), *Living on the Road* (1993), *Rock & Roll Gypsy* (1995), *Big Girl Blues* (1996), *Slidetime* (1998) and *Nothing but the Blues* (2001). In 2002 she signed for M.C. Records and, honing her songwriting skills, she released *The Joanna Connor Band* and several other albums including *Six String Stories* (2016). Renowned for her virtuoso guitar-playing, she has been a fixture at the Kingston Mines club in Chicago since the 1980s, in addition to performing at other venues and festivals.

HOW DID YOU START IN MUSIC?

Listening to music is one of my earliest memories. I remember vividly trying to emulate a song I heard often on the radio because I loved the voice – it was Louis Armstrong and 'Hello Dolly'. I looked that up. It was 1964. I was two. Music found me.

WHEN DID YOU START SINGING OR PLAYING AN INSTRUMENT?

I began guitar at seven.

WHO WERE/ARE YOUR INFLUENCES?

The Beatles, Taj Mahal, the Rolling Stones, Robert Johnson, Ry Cooder, Led Zeppelin, James Cotton, B.B. King, Aretha Franklin, Buddy Guy, Jimi Hendrix, Bonnie Raitt, Weather Report, Joni Mitchell, John McLaughlin, Ravi Shankar, King Sunny Adé.

WHY CHOOSE THE BLUES?

I heard blues from the time I can remember.

HOW WOULD YOU DESCRIBE YOUR APPROACH?

I am a live performing musician. I have a jazz approach to my music, it's never exactly the same and is influenced by my inner being, my band and the audience.

DO YOU WRITE OR COMPOSE YOUR OWN MATERIAL?

I have written many songs. I play a lot of covers though.

HOW DO YOU START MAKING MUSIC? WHAT IS YOUR PROCESS?

I perform a minimum of four days a week for many hours. I have been working steady and nonstop for thirty years.

WHICH DO YOU PREFER – PLAYING LIVE OR BEING IN A STUDIO? WHY?

Live – that's my comfort zone.

HOW DO YOU FIND THE RIGHT MUSIC PRODUCER FOR A RECORD?

I've been producing myself for years. Jim Gaines produced three of my early records. I learned a lot from him.

ARE AUDIENCES DIFFERENT AROUND THE WORLD?

Audiences are extremely different from city to city and for sure around the world. The culture of a place is a big influence, the age of the crowd, even the type of venue.

DO YOU HAVE A FAVOURITE VENUE? WHY?

I have no favourite venue per se: a great night is a great night! Although I am very indebted to and appreciative of the Kingston Mines.

Fitzgerald's Nightclub, Berwyn, Illinois

DESCRIBE YOUR JOURNEY AS AN ARTIST/MUSICIAN/SINGER.

That could be a novel in itself! I moved to Chicago to learn the blues and immerse myself in black culture… it's been a hard-knock life, but I have seen forty-nine states and dozens of countries and raised two kids all along the way. I have been a seeker of being true to myself and becoming a better musician.

WHAT WERE THE HIGHLIGHTS?

Playing with Luther Allison, B.B. King, Robben Ford, Jimmy Page, being on TV several times, seeing so many fabulous countries.

WHAT WERE THE CHALLENGES?

Money is always tight. Being a road act was super-stressful. Being a woman can be lonely in this biz. Being away from my kids was the worst.

IS THERE ONE SONG THAT IS CLOSEST TO YOUR HEART?

There is no song closest to my heart, although I do love the song I wrote for my kids called 'Sixth Child'. But the old 'Walkin' Blues' sure gave my career a boost.

Brooklyn Bowl, London

SHEMEKIA COPELAND

Born in Harlem, New York City in 1979, Shemekia first performed at the Cotton Club at an early age with her father, Texas blues guitarist and singer, Johnny Copeland. At 16, she went on tour with her father as his opening act and began to make a name on the blues circuit.

In 1998, she signed to Alligator Records and released her first album *Turn the Heat Up!* featuring her father's classic number 'Ghetto Child.' Three more albums followed: *Wicked, Talking to Strangers* and *The Soul Truth*. Switching to Telarc International ten years later, the album *Never Going Back* was released and in 2009 she was named "Rising Star – Blues Artist" in *Down Beat* magazine's critics' poll and the next year Living Blues Awards named her Blues Artist of the Year. At the 2011 Chicago Blues Festival, Koko Taylor's daughter, Cookie, presented Copeland with Koko Taylor's crown, and the honorary title "Queen of the Blues". A few years on, Copeland was nominated for a Blues Music Award in the Contemporary Blues Female Artist category, finally winning the title in 2016. Her album, *Outskirts of Love* (2015) reached the charts and was nominated for a Grammy in the Best Blues Album category.

Following the birth of her son, she changed direction, recording her eighth album *America's Child* (2018) in Nashville with guests including John Prine and Emmylou Harris. At the Blues Music Awards in 2019 it won both the Album of the Year and Contemporary Album of the Year titles.

HOW DID YOU START IN MUSIC?

My dad brought me up on stage at the Cotton Club in Harlem when I was ten. I wanted to hide behind the curtain.

WHO WERE/ARE YOUR INFLUENCES?

My father was my biggest influence by far. Females were Koko Taylor and Ruth Brown. Men were O.V. Wright, Sam Cooke and Otis Redding.

WHY CHOOSE THE BLUES?

It choose me. I was born into it. My daddy sang the blues to my mama, and I'll sing the blues to you.

HOW WOULD YOU DESCRIBE YOUR APPROACH?

Above all honest and passionate, I hope. I only sing what I feel and what I believe in.

DO YOU WRITE OR COMPOSE YOUR OWN MATERIAL?

No. I am very fortunate to have an incredible writer, John Hahn, in my close circle of family and friends. He produced a record for my father, and I have known him since I was eight years old. He writes a great deal of my material. And since we speak every day he usually knows what I'd like to sing about. He's my second father and a wonderful writer. We make a great team.

HOW DO YOU START MAKING MUSIC? WHAT IS YOUR PROCESS?

It's continuous. We are thinking about songs all the time. Discussing the world and whatever is going on.

WHICH DO YOU PREFER – PLAYING LIVE OR BEING IN A STUDIO? WHY?

They're both good for different reasons. But nothing beats the thrill of bring in front of a crowd of people who are really into the music. They become part of the music as another living organism.

HOW DO YOU FIND THE RIGHT MUSIC PRODUCER FOR A RECORD?

We listen to lots of records and talk to other artists.

ARE AUDIENCES DIFFERENT AROUND THE WORLD?

People are people. But in some countries they are a little bit more restrained. Though you can still feel a positive vibe off them. They're all good. I'm very fortunate to meet and play for people all around the world.

DO YOU HAVE A FAVOURITE VENUE? WHY?

Yes, but I'm not going to get myself in trouble by telling you and offending other nice venues!

DESCRIBE YOUR JOURNEY AS AN ARTIST/MUSICIAN/SINGER.

Blessed. Lucky to be able to get paid to make people forget their troubles for a little while and just feel good. There are lots of talented artists who are really gifted but can't make a living doing this. I can. And for that I am incredibly grateful.

WHAT WERE THE HIGHLIGHTS?

Playing the White House for President Obama (where I sang backup for Mick Jagger). Performing for the troops in Iraq. The first time I headlined the Chicago Blues Festival. Being nominated three times for Grammy Awards.

WHAT WERE THE CHALLENGES?

Trying to find success in a genre that's still heavily dominated by guitars rather than vocalists.

IS THERE ONE SONG THAT IS CLOSEST TO YOUR HEART?

On the new CD there's a song John Hahn wrote about my son, Johnny Lee, and the world he's inheriting. It's called 'Ain't Got Time for Hate'. That's a message I can live with.

IS THERE ONE ARTIST WHO HAS TRULY INSPIRED YOU?

My father.

HOW DO YOU PROMOTE YOUR IMAGE/YOUR BRAND?

I just try to be myself. Believe it or not, sometimes that's tougher than it sounds.

HOW DO YOU DEAL WITH OBSTACLES SUCH AS AGEISM, SEXISM AND RACISM?

The same way every other woman does. I strongly assert my feelings. I'm not bashful.

IS IT IMPORTANT TO UNDERSTAND THE BUSINESS SIDE OF THE INDUSTRY?

Yes. And to have a strong team around you to do the heavy lifting so you can concentrate on the entertaining.

ARE AWARDS HELPFUL?

Everybody likes to be acknowledged. But in general I don't feel they're very important. Having said that, did I mention my three Grammy nominations (haha)?

WHERE DO YOU SEE YOUR MUSIC GOING NEXT?

I'd like to build on blues tradition but introduce elements from other genres to keep the music alive and growing.

Aurora Blues Fest, Aurora, Illinois

Buddy Guy's Legends, Chicago

DEBBIE DAVIES

Debbie Davies is a pioneering woman of electric blues guitar. A professional musician since the early 80s and a thirty-seven-year veteran of the road, she ranks among the top blues artists in the country. She has received ten nominations for Blues Music Awards and took home the WC Handy award for Best Contemporary Female Artist in 1997. In 2010 she received the Koko Taylor Award from the Blues Foundation. She has released 15 solo albums with her band and two collaborative albums; one with Anson Funderburgh and Otis Grand, and the second with Tab Benoit and Kenny Neal.

Davies cut her teeth playing in blues and rock 'n' roll bands in the San Francisco Bay area before returning to Los Angeles in 1984, where she landed the lead guitar spot in Maggie Mayall and the Cadillacs, an all-female band led by the wife of British blues pioneer John Mayall. In 1988 she was recruited by Albert Collins to join the Icebreakers. During her tenure with Albert, Debbie was invited to perform on John Mayall's 1990 album, *A Sense of Place*, and in 1991 she recorded with Albert Collins and the Icebreakers on the Grammy nominated self-titled release for Point Blank/Virgin Records.

In the summer of 1991 Debbie became lead guitarist for Fingers Taylor's all female blues band, the Ladyfingers Revue, which served as the opening act for Jimmy Buffett's *Outpost* tour. In September 1993 she came out with her debut solo release, *Picture This*, on Blind Pig Records.

Her 2007 Telarc Records release *Blues Blast* is highly acclaimed and includes guest appearances by three high-profile bluesmen: guitarists Tab Benoit and Coco Montoya, and harpist Charlie Musselwhite. In 2009, Debbie Davies released the ground-breaking and acclaimed all instrumental CD, *Holdin' Court* on Vizztone Records. That year also found Davies teaming up with blues singer and harp player, the late Robin Rogers, to tour the country with performances at many festivals.

Davies also joined Tommy Castro's Legendary Rhythm and Blues Cruise Revue that same year, performing both on land and at sea. Debbie Davies is featured on the 2011 release of the revue performing the tune 'All I Found', on Alligator Records.

In 2012, Davies released *After the Fall* on MC Records. The all-original CD also features songs written by Debbie's longtime drummer Don Castagno and a guest appearance by pianist Bruce Katz. In 2013 she self-released a CD of tunes recorded through the years both live and in the studio.

Davies's latest 2015 release, *Love Spin*, on the Vizztone label, is a showcase of originals by both Davies and her songwriting partner, Don Castagno, and includes special guests Terry Hanck, Dana Robbins, Dave Keyes and Jay Stollman.

HOW DID YOU START IN MUSIC?

Growing up in a musical home, I became a music junkie! As a kid I listened to lots of big-band swing albums that my folks played around the house, lots of Frank Sinatra and harmony vocal groups. My dad was a singer in the Hollywood studio scene, so music was always blasting! Mom listened to pop radio all day and played classical music on the piano. As a child I had to have the classical station on the radio beside my bed, or I would not sleep. Of course Mom began teaching us piano when I turned five, but I never felt a total affinity for it. Then, of course the guitar, the Beatles and John Mayall and the Bluesbreakers entered my life, and from then on it was guitar love!

WHO WERE/ARE YOUR INFLUENCES?

On guitar, I guess the Beatles were first, then Eric Clapton, and as I came to realize the music I really gravitated to was called "blues", I worked backwards and got into all the great electric blues players, the Kings, Albert Collins, the Texas cats like Gatemouth Brown, Chicago cats like Buddy Guy and Magic Sam. I also got off on guitar players like Glen Campbell and Roy Clark and kind of just absorbed it all before I got serious about being a player.

WHY CHOOSE THE BLUES?

I think it's the grooves mostly… I love a swingin' shuffle, all the funky grooves… I even consider the older stuff by Muddy Waters or Howlin' Wolf or the like to be very funky in its own way. What guitar player doesn't love to play a slow blues! Of course it's also the passion and raw emotions of the blues that draw me to it. In many ways I am quite shy, so the blues allowed me to unleash all of my emotions and frustrations that needed somehow to be expressed.

HOW WOULD YOU DESCRIBE YOUR APPROACH?

I am an amalgamation of all of my influences: the 60s British blues invasion, *Soul Train*, the swing music I absorbed as a kid, all of the blues greats I have tried to learn my guitar chops from, and in particular the great, bluesy, funky, soulful music of Bonnie Raitt. When I was just beginning to be able to take some comprehensive leads on guitar, Stevie Ray Vaughan hit the scene, so he was a big influence on me too… then Jimmie Vaughan, Anson Funderburgh. I think Texas blues guitar is probably my biggest influence as far as style on guitar goes.

DO YOU WRITE OR COMPOSE YOUR OWN MATERIAL?

Oh yeah. All of my CDs have had originals on them. Some recordings have a combination of originals and selected blues and R 'n' B chestnuts, and some CDs have all original material on them. My longtime drummer, Don Castagno, is a great songwriter, and often contributed his originals too, and then of course we cowrote a number of them.

Buddy Guy's Legends, Chicago

HOW DO YOU START MAKING MUSIC? WHAT IS YOUR PROCESS?

An idea for a song can begin with a guitar riff or with a lyric idea. I try to write down or record an idea immediately: it's so funny how you think you will remember something but you never do! Occasionally a song comes out all at once. I remember writing 'Half-Caf Decaf' while touring in the van… I was writing it out on scrap paper and the music in my head. Very early on I remember sitting with my guitar and the tune 'Livin' on Lies' just poured out: chords, lyrics, everything. For other songs it becomes a work in progress, where I actually have to slave over a tune for a while. Often I would employ Don Castagno to collaborate with and help me with tunes.

WHICH DO YOU PREFER – PLAYING LIVE OR BEING IN A STUDIO? WHY?

I prefer singing in the studio, and playing guitar live.

HOW DO YOU FIND THE RIGHT MUSIC PRODUCER FOR A RECORD?

Hmmm… well, for the most part, especially early on, I had no say in the matter. The record labels would make this choice. On my third Blind Pig recording, *I Got that Feeling*, I got really fortunate to have Jim Gaines produce the record. At times I was able to make my own choices. Duke Robillard was a no-brainer! Then for several recordings, I was able to hire my buddy Paul Opalach to produce. He's one of those multitalented cats who plays all the instruments if needed and works the board! We had some really fun collaborations!

ARE AUDIENCES DIFFERENT AROUND THE WORLD?

Yes, to me audiences change with the climate… the northern countries in Europe and the north-eastern states of the US are all pretty sedate and stiff… tough to move. The southern countries of Europe like Spain for instance, are full of dancing and looseness. It's kind of the same in the southern states in the US. A big exception to the rule is Scandinavia, where they are more than capable of letting loose and going nuts! It's kind of cabin fever for them in the winter! But of course none of this is across the board, just generalizations.

DO YOU HAVE A FAVOURITE VENUE? WHY?

Well, the venues that really have my heart are some of the ones I played early on and got myself going in. Many are no longer with us. There was a joint in San Diego called Blind Melons where we played on a regular basis. It was just off the beach and was always packed with wild, beautiful, crazy energy. I met James Cotton there… he must've been touring in the area and came and sat in with me and my band! It was over the top. Another venue that is no longer with us was the Grand Emporium in Kansas City. I played there with both Albert and my own band. The venue was the essence of soul! Roger Nabor ran that venue before he began doing the Blues Cruises. Speaking of the cruises… I would have to say that the pool stage on the Legendary Rhythm and Blues Cruise is some of my favourite venues.

Around the country today, I would choose the Bradfordville Blues Club in Tallahassee, Florida, for its killer juke-joint vibe and authenticity. Then there is Biscuits and Blues in San Francisco. Despite the difficult load-in, the venue is really dedicated to blues music and artists. The audiences are a mix of local blues lovers and tourists from all over the world! It's a great mix! Not to mention it's in San Francisco! I love being back up there. The Time Out Pub in Rockland, Maine, is always a great time, and was a mainstay for years when I was on the East Coast. The club is, thanks to its promoter Paul Benjamin, a nice exception to the north-east norm: the fans dance their asses off there!

DESCRIBE YOUR JOURNEY AS AN ARTIST/MUSICIAN/SINGER.

Basically I was a girl from a totally musical home who became a music addict at about age three. The guitar became my instrument of choice, and very quickly the electric guitar. But playing electric and being in a band was not something accessible to me growing up. I kind of shelved the dream until after I finally left home and was on my own in northern California trying to pursue a degree in psychology and working day jobs fiercely to afford college! I had an epiphany that my true desire was to be a musician who wanted to play electric guitar. I bought myself my first electric guitar and an amp – used of course – and began the journey. Of course now that gear would be worth so much as vintage gear, if I still had it, haha! Eventually I did get the degree, but at that time it meant nothing. I used my grant and loan money to supplement my income in school, but mostly practised my ass off and sat at the feet of all my favourite blues artists passing through town each night. Somehow I had chosen a little college with a venue for touring blues musicians downtown! I met other players and sat with them as they showed me the concept of learning blues licks off records. I spent hours labouring over the record player, moving the needle back, over and over, until I learned a lick. I fell in love with another guitar player, and we started a blues and R & B band. I was just the rhythm player at first, and we had a lead singer. Eventually I could work in my licks and begin to take solos. Then the singer quit, so I began taking on those duties too. When my boyfriend and I broke up, I ended up in all kinds of bands, working crappy day jobs and playing blues at night. After about seven years of playing I moved back down to LA to enter the big pond and continue my career pursuits. I slept on my sister and her roommate's apartment floor, and went to as many jams as possible. One restaurant called Josephine's in the San Fernando Valley had what I would call "celebrity jams". All of the musicians who were in touring bands, especially with artists such as Bonnie Raitt, John Mayall and Albert Collins, Michael Jackson or whoever, would show up when not on the road to work out and keep their chops up. It took a long time for them to actually let me play. I was the only girl, and I just got asked up at the end of the night. But after a while I was able to be a regular performer at the jam and begin to get to know the players. Coco Montoya, who was touring with Mayall at the time, introduced me to his wife, Maggie, who was putting together an all-female blues band. Simultaneously Coco and I formed a band to play clubs in between the Mayall tours. Through Coco I met Albert Collins, and was eventually asked to be the second guitar player in the Icebreakers. I toured and recorded with Albert for three years, and then went out on my own. That's kind of the abridged version!

WHAT WERE THE HIGHLIGHTS?

The highlights of my career were, of course, touring and recording with Albert Collins while riding the great wave of the blues boom in the 80s and 90s. The joy of having my own band and the great opportunity to record my tunes are another highlight. Maybe, most of all, the opportunity to tour so much of this beautiful planet.

WHAT WERE THE CHALLENGES?

It was tough in the beginning when I was coming up. There was no support from the culture at large for women musicians, and no role models. Bonnie Raitt was the exception to this rule, finally, and became a great influence for me. I realize now how much support from family and society means to a youth and their dreams. Bucking up to the challenge and watching the cultural climate change has made it all worth it! It's been fascinating to watch the culture do a basic 180 as far as its acceptance and support for woman players, especially on electric guitar. There are a lot of great women pickers out there today!

IS THERE ONE ARTIST WHO HAS TRULY INSPIRED YOU?

As I mentioned earlier, I would say I was personally most inspired by Bonnie Raitt. I was watching and listening to a woman playing electric blues guitar, and performing the kind of music that was closest to my heart! Not to mention fronting her own band. Bonnie was doing everything I dreamed of doing, and at the highest level of quality and professionalism. I didn't want to copy her, as I wasn't driven to play slide, but rather wanted to emulate her lead guitar player, Will McFarlane.

Chicago Blues Festival

THORNETTA DAVIS

Born in 1963, Thornetta Davis is a singer and songwriter from Detroit, Michigan. Winner of over thirty Detroit Music Awards, including sweeping the 2017 and 2018 Detroit Music Awards. She first gained attention in 1987, when she became backup singer for the Detroit soul band Lamont Zodiac and the Love Signs. Shortly after, the lead singer left the band and the name changed to The Chisel Brothers featuring Thornetta Davis. In 1996 Thornetta recorded her first solo album *Sunday Morning Music* on the Seattle-based label Sub Pop. Thornetta has opened for legendary blues and R & B greats such as Ray Charles, Gladys Knight, Smokey Robinson, Etta James, Buddy Guy, Koko Taylor, Junior Wells, Lonnie Brooks, Johnnie Johnson and Bonnie Raitt. Her live album *Covered Live at the Music Menu* won Best R & B/ Blues Recording at the Detroit Music Awards 2002. Her latest album, *Honest Woman* (2017), was nominated for a Blues Music Award in the Best Emerging Artist Album category.

THORNETTA DAVIS – IN HER OWN WORDS

You ask, how did I get started in music? Well, I'll always love to sing. Ever since I was a little girl I'd sing around the house to anything, and we always had music playing– Motown, blues, soul music, jazz – and I would just sing to anything. The TV commercials, the musicals on television, Jackson Five – I was Michael whenever I would sing all the Jackson Five tunes with my sisters – but I just love to sing. But I didn't get a chance to really shine until I got into high school. I was always too nervous to audition prior to that, so when I got into high school I found out that I could just take the class Girls' Glee without auditioning. So that's when I really started singing more. I was in Girls' Glee for three years before my teacher really listened to my voice and requested I'd be in a special class. I also started doing talent shows in high school and met some girls, and we ended up forming a group. We called ourselves Chanteuse, and I knew from then on I wanted to be a singer. So we did some shows around the Detroit area, performing Top 40 R & B. Anita Baker and Phyllis Hyman were some of my favourite singers. We did a lot of Gladys Knight, Phyllis Hyman, Linda Baker, Pointer Sisters. But then I would go out and sit in on jam sessions, and there was one particular jam session on the East side of Detroit. I used to go see the soul band, a bunch of white boys, and they called themselves the Chisel Brothers. Well, somebody told them I could sing, and so they asked me would I get up and do background. And eventually, after singing with them so many times background, the audience started yelling out, "Let the girl sing lead." But I only knew one blues song, and that was 'Stormy Monday'. So every time I go back, I sing 'Stormy Monday'. Eventually the leader of the band asked me to join them. He said, "But I don't do Top 40, I do soul music and blues. Can you handle that?" So I went into my momma's records and I pulled out a whole roster of stuff, and my momma even helped me have some older Aretha Franklin tunes and Etta James, and you know, Denise LaSalle and all of the old soul songs that I used to sing or hear when I was a little girl. I started listening to more Etta James and Bessie Smith, and Ida Cox and all of the older blues artists that I had never even listened to before. That's how I became a blues singer. I was a single mom. My daughter was five years old and I wanted to put her in a private school, so I needed money. And so it came along right on time. I started realizing that the music was related to what I had been living as a single mom going in and out of bad relationships. I knew what the blues was, but at the time that I started singing the blues, I used to think of it as my mother's music and I wasn't really into it. But once I started singing it, and feeling the emotion in the music, I realized that I didn't choose the blues. The blues chose me.

I started writing music right after I'd been with the Chisel Brothers for about ten years. They wrote all the music, and we put out *Chisel Brothers Featuring Thornetta Davis*. We did a lot of touring gigging with this particular album, and I learned a lot about singing original tunes, but I didn't write anything until after 1996. I ended up getting signed to a label called Sub Pop. They wanted to have me work with an alternative rock band named Big Chief. I had done background on their album, and the label liked me so much that they decided to want to record me. And so here I am, a blues singer and now turning into an alternative rock artist. It was the mid-90s and that was what was hot at the time, and I didn't want to turn down the opportunity of being on a label. So I decided to record my first solo album, *Sunday Morning Music*. It was released in 1996 and it turned out to be a great experience. At the same time I was in a bad relationship, but that inspired me to start writing some of the songs on *Sunday Morning Music*. I wrote because I was in that situation. One of the songs, 'Cry', which I co-wrote with Al Sutton, ended up on the TV show *The Sopranos*.

So some good things came out of it. I started writing, I started getting more exposure and I started travelling more with Big Chief while I was promoting the album. Only thing is, after that year I wasn't inspired to write any more songs for another album. I just wanted to go back home and raise my daughter. So the label and I decided to part ways. And by the time my daughter graduated in 2000, I decided to form my own band. And we started performing regularly at a local club downtown, the Music Menu. We were there for maybe five years. Every Wednesday night it was a party. And so one day I decided, hey, let's just record one night and see what happens. And it's basically me singing all of my favourite cover songs, stuff that I've been performing for years. That's what we called the album: *Covered Live at the Music Menu*. And that album actually got me out of the city of Detroit, and I started doing tours over in Europe. I started performing in Italy and all over Canada, and everybody would get a chance to hear me.

And so I thank God that I was able to do that particular album, but I was still continuing to write my own music and perform it. I would play songs that were not recorded, and every time I would sing an original tune, I would say, "This is going to be on my next album" – not knowing that it was going to take twenty years to complete *Honest Woman*. But I do believe it was right on time. I'd much rather perform music than going to the studio. That's why it took me so long to record it. I used to think that I needed a producer, so I had the ideal producer in mind, and he was well known, won plenty of Grammys. The songs were good, and I just assumed that if I did get a chance to perform with him, that he'd be interested. But that's not how life goes. And I was kinda disappointed in the beginning, but then I realized that I had to have faith in myself and so I decided to go on to the studio and produce the album myself. I knew what musicians I wanted to work with. I knew how I wanted the songs to go. I knew what I wanted on the songs. And so it took me a while, because I'm an independent artist. I just had to pay for it one song at a time.

But eventually I got the album done, and now *Honest Woman* is better than I thought it could ever be. This album has won awards, it's got me nominated for international awards, and I didn't think that would happen. I like performing all over the world and I'm getting ready to go to Italy again, and Denmark, and all of this off the strength of an album that took me twenty years to write. That's why I know I heard the old saying, it may not be when you want it, but it could be always right on time. And that's how I feel about my musical career. I may not be rich or famous all over the world, but I do this thing for a living and I feel so thankful and blessed to be able to do this.

I've gotten to work with artists like Larry McCray, the producer from Eight Mile, Louie Resto. I've gotten to work with all of Detroit's great artists. Marcus Belgrave is on my album. When I started recording, I didn't think that I'd get Kim Wilson. So if you just step out on faith and go for what you want, anything is possible. 'Honest Woman', I wrote that song for my husband James. I had known of him for twenty years, but we didn't see each other in that light, and at the time that we started dating, it was the right time. And now he's in the band too.

I believe that God has a plan and I pray that I'm just doing what he has planned for me to do. I believe that what you put out you get back. So when God gave me the gift to sing, I wanted to use it to the best of my ability and I don't wanna abuse it. And he's done so many great things for me. I raised a daughter, as a single mom, put her through college, and now she's going to be a mother. I got the husband of my dreams, my health and life partner. I sing for a living and I got the greatest band of friends performing with me and the girls from Chanteuse. Now they sing with me and that's something that I've been dreaming of since I started singing. I don't know where this journey is gonna take me, but I look forward to doing greater things.

Chicago Blues Festival

DEITRA FARR

Deitra Farr is considered one of Chicago 's top vocalists, according to *Living Blues Magazine* (May 1997). Fiery, energetic, and soul-stirring describes this woman, who has over the years been nominated for Traditional Female Blues artist of the year by the W.C. Handy Awards, Female Blues Artist of the year by the Living Blues Critics Awards, the British Blues Connection Awards, and the Les Trophees France Blues awards. In 2015 Deitra was inducted into the Chicago Blues Hall of Fame as a "Legendary Blues Artist". In 2016 the National Southern Soul Foundation gave Deitra "The Most Popular Blues Artist Award". Deitra is the recipient of the 2017 Jus' Blues Music Foundation's Koko Taylor Queen of the Blues Award.

This Chicago native began her career in 1975, singing with local soul bands, before starting her blues career in the early 1980s. When Deitra was 18 years old, she recorded the lead vocals on Mill Street Depo's record *You Won't Support Me*. That record was a Cashbox Top 100 R & B hit in 1976. Over thirty years later, that recording has been re-released and is popular again worldwide.

In 1983, Deitra began her blues career working at the major Chicago blues clubs, such as the Kingston Mines, the Wise Fool's Pub and Blue Chicago. She also toured the US and Canada with the Sam Lay Blues Band. From 1993 to 1996, Deitra was the lead singer with Mississippi Heat, recording two CDs with this all-star group. In 1997, Deitra resumed her own solo career, continuing to sing blues, while reaching back to her soul music roots. After recording on eight previous CD projects with others, she recorded her first solo CD, *The Search Is Over*, for the London-based JSP records. In 2005, Deitra released her second JSP CD *Let it Go!*.

The multi-talented Deitra Farr is also a published writer, poet, songwriter, and painter. A graduate of Columbia College (Bachelor of Arts in Journalism), Deitra has recorded many of her own compositions and has written articles for the *Chicago Daily Defender*, *The Chicago Blues Annual*, and the Italian blues magazine *Il Blues*. Currently she has a column "Artist to Artist" in *Living Blues Magazine*.

In 1990, Deitra represented the Chicago Tourism Bureau in Düsseldorf, Germany and has toured England, Wales, Iceland, Finland, Norway, Canada, Holland, Belgium, France, Switzerland, Monaco, Italy, Slovenia, Greece, Israel, Austria, Latvia, Portugal, Sweden, Mexico, Guadeloupe, Lebanon, Spain, Denmark, United Arab Emirates (Abu Dhabi and Dubai), Qatar, Hungary, Czech Republic, Poland, Scotland, Argentina, Brazil, Croatia, Japan, Macedonia, Serbia, Russia, Armenia and Romania.

Deitra toured Europe with the 2000 Chicago Blues Festival with Lil Ed and the Blues Imperials. In 2003, Deitra completed a six week British tour with Otis Grand and Bobby Parker, as the American Festival of the Blues II. She did the 2004 Chicago Blues Festival

European tour with Jody Williams and Andrew "Jr Boy" Jones. From 2006 to 2010 Deitra has toured with the Women of Chicago Blues project with Zora Young and Grana' Louise. Since 2013, Deitra often tours Europe with Raphael Wressnig's Soul Gift tour, which included Alex Schultz, Enrico Crivellaro, Silvio Berger and Sax Gordon.

Deitra is also performing as a member of the all-star blues group Chicago Wind, along with harmonica great Matthew Skoller.

HOW DID YOU START IN MUSIC?

I started singing as a child. My professional career began in 1975, singing with a large soul band called Central Power System. I was 17 years old.

WHO WERE/ARE YOUR INFLUENCES?

I am influenced by soul music, gospel music and blues. Motown and Hi Records. Diana Ross, Aretha Franklin, Billie Holiday, Muddy Waters, Little Walter, Al Green, Wilson Pickett, Clara Ward, Mahalia Jackson, James Cleveland… many influences of several genres.

WHY CHOOSE THE BLUES?

I loved blues all of my life, thanks to my father playing it in the house. Blues chose me.

HOW WOULD YOU DESCRIBE YOUR APPROACH?

I just do me…

HOW DO YOU START MAKING MUSIC? WHAT IS YOUR PROCESS?

When the words or the melody come to me, I write them down or record them.

WHICH DO YOU PREFER – PLAYING LIVE OR BEING IN A STUDIO? WHY?

I prefer live. I like the energy of an audience.

HOW DO YOU FIND THE RIGHT MUSIC PRODUCER FOR A RECORD?

I self-produce, so the right producer would be someone who allows me to be me.

ARE AUDIENCES DIFFERENT AROUND THE WORLD?

They either love you or they don't. Different nights bring different results.

DESCRIBE YOUR JOURNEY AS AN ARTIST/MUSICIAN/SINGER.

It has been an amazing journey. Blues has taken a girl from the South Side of Chicago all over the world. So far I have sung in 45 foreign countries, which to me is amazing.

WHAT WERE THE HIGHLIGHTS?

My favourite gig ever was singing with a gospel group on the main square of Mexico City. I will never as long as I live forget the emotions of the people.

WHAT WERE THE CHALLENGES?

The challenge for me has been being accepted. I did not fit the stereotypes in a few areas, so some people had trouble accepting me in the blues industry. The real blues legends loved me, and that's why I kept going.

HOW DO YOU PROMOTE YOUR IMAGE/YOUR BRAND?

I spend a lot of time on Facebook. It has opened lots of doors for me.

ARE THERE PRESSURES ON WOMEN TO LOOK A CERTAIN WAY?

The dress code has changed since my career started. You can wear just about anything now. When I started you needed to look like a star… you and the band.

HOW DO YOU DEAL WITH OBSTACLES SUCH AS AGEISM, SEXISM AND RACISM?

I ignore all of it… if it is there. Those issues will always be there.

WHERE DO YOU SEE YOUR MUSIC GOING NEXT?

I'm working on my CD/book project. I move slowly, but it will happen. I will continue to sing where I am wanted.

Chicago Blues Festival

Chicago Blues Festival

IVY FORD

Ivy Ford is a singer, musician, entertainer. Born and raised in Waukegan, Illinois, she is quite the up-and-coming artist of the Chicago blues and live music scene. At 13, Ivy Ford started performing live with Kenosha-based band the Real Deal, managed by Steve Rainey, and since then continues to nurture her niche and calling to the music. She plays the piano, alto saxophone, drums, bass guitar and guitar. In late 2012, Ford joined a local blues band, which in time evolved into Ivy Ford and the Cadillacs. In 2015, she opened for the legendary Buddy Guy at his club in Chicago, and has shared the stage with J.B. Ritchie, Joe Moss, Toronzo Cannon and Tom Holland. She has released four albums to date: *Simply Solo* (2016), *Time to Shine* (2018), *NYE 2018 Live at Mickey Finns Brewery* (2018) and *Harvesting My Roots* (2019). When not fronting her own band, Ivy regularly plays with Chicago Blues Hall of Fame inductee J.B. Ritchie.

HOW DID YOU START IN MUSIC?

It sounds clichéd, but I was probably singing before I could talk. So, from being a toddler, music was always attractive to me. My first time performing for an audience was when I was five years old in kindergarten, and I must admit I sang a Britney Spears song. Since then I jumped at any opportunity to perform that came my way. By the time I reached junior high school I became very involved in musical theatre, and upon graduating high school my intentions were to get a degree in just that. However, it was during that time, and even earlier, when I was around twelve years old or so, my mom was taking me to see live music via local festivals and events that showcased local musicians. One band was called Real Deal. They were out of Kenosha, Wisconsin, and the drummer/band manager, Steve "Rainman" Rainey had seen a promise in me, and quite honestly I believe him taking me under his wing (hiring me here and there to sing) is the biggest factor that laid the foundation for what I do now. I wasn't performing with an instrument then, but by that time I had been teaching myself the piano for a year or two and was in the school band, marching and jazz. It wouldn't be until several years later at twenty that I would pick up the electric guitar, bass and drums. I am 26 years old now.

WHO WERE/ARE YOUR INFLUENCES?

I remember when Alicia Keys came out with her hit 'Fallin''. I was a fan immediately. I believe she was only 16 or so when it came out, so as an aspiring musician, specifically a piano player and also being a multiracial female, I was hooked. I absolutely love Norah Jones for her sound and her writing as well. One of my all-time favourite artists is Lady Day herself, Miss Billie Holiday. My dad turned me on to her when I was a young kid. And actually in hindsight, when I think about it, I remember my mom playing blues records and things back then too. I love Billie Holiday naturally for her voice itself, but it's so much more than that. The phrasing and delivery of how she sings a story to the listener is untouchable. Also, being a woman and a woman of colour in her time must have taken confidence, moxy and all-round mojo, which I know of first-hand; being a woman in the blues myself, I have so much more respect.

Since becoming a guitar player, I think my biggest influences and aspirations are Freddie King, Memphis Minnie, and naturally I love Buddy Guy. I'm lucky to be alive in a time where there are current performers and artists that I'm always in awe of and whose style I love, like Mike Wheeler, Toronzo Cannon, Joanna Connor, Luke Pytel and another Chicago-based artist and friend we lost way too soon: Michael Ledbetter. I'm proud to say I've gotten to play with these artists and always have a "first row seat" to their shows. However there are a few right now that are on my "Ivy's Mix Tape" list. I'm so diggin' Eric Gales these days! Oh and I think I couldn't be a musician if I didn't fangirl and have an admiration for the one and only PRINCE.

WHY CHOOSE THE BLUES?

Really I just kind of fell into it and it fit just right. Like I said, when I first started even singing I was "pop music princess" through and through. However, I was always exposed to all music at a young age. I remember my mom would play everything from Little Milton's 'The Blues Is Alright' to Luther Vandross's 'Never Too Much'.

I started getting my first-hand experience with blues going to open jams locally and sitting in with folks, and like I said, it just felt right. It wasn't long before I was diving in head first, submerging myself in the genre. Plus, blues and roots music *is* an American creation. And its history runs deep with lots of different roots and branches of where it's been, how it has been or is being modified depending on who is playing it and where they're from. Music should tell a story, and blues music is a story of life. It's a social commentary of the everyday people. So I think the audience can relate, because the themes of blues music is so common, and that connection is its magic.

HOW WOULD YOU DESCRIBE YOUR APPROACH?

I pride myself on my showmanship. I stand by on being a good musician, meaning I know my notes, and I'm blessed to have a natural ability to do what I love. When people ask me or say, "So you're pretty good," I jokingly say, "Well they keep paying me to do it, so I must be doing something right." I think I'm lucky because I do genuinely feel confident (at least usually) when I'm on stage, so it allows me to be that catalyst to include my audience, listeners and fans in this experience of my music and performance.

My biggest goal in my music and performances is to make people feel something. Generally I prefer to make them feel good, but I want them to leave my shows feeling they've "been somewhere". There's a certain pulse, heartbeat or meter, let's say, that goes up and down sideways and frontways, and by the end of a show everyone's back into the "station" to step off that train. Of course I hope they want to get another ticket to ride!

DO YOU WRITE OR COMPOSE YOUR OWN MATERIAL?

Yes I do. I started writing as young as twelve years old or so. I was that cliché making music in my mom's basement at one point. I'm proud to say I actually have three albums of my original music. Some of them are not traditional blues, but my most recent album, *Harvesting My Roots*, has been I think the most impactful in my life both personal and professional. It has a more traditional blues quality, while being very appealing to a younger genre and audience, I feel.

HOW DO YOU START MAKING MUSIC? WHAT IS YOUR PROCESS?

I don't have a regime I stick to every time I write. I've written songs where I had a melody in my head first and then added words. Sometimes it's the other way around. I've written my "best" songs all at once within twenty minutes, and for others I've had the lyrics for a few years but still haven't completed a song. You got to take and run with it when something comes to you.

WHICH DO YOU PREFER — PLAYING LIVE OR BEING IN A STUDIO? WHY?

So, when I play live not only is there that pulse thing I was talking about onstage with my fellow bandmates, but your audience has the ability to feed you this energy, and honestly if you ask me, that's a "drug" that gives you a high that is off the charts. I didn't really enjoy per se my first experiences in the studio, but it was really because it's the opposite of performing live. First off, there is no audience, so you have to almost recreate that "playing live" feeling, but all in your head. Plus, recording on a track, your every nuance, good and bad, is like being combed with a fine tooth comb underneath a microscope. Then, because for once you don't have that white noise of bottles clinking on the bar rail, traffic noise outside the stage door or even the humming of a speaker plugged into a faulty outlet, you hear every single flaw. So it's safe to say the experience is, well, intimidating.

But the more I've spent time in the studio the better I've been able to calibrate myself to a point that I actually do enjoy it now. Especially during recording *Harvesting My Roots*, I had a good idea of what kind of sound I was looking for, and I was very confident and direct in what I wanted, so that in itself allowed me to enjoy the process. By then I knew how my voice carried on a studio microphone. I wasn't afraid to listen to myself, vocally or on guitar, so crisply. And it was always a plus that my bandmates and I had been really working hard on coming in with a bang, so we were able to get right to work. Dave Axen (drums) and Willie Rauch (bass) are honestly two of the greatest people I know. We genuinely enjoy each other's company, conversations and jokes. Oh, and that's right, they're really first-class musicians.

HOW DO YOU FIND THE RIGHT MUSIC PRODUCER FOR A RECORD?

Well, considering I've yet to trust someone else to produce my work, I'd say it can be a pretty labouring task. Since two years old I've always known what I want, when I want, and plan on doing it myself to ensure that it happens. The same goes with producing a record. A producer's job is to basically be "the coach", calling the plays, and they can also be the one that picks up the cheque, so then in some ways they're entitled to do so. So in picking a producer you have to trust that not only they have your best interest in mind as an artist, but also that they can deliver. It's one thing to talk the talk, but the proof is in the pudding. For example, say you as an artist write a song and you want to record it solo on acoustic guitar, a producer could insist that you pick it up on electric, add horns, backup singers and cowbell. OK, maybe that's a little drastic, but it could happen. Now you could say no, but then remember they're the ones that are pulling out their wallets to front that project, so things could get "funny". I know there are great producers out there, but what I'm saying is sometimes it might be best to try and do something on your own and give yourself a chance to find yourself on your own time without other hands in the kitchen. That way you know exactly who you are and what you want, when say a producer does approach you. Then you'll be ready.

ARE AUDIENCES DIFFERENT AROUND THE WORLD?

Audiences can be different depending on the time of day, haha. I will say this: blues and Americana music is definitely more appreciated overseas. Not that people don't like what I do when I'm close to home, or even just in the States generally. But there's a gratitude from fans I meet from other countries that is greater than folks that live close. It could be that "local" audiences feel they already get the milk "for free", so they don't have to buy the cow. Again, there are many exceptions to this ironic circumstance, but I know that, for me, I'm more respected when I "leave home."

DO YOU HAVE A FAVOURITE VENUE? WHY?

Buddy Guy's Legends. It's the world's premier blues club. Admittedly, my very first show in Chicago with my own band was there. January 11th, 2015, I opened for Buddy Guy himself. I didn't know that night would be the first of several on which Buddy would get on stage with me and share a tune or two with me. The last time I was at Legends Buddy said to me, "They kept asking me to get on stage with you, but I didn't want to. Girl, I was scared, because you play that guitar like I don't know what."

Another greatest moment and venue that holds a special place in my heart is the Orpheum Theater in Memphis, Tennessee. We competed in the 2019 International Blues Challenge. We ranked top 8 in the world and therefore got a twenty-five-minute showcase set. What a stage, what a theatre, what a night! And of course I got to share my original music, which was to become my current album, *Harvesting My Roots*, with many that night!

DESCRIBE YOUR JOURNEY AS AN ARTIST/MUSICIAN/SINGER.

It's still ongoing. Of course there's ups and downs. I'm lucky I usually have more of the former than the latter. Although a lot of success can result from being in the right place at the right time with the right people, it's just as important to make sure you're applying yourself. Taking on every opportunity big or… well actually every opportunity is big to "show up and show out". The more I perform and the more I write, compose and produce, the more I find new things about myself. Therefore I like to think I just keep getting better.

WHAT WERE THE HIGHLIGHTS?

The first one has to be opening for Buddy Guy as my initial break into the Chicago circuit. Most recently I just opened for Robert Cray at the Arcada Theater in St Charles, Illinois. Also, each time people come to me and reach out to let me know what their favourite song is of mine. When they put in requests of songs that I wrote. The "little" things that fans sometimes think are irrelevant and don't mean much to me, like saying "I had a job interview and I played your song 'Time to Shine', because it really just lifted me up and prepped me for a confident interview", are really the memories that last a lifetime. That's what keeps me going and feeling like I'm doing something right.

WHAT WERE THE CHALLENGES?

Well I'd be lying if I said the challenges don't entice me. Maybe it's the competitive or personal drive that I've had since being about five years old. They're clichéd but true. I definitely have to push through sometimes being such a young person in this genre. There's been times when people I work with may not take me as seriously right out of the gate because I am so young. They quickly realize I mean business when it comes to showtime, contracts, what I do. Being a female guitarist can be a double-edged sword. More often than not, I'm fortunate in that people think it's really cool and impressive, because you don't see as many female electric-guitar players. Some people get their nose out of joint, but usually it's other male guitarists who quite honestly are just intimidated by us women! However, their insecurities have nothing to do with us. The real kickass guitar players ain't worried about anyone dimming their spotlight – you wanna know why? Because they are too busy being rock stars and being great. I love it!

IS THERE ONE SONG THAT IS CLOSEST TO YOUR HEART?

There are many, just depends which way my heart is feeling. However, one that is always close is one of mine, 'Whiskey Love'. It's on my recent album *Harvesting My Roots*. Funny thing is, I originally recorded it about four or more years ago, and it had a different feel completely. Also, I really drink whiskey. But the themes and words are very reflective of experiences that have happened and do happen in my life. I'm sure many others can relate, and they must do, because that's probably one of my fans' favourites.

IS THERE ONE ARTIST WHO HAS TRULY INSPIRED YOU?

There are many. I have a two-year-old daughter, Vivian. I played just as much as usual while being pregnant up until about three weeks before I gave birth. My last show was at Navy Pier. She was born July 16th, and about three or so weeks later she was with momma at the Crossroads Blues Festival. So I'm a professional musician, a woman and a mom. Another world-renowned artist, Joanna Connor, was doing the same thing when she was my age. Only difference is she had two children. She is still rockin' and bluesin' more than ever, and actually, when I was 19, before I knew who she was and way before I knew I would be looking after a two-year-old, I opened up for her too. I'm honoured now to be able to call her a peer and be considered an equal. Through the luxury of modern technology and social media, Joanna and I do get to share conversations and see each other's accomplishments and travels.

HOW DO YOU DEAL WITH OBSTACLES SUCH AS AGEISM, SEXISM AND RACISM?

Honestly, I just go and do the damn thing. Usually the people "in the business" that I want to be working with do not create a problem from any of these perspectives. And that's cool because all three and more apply: I'm twenty-six years old and started playing live music at darn near twelve, so there's that. Yes, I am a woman, chick, girl or whatever other nickname you call females. I am a person of colour. I'm African-American and Caucasian. So I catch a mean tan in the summertime and look peaked and sickly in the middle of winter because of less sun exposure (but who doesn't have vitamin D deficiency in the Midwest?).

I try not to let those issues get to me when ignorant people present a problem. Maybe I'm naive, but I am definitely strong-headed, or maybe, like I said earlier, I don't mind the challenge. I mean, if you don't have to work for something a little bit and it doesn't make you anxious or nervous, is it really worth it? But lucky for me, in the big opportunities that I get, that's not even a factor.

IS IT IMPORTANT TO UNDERSTAND THE BUSINESS SIDE OF THE INDUSTRY?

You are your best advocate. How can you protect yourself if you don't know what the heck is going on? Again with the clichés, we've all heard the stories of artists making all this money from recordings, etc., etc., but they never see a dime. It is important to understand it and not be afraid to stand up for yourself, ask questions or disagree with something you don't like. What's the worst that can happen, someone tells you "no" in response? Well then it wasn't meant to be, and now you can go to the next one.

ARE AWARDS HELPFUL?

I'm not gonna lie: they are nice. As an artist, it does make you feel some sort of validation of what you're doing aside from still working and performing. They are not everything and, depending on the award, you're at the mercy of a select group's "opinion" of you. So don't be afraid to appreciate an award that you get. But on the flip side, don't make yourself miserable or feel inadequate just because you may not have won an award. The world goes on, people still listen to music and more than likely they're still coming to your shows and buying your music, so take a deep breath, exhale, #keepcalmandblueson.

WHERE DO YOU SEE YOUR MUSIC GOING NEXT?

The sky is the limit. I want to keep on pushing the boundaries and limits of the blues genre in order to broaden its audience. Like I said, now that I'm starting to almost enjoy the recording and studio process, I feel inspired to write more and do my music. I look forward to the life experiences to come. My ultimate goal is to only play and perform because I want to, not because I need the work. So I'm striving to obtain and maintain a sense of conventionalism and stability with a career choice that for most would terrify them. I don't want to jinx myself, but I think I'm on the right path and the combination of luck, opportunity and perseverance is helping me to accomplish those things.

Chicago Women in the Blues at Reggie's, Chicago, Illinois

Blues Heaven Festival, Frederikshavn, Denmark

RUTHIE FOSTER

Ruthie Foster was born in 1964 and grew up in Gause, Texas. She was in the church choir singing solo by the age of 14, and subsequently went to college to study music and sound engineering. She then joined the Navy, where she performed with the Navy Band. After leaving the Navy, Foster moved to New York, where she began playing in folk clubs, eventually signing a deal with Atlantic Records. In 1993 she returned home to care for her sick mother for a few years, before resuming her music career and releasing her first album, *Full Circle*, in 1997.

In 2010, her album *The Truth According to Ruthie Foster* received a Grammy nomination for Best Contemporary Blues Album. In 2012, *Live at Antone's* won the Blues Music Awards' DVD of the Year Award. Other notable awards include: Contemporary Blues Female Artist of the Year 2010 (Blues Music Awards), Blues Artist of the Year (Female) 2010 (Living Blues Critics' Poll), Koko Taylor Award for Traditional Blues Female Artist of the Year 2011, 2012, 2013, 2015, 2016, 2018, 2019, and induction into the Texas Music Hall of Fame 2019 (Austin Music Awards).

HOW DID YOU START IN MUSIC?

I started singing gospel in churches around Texas as a young girl. I learned to play piano and at ten years old taught myself guitar.

WHO WERE/ARE YOUR INFLUENCES?

I listened to a lot of Mahalia Jackson, Aretha Franklin. Also, Phoebe Snow, Stevie Wonder and many others.

WHY CHOOSE THE BLUES?

The blues chose me!

HOW WOULD YOU DESCRIBE YOUR APPROACH?

I approach everything I sing or play with the utmost compassion for the song itself with every performance.

DO YOU WRITE OR COMPOSE YOUR OWN MATERIAL?

Yes.

HOW DO YOU START MAKING MUSIC? WHAT IS YOUR PROCESS?

I usually start with playing an instrument first, guitar or sometimes piano. I add lyrics as I go. But it's not unusual to start with a title once in a while.

WHICH DO YOU PREFER – PLAYING LIVE OR BEING IN A STUDIO? WHY?

I prefer live audience over singing in a studio. With a live audience I get immediate feedback, and it's more interactive.

HOW DO YOU FIND THE RIGHT MUSIC PRODUCER FOR A RECORD?

Every producer has a signature sound, whether that's the result of the group of musicians they hire or their particular recording process. I look for what a producer can bring to my own music.

ARE AUDIENCES DIFFERENT AROUND THE WORLD?

Yes! They truly are, depending on the venue, the culture, demographics and so on.

DO YOU HAVE A FAVOURITE VENUE? WHY?

I have several. They know who they are and why!

DESCRIBE YOUR JOURNEY AS AN ARTIST/MUSICIAN/SINGER.

I started out as a pianist/singer and songwriter of mostly gospel music in churches and surrounding communities in Central Texas as a pre-teen. Afterwards, I was mostly a self-taught guitar player while learning folk, blues and soul music and also writing original songs. I studied music and graduated with a commercial music degree, with emphasis on voice. I then joined the military and became a vocalist for the Navy Band Pride in Charleston, South Carolina, doing all genres from big band to pop and soul music. I moved to New York in the late 90s and was signed with Atlantic Records. I honed the craft of songwriting while doing a lot of vocal session work. I then moved back to Texas in the 90s and started recording my own music again, and I have been since.

WHAT WERE THE HIGHLIGHTS?

Signing with a major record label, Atlantic Records, and getting the chance to live and work as a musician in New York City and record with various entertainers like Nona Hendrix, Robert Cray. Of course being nominated for three Grammy Awards is a big highlight!

WHAT WERE THE CHALLENGES?

My challenges have been learning how to keep my focus. I have a lot of hats that I wear in my life. I'm a mother. I like to keep up and visit with my family when I'm not travelling with music.

IS THERE ONE SONG THAT IS CLOSEST TO YOUR HEART?

There are many, but I will always enjoy performing 'Phenomenal Woman'. It's a poem written by Maya Angelou (set to music by Amy Sky). It's a beautiful anthem about empowerment for women.

IS THERE ONE ARTIST WHO HAS TRULY INSPIRED YOU?

Mavis Staples.

HOW DO YOU PROMOTE YOUR IMAGE/YOUR BRAND?

I try to put out quality music that I truly believe in and hope that it makes a difference in somebody's life, even if just for the ninety minutes that I'm onstage. I make music that moves me and hope that it does the same for others.

HOW DO YOU DEAL WITH OBSTACLES SUCH AS AGEISM, SEXISM AND RACISM?

Those are only obstacles if one allows them to become so. Any situation concerning ageism, sexism or racism could, and has in my life experience, become an opportunity to educate. You teach people how to treat you.

IS IT IMPORTANT TO UNDERSTAND THE BUSINESS SIDE OF THE INDUSTRY?

Absolutely. I'm still learning!

ARE AWARDS HELPFUL?

Though I'm grateful for being acknowledged by my peers in this industry via awards and recognition, I've found that they are not necessary and in no way proof of anyone's worth as a great musician.

WHERE DO YOU SEE YOUR MUSIC GOING NEXT?

Wherever it wants to go. I'm staying open to all possibilities.

Chicago Blues Festival

Brooks Blues Bar, London

DANA GILLESPIE

Dana Gillespie was born in 1949 in Woking, Surrey. She began recording in the mid-1960s, starting out in the folk genre before branching out into pop, achieving success with her 1965 single 'Thank You Boy'. Since then she has released nearly seventy albums, mainly in the blues genre, her first musical love. A brief foray into rock in the 70s saw David Bowie write the song 'Andy Warhol' for Gillespie, released on her album *Weren't Born a Man* (1973).

In addition to her music career, she has also worked extensively as a stage and film actress, primarily in the 1970s and 1980s. For three years she sang with the Austrian Mojo Blues Band, and now fronts the London Blues Band. She began releasing blues records with Ace Records in 1982, with *Blue Job*, and has continued recording for them ever since, with albums including, among others: *Below the Belt* (1984), *Sweet Meat* (1989), *Experienced* (2000), *Staying Power* (2003), *Live with the London Blues Band* (2007), *I Rest My Case* (2010), *Cat's Meow* (2014) and her latest release *Under My Bed* (2019).

She founded a charity blues festival on the Caribbean island of Mustique, which is held annually in the first week of January and has attracted many high-profile blues performers. She was voted Top British Female Blues Vocalist by the *British Blues Connection* and *Blueprint* Magazine between 1992 and 1996 and has now been elevated into their Hall of Fame.

HOW DID YOU START IN MUSIC?

I was lucky to be growing up in the 60s in London, so I started my career as a drummer in a band, and then a folk singer as I couldn't afford my own band – and anyway folk was "in" at this time, so I could go out and strum my twelve-string guitar in folk clubs. I had piano lessons from the age of seven, and also learned the viola while at school, but moved on to guitar as I needed to accompany myself to get gigs. David Bowie taught me some of my first chords, learned on an old nylon-string Spanish guitar. A bit later I moved on to much better instruments!

WHEN DID YOU START SINGING OR PLAYING AN INSTRUMENT?

I started writing songs from the age of eleven, so I needed to sing them in order to get them heard. I heard an LP by a drummer called Sandy Nelson, and he spurred me on to drumming, but then came Joe Morello who played with the Dave Brubeck Quartet. I also started learning Brubeck on piano from the age of twelve.

WHO WERE/ARE YOUR INFLUENCES?

Life was my main influence, as the 60s were so great. I was listening to blues, folk and jazz, but if I had to take just a few LPs onto a desert island with me, I'd take Howling Wolf, Muddy Waters, Bessie Smith and Etta James… the usual suspects. But this quartet moved me enough to check out all the other great performers, too numerous to name.

WHY CHOOSE THE BLUES?

Blues seemed the most real type of music that seems to come straight from the heart, via sweat, sex, fun and broken hearts, and this was a perfect vehicle for growing up to.

HOW WOULD YOU DESCRIBE YOUR APPROACH?

Approach to what? Life? Music? I've always been fearless when it comes to what I love, and music has always been my God since my earliest memories.

DO YOU WRITE OR COMPOSE YOUR OWN MATERIAL?

The only way I could get my songs heard was by singing them, and I was signed as a songwriter to many different publishers from the age of sixteen. It is very rare for me to sing someone else's material, unless the words convey what I would've said myself. I like to keep things real, which means I'd never sing a song like 'I'd Rather Go Blind', as there is no way I'd give up my eyesight just because some man I was involved with was seen with another woman. That's a load of bollocks, as I'm no longer fooled by transitory love situations… one of the joys of getting older!

HOW DO YOU START MAKING MUSIC? WHAT IS YOUR PROCESS?

Everything starts with the song and what emotion it will convey. Often I am given backing tracks with no melody but just chord changes, and I love dealing with this and working out what fits best, and it's a really good feeling when the right words come out too. A bit like doing a crossword puzzle but with an end in sight. When I'm in a wicked mood then I like to write songs that are a bit over the top, like 'Fck Blues' (the only thing that's missing is you!) or 'Come on if You're Coming'. This whole thing of risqué blues came about because I went to Ace Records in 1980 and said I wanted to do an LP of this old type of blues, and I told them I wanted to call the LP *Blue Job*! Thankfully they had a sense of humour and said yes, but most blues listeners have a sense of humour!

WHICH DO YOU PREFER – PLAYING LIVE OR BEING IN A STUDIO? WHY?

I like both equally. I've made or been involved with nearly seventy albums in my career, so studio life is where I feel very comfortable, but there is a really good feeling when you know you've done a great gig – but then I have the cream of the UK blues scene in the London Blues Band, and when I work in Europe with the Joachim Palden Trio then

I know I've got the best of boogie players, so it's the musicians that lift me up when it comes to a "live" gig.

HOW DO YOU FIND THE RIGHT MUSIC PRODUCER FOR A RECORD?

In the mid-60s I did an LP with Mike Vernon of Blue Horizon fame, and I since went on to do three more LPs with him – one a decade! But now I prefer to produce myself, as I know what I want, and anyway I get to mix with a great man called Dominique Brethes at Wolf Studios in Brixton. I've been working with him for about thirty years, so it's good when you know you can trust someone else's ears. For the last two CDs I did for Ace Records, I've been co-producing with Jake Zaitz, who also plays guitar in the London Blues Band, and when you know someone really well, it just makes the whole production thing easier and more fun.

ARE AUDIENCES DIFFERENT AROUND THE WORLD?

Basically audiences are the same everywhere, and I've been really lucky through the years to say that I've played all over the world. However, in places like South Korea they clap on the 1 and the 3 – as do the Germans sometimes – but most countries get it right and clap on the 2 and the 4.

DO YOU HAVE A FAVOURITE VENUE? WHY?

I haven't got a favourite venue, although in the early 70s there were far more blues gigs in pubs which had fantastic atmospheres. But now these venues have been turned into poncy wine bars. Shame!

DESCRIBE YOUR JOURNEY AS AN ARTIST/MUSICIAN/SINGER.

I'm just happy to be doing what I always wanted to do, which is sing and write songs, and I've been doing this since I was fifteen, so I've been at it fifty-five years. Lucky me!

WHAT WERE THE HIGHLIGHTS?

There are two gigs that stand out in my memory. One was when I was support act to Bob Dylan in '97. He is such a gentleman, and it's always good to do huge venues, but I'm also happy at the 606 Club in Chelsea, where I often perform – in places like this I can talk more to the audience, in between the songs. However, the most memorable of all my gigs has to be the 70th birthday of Sai Baba, the Indian holy man, and there were nearly a million people in the audience, so it was bigger than Woodstock! They had never heard blues before, so there was a pioneering spirit to it. I also played with my blues band there for his 75th birthday. It was an honour to play in India, and I was the first Western blues band ever to tour there, with twenty-two concerts all over, staying in marvellous hotels. There was the added bonus of the feeling that I was sort of preaching the blues, as not many people had heard of this type of music then, which was about twenty years ago.

WHAT WERE THE CHALLENGES?

The one challenge is to find a decent agent, as they are as rare as rocking horse shit! Where are they?

IS THERE ONE SONG THAT IS CLOSEST TO YOUR HEART?

As I said, I don't often do songs that I haven't written myself, but there is one that always gets a great reaction, and that is 'St Louis Blues'. Everyone knows it, but nearly no one sings it, and it's one I know always gets a good reaction.

HOW DO YOU PROMOTE YOUR IMAGE/YOUR BRAND?

I don't promote as well as I should, as I'm not into all that social media world, but I

Brooks Blues Bar, London

wish I had someone to do it for me, as I'd rather look at a sunrise or read a book than sit and stare at a screen – but don't forget I'm old school!

ARE THERE PRESSURES ON WOMEN TO LOOK A CERTAIN WAY?

At my age, I don't get any pressure, but I didn't get much when I was younger either, only when I did some of my Hammer films in the 70s did anyone care about how I looked, and it was usually to do with my bust! I've never judged anyone by how they look, but then I'm not a man, and men fall in love with their eyes, whereas women fall in love with their ears.

HOW DO YOU DEAL WITH OBSTACLES SUCH AS AGEISM, SEXISM AND RACISM?

I guess the only thing I might have to deal with is when to let the henna grow out of my hair, as women with white hair don't exist in this business, except for Emmylou Harris – but she went white in her twenties. I don't encounter racism in the blues, but I don't often go to America, where it might be around – but Europe is pretty cool about things like race.

IS IT IMPORTANT TO UNDERSTAND THE BUSINESS SIDE OF THE INDUSTRY?

Can one ever understand it? It's not my forte, but I get by…

ARE AWARDS HELPFUL?

Awards are helpful only if you win them, but there's not much happening in the blues world and it's usually dominated by Americans.

WHERE DO YOU SEE YOUR MUSIC GOING NEXT?

As long as I can keep writing songs, recording and doing gigs, then I'm happy. That's been my life since I was sixteen, and so I don't know or want anything else.

TIA GOUTTEBEL

Tia is a French blues singer and guitar player. She started touring with her own band, Tia & The Patient Wolves, in 2002. She recorded several EPs and two albums, *Foggy Head, Warm Heart* (2007) and *Travellin' with My Guitar* (2011). Later came *Lil' Bird* (2017) under her sole name, Tia. She received the Cognac Blues Passions Award in 2012. Today, while still heading her own band, Tia & Her Band, she also tours solo, and as a duo, Tia & The Groove Box, with percussionist Marc Glomeau.

Besides, in 2012, she started playing with Gilles Chabenat (hurdy gurdy) and Marc Glomeau (percussions) in a trio called Hypnotic Wheels – which later became Muddy Gurdy – recording two albums so far, *Hypnotic Wheels* (2014) and the critically acclaimed *Muddy Gurdy* (2018). They won the Coup de Cœur Musiques du Monde (World Music Award) from the prestigious Académie Charles Cros and were finalists for the Blues Prize from the just as prestigious Académie du Jazz.

Throughout her career, she performed at festivals in France, Belgium, the UK, the Netherlands, Switzerland, the US and Poland. She has opened for Charlie Musselwhite, Ben Harper, John Mayall, Jimmy Johnson, Angela Brown, Beverly Jo Scott and many more. She also shared the stage with the likes of Joe Louis Walker, Tad Robinson, Alex Schultz, Kirk Fletcher, Cedric Burnside, Skip Martin (Kool & The Gang), Murali Coryell, Rick Estrin, Al Blake, Lynwood Slim and Larry Garner.

TIA GOUTTEBEL – IN HER OWN WORDS

I started playing music when I was six. My mum asked us – my two sisters and I – if we wanted to try out an instrument. She wasn't a musician herself, hadn't learnt music, but she had the desire to offer us a chance to take up sport or music. I picked the guitar. She enrolled me in a two-day workshop to discover the instrument – how magical for a six-year-old girl! I enjoyed it so much that she bought me a little classical guitar. I still remember exactly how I felt! As soon as I got my guitar I went to the balcony of our flat and screamed: "I have a guitar!" I attended the conservatory for several years, until I was kicked out when I was ten. I never really understood why. I really wanted to continue, so my mother found a private school.

Several years later, at the lycée, I was, once again, following a classical form of teaching. I felt so uncomfortable that I quit school. I did take the final exam though, the *baccalauréat* as an external candidate. I had to analyse several classical works and sit a practical exam with my instrument. I went in front of the examiners with my electric guitar and played a song recorded by B.B. King – something unheard of for them! In France, musical styles are very compartmentalized. It was kind of unreal. The

Chicago Blues Festival

TIA GOUTTEBEL

Tia is a French blues singer and guitar player. She started touring with her own band, Tia & The Patient Wolves, in 2002. She recorded several EPs and two albums, *Foggy Head, Warm Heart* (2007) and *Travellin' with My Guitar* (2011). Later came *Lil' Bird* (2017) under her sole name, Tia. She received the Cognac Blues Passions Award in 2012. Today, while still heading her own band, Tia & Her Band, she also tours solo, and as a duo, Tia & The Groove Box, with percussionist Marc Glomeau.

Besides, in 2012, she started playing with Gilles Chabenat (hurdy gurdy) and Marc Glomeau (percussions) in a trio called Hypnotic Wheels – which later became Muddy Gurdy – recording two albums so far, *Hypnotic Wheels* (2014) and the critically acclaimed *Muddy Gurdy* (2018). They won the Coup de Cœur Musiques du Monde (World Music Award) from the prestigious Académie Charles Cros and were finalists for the Blues Prize from the just as prestigious Académie du Jazz.

Throughout her career, she performed at festivals in France, Belgium, the UK, the Netherlands, Switzerland, the US and Poland. She has opened for Charlie Musselwhite, Ben Harper, John Mayall, Jimmy Johnson, Angela Brown, Beverly Jo Scott and many more. She also shared the stage with the likes of Joe Louis Walker, Tad Robinson, Alex Schultz, Kirk Fletcher, Cedric Burnside, Skip Martin (Kool & The Gang), Murali Coryell, Rick Estrin, Al Blake, Lynwood Slim and Larry Garner.

TIA GOUTTEBEL – IN HER OWN WORDS

I started playing music when I was six. My mum asked us – my two sisters and I – if we wanted to try out an instrument. She wasn't a musician herself, hadn't learnt music, but she had the desire to offer us a chance to take up sport or music. I picked the guitar. She enrolled me in a two-day workshop to discover the instrument – how magical for a six-year-old girl! I enjoyed it so much that she bought me a little classical guitar. I still remember exactly how I felt! As soon as I got my guitar I went to the balcony of our flat and screamed: "I have a guitar!" I attended the conservatory for several years, until I was kicked out when I was ten. I never really understood why. I really wanted to continue, so my mother found a private school.

Several years later, at the lycée, I was, once again, following a classical form of teaching. I felt so uncomfortable that I quit school. I did take the final exam though, the *baccalauréat* as an external candidate. I had to analyse several classical works and sit a practical exam with my instrument. I went in front of the examiners with my electric guitar and played a song recorded by B.B. King – something unheard of for them! In France, musical styles are very compartmentalized. It was kind of unreal. The

Chicago Blues Festival

TIA GOUTTEBEL

Tia is a French blues singer and guitar player. She started touring with her own band, Tia & The Patient Wolves, in 2002. She recorded several EPs and two albums, *Foggy Head, Warm Heart* (2007) and *Travellin' with My Guitar* (2011). Later came *Lil' Bird* (2017) under her sole name, Tia. She received the Cognac Blues Passions Award in 2012. Today, while still heading her own band, Tia & Her Band, she also tours solo, and as a duo, Tia & The Groove Box, with percussionist Marc Glomeau.

Besides, in 2012, she started playing with Gilles Chabenat (hurdy gurdy) and Marc Glomeau (percussions) in a trio called Hypnotic Wheels – which later became Muddy Gurdy – recording two albums so far, *Hypnotic Wheels* (2014) and the critically acclaimed *Muddy Gurdy* (2018). They won the Coup de Cœur Musiques du Monde (World Music Award) from the prestigious Académie Charles Cros and were finalists for the Blues Prize from the just as prestigious Académie du Jazz.

Throughout her career, she performed at festivals in France, Belgium, the UK, the Netherlands, Switzerland, the US and Poland. She has opened for Charlie Musselwhite, Ben Harper, John Mayall, Jimmy Johnson, Angela Brown, Beverly Jo Scott and many more. She also shared the stage with the likes of Joe Louis Walker, Tad Robinson, Alex Schultz, Kirk Fletcher, Cedric Burnside, Skip Martin (Kool & The Gang), Murali Coryell, Rick Estrin, Al Blake, Lynwood Slim and Larry Garner.

TIA GOUTTEBEL – IN HER OWN WORDS

I started playing music when I was six. My mum asked us – my two sisters and I – if we wanted to try out an instrument. She wasn't a musician herself, hadn't learnt music, but she had the desire to offer us a chance to take up sport or music. I picked the guitar. She enrolled me in a two-day workshop to discover the instrument – how magical for a six-year-old girl! I enjoyed it so much that she bought me a little classical guitar. I still remember exactly how I felt! As soon as I got my guitar I went to the balcony of our flat and screamed: "I have a guitar!" I attended the conservatory for several years, until I was kicked out when I was ten. I never really understood why. I really wanted to continue, so my mother found a private school.

Several years later, at the lycée, I was, once again, following a classical form of teaching. I felt so uncomfortable that I quit school. I did take the final exam though, the *baccalauréat* as an external candidate. I had to analyse several classical works and sit a practical exam with my instrument. I went in front of the examiners with my electric guitar and played a song recorded by B.B. King – something unheard of for them! In France, musical styles are very compartmentalized. It was kind of unreal. The

examiners enjoyed my performance. As for me, I enjoyed explaining to them what I knew about the blues, who B.B. King was, etc. I was glad to have an audience who, for once, listened to my view of music. And I passed!

I discovered the blues with musicians like Muddy Waters, Big Bill Broonzy, Bessie Smith… It made me feel good, a wonderful sensation, very soothing. I still love that direct emotion. At the time none of my friends were listening to the blues, except for a young guy, Ivan, whom I had met at a gig. We became close friends, and I don't know how, but we always ended our nights out in the green rooms with the musicians!

One night we attended a performance by Magic Slim. We had nobody to drive us back, so we asked the musicians if they could help us. They were so nice to us, and even invited us for dinner, telling the organizers that we were cousins of theirs – an anecdote which still makes me smile today! Honestly, I think that the blues gave a meaning to my life.

My influences? There are so many! Not only in blues but also in gospel, soul, funk, rhythm and blues and rock and roll. If I had to pick a few, I would name Magic Sam, Buddy Guy, and Freddie King for their music, the energy they put into their singing and their guitar playing. I would add Eddie Taylor, Luther "Snake Boy" Johnson and Robert Lockwood Jr for their discreet although essential role in blues music and their rich guitar playing, B.B. King for his humanity, Little Esther, Etta James, Candi Staton for their voices – so unique! – Nina Simone, Mavis Staples and J.B. Lenoir for their engaged lyrics, Sam Cooke, O.V. Wright, Skip James and Al Green for their incredible singing, the harp players Sonny Boy Williamson, Little Walter, Carey Bell, George Smith… Mississippi Fred McDowell, Jessie Mae Hemphill and R.L. Burnside introduced me to North Mississippi hill country blues, a form of blues which became essential in my life later on.

I also love many contemporary musicians, such as James Hunter (from the UK), Billy Boy Arnold, Jimmie Vaughan, Sue Foley and Harrison Kennedy (from Canada), John Boutté, Kim Wilson, John Nemeth, Rusty Zinn, Marquise Knox, Cedric Burnside, Tad Robinson, Carolyn Wonderland, Alabama Shakes… As well as European performers, like the Belgian Marc Tee and Big Dave, the French Youssef Remadna, Nico Duportal, Don Cavalli, Theo Lawrence, Anthony Stelmaszack and Malted Milk, the British Big Joe Louis and George Sueref, and so many more.

We didn't have the internet when I started listening to the blues. I used to listen to Patrick Verbeke's wonderful radio show. A musician himself, he always invited people who were on tour in Paris. He used to tell stories about the songs, about the musicians… I was hooked! I also spent quite some time in the library and, of course, at record stores.

After the lycée, I attended university for… two weeks! Something very special happened to me then: I met a band of musicians after their gig in my hometown of Clermont-Ferrand, in central France. They were from Louisiana and Chicago, and most were old enough to be my parents. I had brought my guitar. I was already playing electric guitar at the time, and had started to learn some blues songs. They asked me:

"What are you doing tomorrow? You should come with us!" I was just barely eighteen at the time, and the situation at home was pretty tough. So the following day I hit the road with them. It was magical! They encouraged me to sing, so I started singing. Blues music is based on a true oral tradition – people pass it on to other people. Even though it lasted just a couple of weeks, I learned and understood so many things. I was lucky to experience this adventure on the road with these older black bluesmen and women.

When I play and sing, I try to be myself, to be as sincere as I can. I don't want to imitate the people I love. I want to sound like Tia. I sing the stories I live. And if I do sing and play a cover, I choose lyrics which suit me or change them if needed. You will never hear me singing that I used to pick cotton or things like that. Sometimes I adapt the lyrics. For example, with J.B. Lenoir's 'Down in Mississippi' I sing "…down in Mississippi where *he* was born."

I started performing with my band, Tia & The Patient Wolves, in 2002. We toured a lot, played in clubs and cafés at first, and at festivals later on. I recorded several EPs and two albums with this band. We mostly did covers.

I didn't enjoy studio work back then. It is very different now: I have come to love it. Maybe because I am more experienced, even though I am conscious that we learn all our lives, which is a good thing as we never get bored! With live music, you share one moment in the same room with the audience, and it's already over. Recording in the studio, for me, is like painting a picture. The result is there to stay. It is the picture of a moment. It is also very pleasant to see the evolution of a song – from the start, when you compose, alone in your bedroom, to the final version with the band.

When I compose and write lyrics, I tell stories, I talk about people, places, feelings… I use images, play with words, give double meanings. That is one of the aspects I really love in blues music: the language. Blues artists had no other choice but to find alternate ways to say what they really wanted to say. In 2017, I was ready to get more personal. That is when I recorded *Lil' Bird* under my sole name, Tia. I wrote most of the songs. My partner, Marc Glomeau, helped me for the pre-production. Most of the time I have ideas for the music (or at least an atmosphere), the rhythm and the lyrics at the same time (the rhythm is probably the most important thing in music). I try to follow through with my idea till it ends with the recording. But I also allow myself to listen to other musicians' ideas, like Marc's, who also happens to be a percussionist.

I also really love playing live. I love to travel, to meet new people, to perform in new venues. It is a life that is very rich, both socially and emotionally. We share something special with other people.

Audiences can be very different from one area to another, even within one country. In France, the audience won't be the same in the north, where I lived for a while, or in the centre, where I live now. There are several venues in particular where I love to play. One of them is in Belgium, in an old farm, La Madelonne, lost in the countryside. The venue is run by Claude Lentz, a guy who is passionate about his work. So many masters have performed there over the years – Dizzie Gillespie, Memphis Slim, Dexter Gordon and so many more. The atmosphere is crazy, and the people love and respect music.

I particularly enjoy smaller and medium venues, which allow us to be close to the audience. Sensations are so different at bigger venues or at festivals. But as I said earlier, every gig is different. I also think that the owner or manager helps creates part of the atmosphere.

These past few years many great things happened to me. In 2012 I was the very first woman to receive the prestigious Cognac Blues Passions Award. It gave me the opportunity, the following year, to perform on the main stage – a huge stage, in front of 7,000 people. I opened for a great legend, Charlie Musselwhite, who was performing with Ben Harper at the time.

In 2017, I recorded a second album with the Hypnotic Wheels trio, which, since then, changed its name to Muddy Gurdy. We travelled to North Mississippi to record with very special guests: Cedric Burnside, Shardé Thomas, Cameron Kimbrough and Pat Thomas. We recorded in live conditions, just like they used to do with field recordings, in different places such as Dockery Farms in Cleveland – where the blues supposedly was born – B.B. King's Club Ebony in Indianola, and the private homes of friends who had special links with the blues in Como. The album was released and distributed by the American label VizzTone. It is a very special project, as we do something that has never been done before: play the blues with a hurdy-gurdy. It is new, but at the same time connected to the roots.

That same year I received an email from blues great Joe Louis Walker. He asked me to call him as soon as possible. He had watched some videos of me on YouTube. He told me he loved the way I play, especially Magic Sam's 'Lookin' Good', that Magic Sam would have been very proud of me. And he asked me if I wanted to join him to perform at the Mustique Island Blues Festival. Other great bluesmen would be there, on that small Caribbean island, such as Rick Estrin, Murali Coryell, Ian Siegal, Skip Martin (from Kool & the Gang), Amar Sundy. Needless to say, I spent two amazing weeks all together, performing every night and enjoying our days in luxury houses on an island in paradise. When I thanked Joe after the festival, he answered that I deserve it, that it was his turn to help the youngest the way elders had helped him.

I travelled back to the United States one year after our Muddy Gurdy recording. I wanted to go back to Mississippi, a place where I love to spend time. I also attended the Blues Music Awards for the third time and shared a table with the VizzTone team, Muddy Gurdy's American label. Both co-founders were there: Richard Rosenblatt and Bob Margolin, who used to be Muddy Waters's guitar player, as well as partner and publicist Amy Brat. That same week in Memphis I had the chance to share the stage with Bob for several songs. He later wrote me a note I will never forget: "When we played together in Memphis last week, with you leading us, you took me all the way with both your deep blues guitar playing and your singing, which is *you*, both deep blues and French. You are a blues player of the world, and I can tell you for sure because I knew him: Muddy Waters is smiling and dancing when you play."

Each visit to the US has been a new stage in my apprenticeship. I have been very lucky to be able to meet great musicians, to learn from them, even when I was just watching them. Because even that teaches you something. One day, while in Los Angeles, I happened to be in the studio with the Mannish Boys (the all-star band featuring Finis Tasby, Arthur Adams, Kirk Fletcher, Bobby Jones, Kid Ramos, Nick Curran, Franck Goldwasser, Fred Kaplan, Jimi Bott, Willie J. Campbell…) as they were recording. Kirk later invited me to his jam in Santa Monica – another incredible moment! At the end of the jam, drummer James Gadson (drummer for Bill Withers and so many others…) came to me, shook my hand and said: "Please, never stop playing music."

I have worked hard to get where I am today. It has not always been *la vie en rose*… In music, just as in every other professional environment, being a woman can mean having to struggle. Even though most of the people I meet are wonderful, I too have had to deal with chauvinistic attitudes.

One example: I once started talking with a blues producer, telling him about my music, my career. He glanced at the CDs, photos and other material I had given him, looked up at me and said: "You are very beautiful." I wasn't expecting that kind of answer! I hate it when someone diverts from talk about my work to my looks.

Another example: I was at the beginning of my pregnancy. I was feeling really tired before a very important gig on a big stage. The people at the festival didn't allow me to use our dressing room, which was reserved… for a male band! Me and my band only had a little tent to accommodate us, without even access to a bathroom! It was summertime, and it was hot. I had to get dressed in another tiny tent, in the dark…

More generally, some people have built their own image of what a blues female singer should sound like, should look like, should be… Why? Aren't we all different, just like our male counterparts? It is very important that we grow within our own personality, that we manage to be who we really are, deep inside ourselves. When I see Robert Cray or when I see Buddy Guy, I see two incredible musicians who have their own attitudes, sounds, personalities. Why should it be different for women?

Photograph: Alain Hiot, Availles
Blues Festival, France

107

Chicago Blues Festival

DIUNNA GREENLEAF

Diunna Greenleaf is a blues singer and songwriter born in Houston, Texas, in 1957. Her parents, Ben and Mary Ella Greenleaf, were active in the gospel scene, and her singing was influenced by the likes of Koko Taylor, Aretha Franklin, Rosetta Thorpe, Sam Cooke and Charles Brown. In 2005, Greenleaf and her backing band, Blue Mercy, won the International Blues Challenge in Memphis, Tennessee, and two years later they released their debut album *Cotton Field to Coffee House*, which won Best New Artist Debut at the Blues Awards in 2008. The follow-up album, *Trying to Hold On*, was released in 2011. She has performed live at numerous international festivals. Diunna Greenleaf was President of the Houston Blues Society for three years, and is one of the founders of the Friends of Blues Montgomery County, as well as a patron of the Blues in Schools Program and the annual annual Houston Blues Society Founders Day.

HOW DID YOU START IN MUSIC?

I really was born into it. My father, Ben Greenleaf, led a gospel quartet called the Spiritual Gospel Singers of Houston, Texas. He and his cousin Joe Johnson also produced and promoted gospel music concerts in the Houston Metropolitan area (usually at Lyons Unity Baptist Church and the Houston Auditorium and other *churches*). Just as importantly, he was a vocal coach for young men who were interested in studying and singing gospel music. Some of his students were: a young group called the Highway QCs, Joe Tex, Cecil Shaw and the Shaw Singers and a young Bobby Womack. (Bobby told me this himself.) The Highway QCs were a group of teenagers that included Taylor Jr, Johnny Taylor and Sam Cooke.

WHEN DID YOU START SINGING OR PLAYING AN INSTRUMENT?

I cannot remember a time when I did not sing.

WHO WERE/ARE YOUR INFLUENCES?

My mother, Mary Ella Greenleaf , Mahalia Jackson, Rosetta Tharpe, Aretha Franklin, Koko Taylor, B.B.King, Dinah Washington, Dorothy Love Coats, Howlin' Wolf and Johnny Adams.

WHY CHOOSE THE BLUES?

You just know some of my blues. I write and sing in several different genres. I came in on the historical side of the music, trying to teach others about traditional African American music. Because there were so few of our youth who knew and appreciated the blues, I wanted to show them the diversity, range, beauty, strength and overall appeal of this art form. I also wanted them to recognize the fact that although they were unaware of it, blues was incorporated into much of the music that they embrace today.

HOW WOULD YOU DESCRIBE YOUR APPROACH?

I write about what and who I see, hear and feel.

HOW DO YOU START MAKING MUSIC? WHAT IS YOUR PROCESS?

I just let it roll. It comes into mind and I write it down.

WHICH DO YOU PREFER – PLAYING LIVE OR BEING IN A STUDIO? WHY?

Live, because of the audience interaction.

HOW DO YOU FIND THE RIGHT MUSIC PRODUCER FOR A RECORD?

Good question. I usually do it myself.

ARE AUDIENCES DIFFERENT AROUND THE WORLD?

Yes, some are very vocal and others are politely quiet during the performance and then erupt at the end.

DO YOU HAVE A FAVOURITE VENUE? WHY?

Yes, a couple. Sound quality, professionalism and expertise of staff, as well as safety, lighting and ease of movement, are all important factors.

DESCRIBE YOUR JOURNEY AS AN ARTIST/MUSICIAN/SINGER.

Several of my parents' old friends were trying to get me to sing: Ed "Papa" Berry, Katie Webster and Teddy "Cry Cry" Reynolds, who were all part of the blues scene; Mr Crain, who was a longtime member of the gospel group the Soul Stirrers. (His son, Steve Crain, and I worked in offices next to each other at Texas Southern University for years. He knew who I was, but I did not know who he was for two years until he told me.)

WHAT WERE THE HIGHLIGHTS?

1. Being the first woman to win first place in the International Blues Challenge Band category (another woman did not win first place for eleven years). Leading the band Blue Mercy for what is now more than twenty-five years. Additionally, winning three Blues Music Awards (two of them the Koko Taylor Award for Best Traditional Blues Female).

2. Performing around the world and engaging with people from various ethnic, socio-economic, religious and political backgrounds.

3.Having the honour to meet, perform with, tour with, become friends with and be advised by several of my heroes and sheroes (in the blues music industry), e.g. B.B. King, Koko Taylor, Katie Webster, Robert Lockwood Jr, Pinetop Perkins, Ruth Brown, Linda Hopkins, Gatemouth Brown, I.J. Gosey, Bob Margolin, Luther Allison, Ed "Papa" Berry, Sherman Robertson, Hubert Sumlin, Joe Kubek, Anson Funderburgh and Sam Myers to name a few. There were many others, but these are among the closest.

WHAT WERE THE CHALLENGES?

Besides sexism, racism, ageism, there is the struggle to keep unscrupulous individuals out of your circle. There are changes in the industry due to government funding, airline travel, warnings of terrorism in many areas, changing international requirements for US entertainers, in addition to the life challenges of individual band members.

IS THERE ONE SONG THAT IS CLOSEST TO YOUR HEART?

Three: 'Trouble in Mind', 'It Hurts Me Too' and 'Hard Times'.

IS THERE ONE ARTIST WHO HAS TRULY INSPIRED YOU?

Koko Taylor.

HOW DO YOU PROMOTE YOUR IMAGE/YOUR BRAND?

Through my website, www.diunna.com, Facebook and Instagram.

HOW DO YOU DEAL WITH OBSTACLES SUCH AS AGEISM, SEXISM AND RACISM?

On a case-by-case, day-by-day basis.

IS IT IMPORTANT TO UNDERSTAND THE BUSINESS SIDE OF THE INDUSTRY?

Yes. At least you know when you are being dealt with fairly or when you are being screwed.

ARE AWARDS HELPFUL?

I have not felt a marked benefit after receiving any, except the 2005 Blues Challenge.

WHERE DO YOU SEE YOUR MUSIC GOING NEXT?

To the top of the charts, baby!

Chicago Blues Festival

ANNE HARRIS

Born in Yellow Springs, Ohio, Chicago-based singer-songwriter and fiddle player Anne Harris has been crafting and evolving her unique sound for over a decade, producing six indie studio records and playing countless performances in the US and abroad. Her collaborations, live and in studio, span a large and diverse group of artists, including Los Lobos, Anders Osborne, Living Colour, Amy Helm, Walter Trout, Cracker, Vieux Farka Touré, Guy Davis and Jefferson Starship. Notably, her work with trance-blues innovator and multi-Blues Music Award winner, Otis Taylor, with whom she recorded and toured internationally for nine years, gained her international acclaim.

Harris's most recent release, *Roots,* is a collection of acoustic, instrumental fiddle pieces paying homage to the influences in American folk and roots traditions that have been an integral force in shaping her sound. Current side projects include Harris James, a collaboration with alt-blues artist Markus James, J.P. Soars's Gypsy Blue Revue featuring Jason Ricci and Anne Harris, and Gumbo, Grits & Gravy, a trio featuring Guy Davis, Anne Harris and Marcella Simien. Anne appeared on screen as the star of *The Musician*, a short film by acclaimed director Mark Schimmel, for which she also provided the musical score.

HOW DID YOU START IN MUSIC?

I began taking violin lessons when I was eight. But I had been begging my parents since I was around three and my mother took me to see the movie version of *Fiddler on the Roof*. She said I watched, transfixed, and kept telling her after, "Mommy, that's what I want to do!" I was classically trained and played in my school orchestra and in small ensembles. My school system had very strong music and theatre programmes, and support for the arts in general was just incredible in our community. At home, while I was growing up, my parents were music lovers, and my dad had a huge and diverse LP collection. At any given time there might be Stevie Wonder, Mahalia Jackson, Little Walter, Count Basie, The Beatles, a musical, an opera… you name it. So my ears were filled with all kinds of music. During my teenage years, funk, R & B, rock and soul became my go-to. But then I got into different music from around the world – Ireland, Scotland, Africa (specifically Mali and Senegal), India. I also began diving into American folk and roots traditions. I moved to Chicago in the 90s, began playing with different bands and started my own project, an American roots band. I had also started listening to blues with a keener ear than when I was growing up, because now I was in a blues epicentre. The incredible wealth of blues artists there, and the clubs, festivals and many radio programmes that supported the music felt truly special. Then in 2008 Otis Taylor heard me playing at Buddy Guy's place, at a kickoff party for the Chicago Blues Fest. He asked me to sit in with him during the festival, and it seemed to go pretty well, gradually leading to a job. I toured nationally and internationally and recorded with him for nine years. At this point I became fully immersed in the blues, learning all I could and playing with so many incredible artists. This became my new home base, and the filter through which I began to channel the other types of genres I was influenced by. Although the blues found its way into my soul a little later, it resonates like nothing else and is at the heart of all modern music.

WHICH DO YOU PREFER — PLAYING LIVE OR BEING IN A STUDIO? WHY?

I prefer playing live to playing in a studio. When you play live the interaction between you and the audience becomes a whole expanded energy space, and you never know what's gonna happen. That's the magic, and you can only experience that in the moment.

ARE AUDIENCES DIFFERENT AROUND THE WORLD?

Playing in many different countries I have noticed that there are differences in the audiences. I think that Americans in general are extremely vocal, loose and love to

Chicago Women in the Blues Festival, Reggie's, Chicago

Blues on the Fox Festival, Aurora, Illinois

get right up in it. I love that, because you can gauge what they're feeling. Sometimes Europeans can be a little more restrained in their behaviour, but their passion for the blues is *serious*, and humbling.

IS THERE ONE ARTIST WHO HAS TRULY INSPIRED YOU?

As far as influential fiddle players, I'd have to say Sugarcane Harris, Papa John Creach and Regina Carter. They are all very different artists, but in their approach to the instrument they all have such unique and individual voices. I love that, and it's my goal to have my own unique sonic fingerprint as well. They all draw from myriad styles, and each blend these seamlessly in their own way.

WHAT WERE THE CHALLENGES?

The challenges of being a professional musician are many. But I feel that I am called to use the energy of sound to help lift the vibration in some small way. The ability to make people feel better, I hope, and to connect people through music is an incredible honour, and a gift for which I feel humbled, grateful, and blessed.

Chicago Blues Festival

UVEE HAYES

Uvee Hayes was born in Mississippi, but moved to St Louis, Missouri, after marrying the broadcaster Bernie Hayes. She has appeared and performed on shows with Bobby Rush, Tyrone Davis, Ike Turner, Little Milton Campbell, Oliver Sain, Syl Johnson, Clifton Davis and countless artists and musicians around the country. She has recorded nice solo albums: *I.C.U.U.V.* (1984), *On My Own* (1998), *Sweet & Gentle* (1998), *There'll Come a Time* (2001), *Play Something Pretty* (2009), *True Confessions* (2011), *In the Mood* (2014), *Nobody But You* (2017) and *From a Woman's Point of View* (2018) and has appeared on many other recordings. In addition to her singing career she is a psychological examiner for the St Louis Public Schools.

HOW DID YOU START IN MUSIC?

I was always a music fan, and while in high school I began to imitate James Brown, who was one of my favourite artists. I loved his style and presentation.

WHO WERE/ARE YOUR INFLUENCES?

James Brown, Muddy Waters, Howlin' Wolf, Dinah Washington, Mary Wells, Etta James.

WHY CHOOSE THE BLUES?

I grew up listening to the blues on the radio, and my culture and immediate environment was saturated with the blues.

HOW WOULD YOU DESCRIBE YOUR APPROACH?

I sing from the heart, and receive joy when I see the positive reactions of the audiences.

DO YOU WRITE OR COMPOSE YOUR OWN MATERIAL?

I have several writers and arrangers, from Chicago, St Louis, New Orleans and Memphis.

HOW DO YOU START MAKING MUSIC? WHAT IS YOUR PROCESS?

I listen to my producers and after a lot of practice and rehearsals it starts to come natural.

WHICH DO YOU PREFER – PLAYING LIVE OR BEING IN A STUDIO? WHY?

Live, because I am able to interact with the audience. The studio is for perfection and mood.

HOW DO YOU FIND THE RIGHT MUSIC PRODUCER FOR A RECORD?

I am fortunate enough to have producers call me and offer me tunes.

ARE AUDIENCES DIFFERENT AROUND THE WORLD?

Every audience is different. In every city and every state.

DO YOU HAVE A FAVOURITE VENUE? WHY?

I can adjust to any venue. Sometimes I set the mood in a special, intimate venue, but I adapt to them all.

DESCRIBE YOUR JOURNEY AS AN ARTIST/MUSICIAN/SINGER.

It has been long but fun. From high-school talent shows to college choirs and small combos in and near my hometown, I have learned to become a part of the crowd and try to learn from every experience.

WHAT WERE THE HIGHLIGHTS?

Having the audiences show positive responses to my music and my performances.

WHAT WERE THE CHALLENGES?

Warming up to new crowds who don't know me or know what to expect.

IS THERE ONE SONG THAT IS CLOSEST TO YOUR HEART?

There are too many to try to select one, but Mitty Collier has several that I really love.

IS THERE ONE ARTIST WHO HAS TRULY INSPIRED YOU?

Howlin' Wolf.

HOW DO YOU PROMOTE YOUR IMAGE/YOUR BRAND?

Live personal appearances in local venues, and on social media. I also interact with media such as newspapers and magazines.

HOW DO YOU DEAL WITH OBSTACLES SUCH AS AGEISM, SEXISM AND RACISM?

I have learned to go with the flow. When I see a situation that I can change, I change it. Things I have no power over I deal with in a respectful and calm manner.

IS IT IMPORTANT TO UNDERSTAND THE BUSINESS SIDE OF THE INDUSTRY?

The industry is all business, but I deal with the human side as well. I love people, and I know that negotiating is the key to success.

ARE AWARDS HELPFUL?

Awards are very helpful in building my confidence. It is a motivation that is essential to my growth.

WHERE DO YOU SEE YOUR MUSIC GOING NEXT?

Wherever it takes me. I want to keep up with the trends, yet remain true and faithful to my roots. I am open to new movements but I love what I am doing.

City Winery, Chicago

Chicago Blues Festival

LYNNE JORDAN

In a city (Chicago) brimming with classic blues and jazz divas, Lynne Jordan stands apart. Not only do her soaring vocals dip effortlessly into blues, jazz, funk, rock and even country but her bawdy personality wins over any crowd. Her talent so dazzled the Second City that the late Chicago film critic Roger Ebert declared her his "favorite diva." Backed by her sizzling band The Shivers, Jordan quickly developed into a Chicago institution, playing jazz and blues clubs, swanky lounges and even the charity circuit throughout the country. She brought her special brand of storytelling, raw humour and performance to New York and Atlanta with her sold-out show, *A Musical Tribute to Nina Simone*.

Growing up in Dayton Ohio, Jordan came from a family of church-going singers who encouraged humility. She down-played her big voice until she was singled out to star in school musicals. Arriving in Chicago to study at Northwestern University, Jordan promptly changed her major from journalism to theatre and has been performing non-stop ever since. She performed as an Arts Ambassador representing the City of Chicago in Moscow and Kyiv and has graced stages throughout Europe and South America and is currently featured in the jazz opera *Don't Worry, Be HaRpy* by French composer Isabelle Olivier. The show returned to Paris for a third tour in June 2016. She has released two CDs to date and is featured on recordings by Tom Waits, Urge Overkill and several compilations, most notably a tribute to Janis Joplin: *Blues Down Deep: Songs of Janis Joplin* which also featured Etta James, Otis Clay, Taj Mahal and Koko Taylor.

Lynne has written a one-woman show, *A Great Big Diva*, about her life and her experiences out there in show business.

HOW DID YOU START IN MUSIC?

I started singing in choir as a child, but was always too shy to sing out. In high school I starred in musicals, but upon graduation I wanted to be a journalist and pushed music aside. Then a friend pushed me onto the stage and I started singing with a band while I was at Northwestern, but I didn't truly pursue music until Linda Cain hooked me up with an audition-type gig at Blue Chicago. She spotted me sitting in with Pete Special (who was an old neighbour that I ran into years later at a restaurant he was playing). From there I played with Pete's band, and he decided that the band could centre around me. As time went on, I just kept gigging, and soon my career just happened by popular demand. I started doing a lot of corporate and private work. I have worked with my present band now for over twenty years.

WHO WERE/ARE YOUR INFLUENCES?

Always a hard question for me. I draw upon almost everyone and everything – quite like an actor uses life experiences to form characters. I will try to name early influences: Janis Joplin, Nina Simone, Aretha Franklin, Moms Mabley, Etta James, Alberta Hunter, Bette Midler, the Baptist preachers (my grandfather was a preacher), classic blues performers.

WHY CHOOSE THE BLUES?

Blues has always come natural to me, and the approach to singing, the freedom in performing, has always been a part of my singing DNA.

HOW WOULD YOU DESCRIBE YOUR APPROACH?

Organic. I also find the character of the song, and of course I try to find my own personal experience and feel the emotion or playfulness of any song I sing.

DO YOU WRITE OR COMPOSE YOUR OWN MATERIAL?

Not much. For some reason I have not done much songwriting. I am a good writer, so I don't really know why I haven't done more so.

WHICH DO YOU PREFER – PLAYING LIVE OR BEING IN A STUDIO? WHY?

I love live performing because of the immediate contact and relationship with the audience, but I *love* studio work – everything about it, the technology, the intimacy of voice to microphone in the studio, but I sometimes find it a challenge to recreate the same energy as a live performance. I get there, but it sometimes takes me a minute…

ARE AUDIENCES DIFFERENT AROUND THE WORLD?

Yes. Some audiences are more polite – they don't get vocal right away. I think it's a matter of respect for the artist, but I like a spirited audience. Obviously some work requires a listening audience…

DO YOU HAVE A FAVOURITE VENUE? WHY?

City Winery, because the philosophy of the place is that performers are treated like artists, not purely as a vehicle to sell drinks and admissions.

DESCRIBE YOUR JOURNEY AS AN ARTIST/MUSICIAN/SINGER.

As I described earlier, I went from singing a choir as a child to gigging with my band. As the work slowed down I started doing smaller intimate concerts, and I finally started writing my one-woman show. It includes monologues and music, video projections and sound. I also started working with other artists such as Corky Siegel and the French composer Isabelle Olivier. I was cast in her jazz opera *Don't Worry, Be HaRpy* – that experience changed my life, as it built my confidence when it comes to being totally free in improvisation, and I really got to incorporate my acting skills as well.

WHAT WERE THE HIGHLIGHTS?

Travels to Europe and live concert settings where the audience and I are in complete sync.

WHAT WERE THE CHALLENGES?

I was always able to get work when I was younger, but as I aged I found that the work became scarce at times. But I will never stop. I diversified.

IS THERE ONE SONG THAT IS CLOSEST TO YOUR HEART?

'Feeling Good'.

IS THERE ONE ARTIST WHO HAS TRULY INSPIRED YOU?

Nina Simone.

HOW DO YOU PROMOTE YOUR IMAGE/YOUR BRAND?

Social media. It is not a calculated thing. I just keep it real. I have always had the intuitive sense to keep a mailing list from the very beginning. You have to build a fanbase and organize enough to be able to call upon them to come out and support you.

HOW DO YOU DEAL WITH OBSTACLES SUCH AS AGEISM, SEXISM AND RACISM?

Oh man. I started as a younger, thinner artist, and I definitely see the work diminish as I get older, fatter and less mobile…

ARE AWARDS HELPFUL?

Yes. They add to the resume and profile of the artist.

Chicago Blues Festival

Chicago Blues Festival

MARY LANE

Mary Lane was born in 1935 in Clarendon, Arkansas, and learned how to sing as a child on the street corners and cotton fields. In 1957 she relocated to Chicago as one of the millions of African Americans to move from the South to the North during the Great Migration. She established herself on the blues circuit there by singing in clubs with the likes of Howlin' Wolf, Elmore James, Magic Sam and Junior Wells. She recorded her debut single with Morris Pejoe and his band, 'You Don't Want My Lovin' No More' in the 1960s, but did not record anything else until 1997's album *Appointment with the Blues*, despite remaining a well-known and respected presence on the Chicago Blues Scene. It took more than two decades for her to record her follow-up album *Travelin' Woman* (2019), the first release for the new label Women in the Blues Records. She has been inducted into the Chicago Blues Hall of Fame and is the subject of the documentary *I Can Only Be Mary Lane*.

This is an edited version of an interview by David Whiteis, which appeared in *Living Blues Magazine* in July 2019.

With a new CD, a rejuvenated performing schedule and a raft of fresh publicity, octogenarian Mary Lane is being touted in some quarters as a rare twenty-first-century blues "rediscovery". Once again, though, that term (and the unspoken patronization behind it) is misguided. Her Chicago-area career extends back to the 1950s; before that, while living in the South, she appeared on bandstands with the likes of Robert Nighthawk, Howlin' Wolf and Joe Hill Louis. Like so many who've come before her, Mary Lane could easily record a blues with the all-too-appropriate title "How can you 'discover' me when I've never been away?"

She was born in Clarendon, Arkansas, in 1935. "Little country town," she recalls. "Just a few stores, little juke joints and stuff like that. My father lived in a place called Elaine, Arkansas, out from Helena. He lived out on a farm, and we used to go see him, me and my sister and my brother, every year we'd go there. We used to do a lot of picking cotton, and in the cotton field my father just liked to sing all the time. I picked it up from him – Charlie Lane."

(Elaine was an even smaller town than Clarendon, but it loomed large and ominous in Delta history. In 1919, in the wake of a unionizing effort among local sharecroppers, an estimated 100 to 237 African Americans were killed, along with five white men, in what the *Encyclopedia of Arkansas* refers to as "the Elaine Massacre… the deadliest racial confrontation in Arkansas history and possibly the bloodiest racial conflict in the history of the United States".)

Life in the cotton fields was arduous, but back in Clarendon, young Mary sometimes found other ways to make money. She has remembered singing and dancing for change on street corners, sometimes backed up by a guitarist named Al Montgomery. "They throwin' quarters and dollars and stuff in the bucket," she told one interviewer. "I was still singin'."

She inched a little closer to the big time after she moved to Brinkley, Arkansas. "My uncle had a club there, by the railroad tracks, called the White Swan. I used to go there on a weekend when [Howlin'] Wolf would be there. It was Wolf, James Cotton, Junior Parker, Oliver Sain [probably on drums]. Hubert Sumlin was his guitar player, and Willie Johnson. I may have been about seventeen, I can't remember exactly. I used to go and listen to Wolf and them every weekend.

"So one weekend they came back down there, and they put me up on the stage. There was one song that I had heard Elmore James do, 'Dust My Broom', and I did that song. That was a song James Cotton used to do all the time. When I did the song, Wolf and them say, 'Uh-oh!' Said, 'Mary Lane can beat you singing 'Dust My Broom'!' And everybody just laughed at it and everything, so from that night on, whenever he come to town, I would do something with him. He was playing a lot in West Memphis, Arkansas, Wolf was, and a couple of times I left from Brinkley and did some tunes with him in West Memphis.

"The first time I met Robert Nighthawk," she continues, "I was in a place called Marvell, Arkansas; that's where my sister lived. There was two little clubs, one on this side and one on this side – on the ground, they didn't have no steps, you just walk right off the ground right in the club – and by the time we got up there, Robert was playing that slide and everything, everybody was dancing and goin' on. I just went over there and got the mic, and boy, I started to singing, and everybody started to hollerin' and clappin' and goin' on. And [then] every week, I was up there singing with Robert Nighthawk." (She has also remembered working with Joe Hill Louis, whom she knew from his appearances with Sonny Boy Williamson on Helena radio station KFFA's famed *King Biscuit* show.)

Those little country jukes were pretty bare-bones, but unlike some of her contemporaries, Mary doesn't remember them as particularly forbidding. "They were nothing like the clubs up here," she attests. "They didn't have no bar and stuff like that, just little stools you sit on, and the band, when they played, they didn't have no stage or nothing, just played, 'round on the floor. All that fighting and shooting and everything, I didn't see none of that. Everybody just drink their beer, listen to the music, smoke their cigarettes, reefer, whatever they smoking, and that was it. I never did see no fights and stuff down there when I was comin' up."

In 1957 or so, she moved to Illinois and settled in the city of Waukegan, about halfway between Chicago and Milwaukee. That's where she met Morris Pejoe, a singer/guitarist originally from Louisiana who'd released a few sides on Checker, Vee-Jay, and Abco. "[Pejoe] played at a club in Waukegan called Shug's," she says.

The Waterhole, Chicago (pictured with Billy Flynn and Eddie Taylor, Jr)

"I used to go down there on weekends and sing with him and Cassell [Burrows], that was his drummer. My sister had a daughter by Cassell, and I used to go down there and sing with Morris. Then I decided to come over to Chicago, and I've been over here since."

Mary and Morris Pejoe soon married, and they carried on as a team for several years. Although his records are now prized by collectors, she says that at the time he wasn't much of a celebrity around Chicago. "He was playing [mostly] in Waukegan," she maintains. But she does remember working with him, Freddie King, and G.L. Crockett ('It's a Man Down There') in Chicago at the Squeeze Club at 16th and Homan, and in earlier interviews she recalled performing at Silvio's on Lake Street, and at a club called Bobo's on Congress Parkway (now Ida B. Wells Drive), where she rubbed shoulders with the likes of bass players Aron Burton and Willie Kent. She remembered playing cards with Elmore James, hanging out – and occasionally singing – with Magic Sam, and, at least for a while, living with Pejoe in a hotel on Washington Boulevard, where Burrows was also staying.

In about 1963 (some sources suggest '66), she appeared with Pejoe on what looked for a long time as if it was going to be her only recording, a 45 r.p.m. on the obscure Friendly Five label. 'You Don't Want My Loving No More' found Mary laying her vocals over Pejoe's rendition of King's 'Hide Away'. Her voice was strong and youthful, higher toned than it is today, and the lyrics sound as if they might have been improvised on the spot – a technique she says she still uses in the studio. The flip, 'I Always Want You Near', was a slow-rolling blues bailad, again showcasing Mary's voice at its most full-bodied, seasoned by a subtle vibrato and sparked by Pejoe's guitar work (he's misidentified as Morris "Pejae" on the label). Both songs are credited to "Little Mary", the stage name she usually went by in those days. She remembers a bass player named Louis, who she says was guitarist Hip Linkchain's brother, playing on those sessions; she doesn't recall the rest of the personnel, but most accounts credit Henry Gray as the pianist, and possibly Robert "Huckleberry Hound" Wright as the drummer.

After her relationship with Pejoe ended, Mary soldiered on. The precise chronology is a little uncertain, but she worked for a time at the Avenue Lounge on Madison Street, on shows that included guitarist Lonnie Brooks, saxophonist Abb Locke, and vocalists Denise LaSalle (riding the success of her local hit 'A Love Reputation') and Barkin' Bill Smith. She worked as a waitress at Pepper's Lounge after it moved from 43rd Street to 1321 South Michigan Avenue, and she performed – or at least sat in – at such South Side venues as Brady's (she remembers singing with Little Johnny Christian, Vance Kelly, Roy Hytower and others), the Checkerboard (with guitarist Bobby "Slim" James) and Theresa's Lounge. "I used to work down to Theresa's with John Primer, Sammy Lawhorn, and all of 'em," she recalls. "I remember Herman Applewhite used to play [bass] down there; his brother Nate used to play drums. Sammy Lawhorn, that was my buddy. He would be sittin' up on his amp, playing – he could play some blues! – he'd sit up there and go to sleep, wake up, still be in the key you're singin' in! I look at him and say, 'Gooood!' I loved Sammy."

Looking back, though, she says now that she really doesn't consider herself to have been working all that much in those days. "I guess every now and then I'd go out," she avers. "I'd go out to clubs and sing with peoples. I used to work with Hip Linkchain, too, him and his sister May B. Mae [actually Eddie King's sister], I used to work with them."

Finally, in 1997, Mary released *Appointment with the Blues*, her first album under her own name. Producer Kirk Whiting, who had met her at a gig with Willie Kent in a West Side club, provided her with a no-nonsense, straight-ahead Chicago backing and issued the disc on his Noir imprint. She insists she wasn't looking for any more recording opportunities after that ("It really didn't even make me no difference—after I waited so long to do a whole CD and everything, it really didn't matter with me"), although Wolf Records did include her on its 1998 anthology, *Chicago's Finest Blues Ladies*. She continued to appear around town (increasingly on the predominantly white North Side circuit), she spent some time with the band Mississippi Heat, and she made one European sojourn with Jimmy Johnson ("I'll never fly no more").

Then a few years ago, almost two decades after *Appointment* made its appearance, veteran Chicago producer Jim Tullio got wind of her and summoned her into the studio for what he originally intended as a one-off session. "He said he wanted to do two tunes," she says. "He was going to do two tunes for me, free. We did two tunes, and they come out so good that he just wanted to do a whole CD. He had the music, and I just come up with the lyrics and everything."

The result was 2018's *Travelin' Woman*, a disc that places her in a musical setting that, while still blues-based, is more modernist than the sparse, shuffle-driven West Side sound she's most at home with. By her own admission, it took a while to adjust: "That's all a different [style] from what I've been used to singing. As I did it, I come to like some of the music that I have on there. One of the songs, 'Let Me into Your Heart', it took me six months to get that one together because with the way the music is [a 3/4 soul ballad], I had to come up with something to fit the music."

In the wake of the CD's release (she also contributed to West Tone's *Chicago/The Blues Legends/Today!* in 2018), Mary has suddenly found herself the subject of numerous radio and TV interviews and a documentary film, *I Can Only Be Mary Lane* (directed by Jesseca Ynez Simmons), and gigs have picked up considerably. She'll be appearing at the King Biscuit festival this fall, and although she still won't fly, she says that offers from overseas continue to come in. She has already dropped a follow-up to *Travelin' Woman*; titled *The Real Mary Lane*, it's a somewhat more traditionally oriented five-song CD produced by Michael Bloom and issued on the Random imprint. Life can still be a struggle, though ("Most of the time I be here all the week, I ain't doing nothing, I go down and try to sell a few CDs to pay a phone bill, to pay a light bill or something"). After all these years, she's not about to let optimism – false or otherwise – blind her to the realities of life in the music business, even for an 83-year-old blues diva basking in an almost unprecedented latter-day glow of public recognition.

"I been out here too long," she maintains, her expression an inscrutable mix of weariness and resolve. "If I live to see the 23rd of November, I'll be 84 years old. I did shows with everybody, I appreciate all the publicity I get, but if this record don't do nothing for me, I'm through. I'll sit down and enjoy my grandkids and listen to my music and look at my films that I made and be satisfied, and thank God. So like I say, I don't worry about it no more. Just try to *live* and be right by peoples and keep on living. That's all I can do."

Chicago Blues Festival

LARKIN POE

Larkin Poe is comprised of Nashville-based sisters Rebecca and Megan Lovell, who named the band after their great-great-great-grandfather, a cousin of writer Edgar Allan Poe. Steeped in the traditions of Southern roots music, the Atlanta-born sister duo recently released their self-produced fourth album *Venom & Faith*. The album showcases their mastery in orchestrating, harmonizing and breathing new life into the musical heritage of their upbringing as the band emerges rattling, stomping and sliding into a modern-day depiction of what roots rock should sound like. *Venom & Faith* is the follow-up to their 2017 album *Peach*, which was nominated for a Blues Music Award.

Larkin Poe have performed at such esteemed festivals as Glastonbury (twice), Lollapalooza, and Bonnaroo; have opened for and been in the backing band of Elvis Costello and Conor Oberst; supported the likes of Bob Seger, Queen, and ZZ Top; and were featured guest performers on Keith Urban's *Graffiti U* tour this past year.

HOW DID YOU START IN MUSIC?

Our mother put us in classical violin lessons at ages three and four, so that was our first taste of music. Bless our mom for her fortitude in enduring little girls scratching away at the violin and, later, banging away at the piano. In our early teens we were introduced to roots music and it was all over for the classical training – we were captivated by folk, blues and bluegrass. We switched our violins for banjos, mandolins and dobros and began experimenting with improvisation and songwriting.

WHO WERE/ARE YOUR INFLUENCES?

RL: Growing up, our father was always spinning the great classic rock records for us – Pink Floyd, Fleetwood Mac, the Eagles, Led Zeppelin, the Rolling Stones, the Allman Brothers… So we've always had a great love of 60s and 70s rock that's found its way into the sound of Larkin Poe. I'm also really inspired by the music of Chris Whitley; he's my ultimate.

ML: I've been thankful to have grown up listening to so many iconic slide players; from Jerry Douglas to David Linley to Duane Allman to Bonnie Raitt. More recently, I've been loving Derek Trucks and the beautiful delta blues slide players, Son House, Elmore James, Bukka White, among others.

WHY CHOOSE THE BLUES?

There's a raw soulfulness in blues music that is unrivalled. We're always struck by the timelessness of blues lyrics and melodies; we're listening to songs written a hundred years ago, but they're still completely relevant. It's music played with humanity and written from the heart – beautiful!

DO YOU WRITE OR COMPOSE YOUR OWN MATERIAL?

We write most of Larkin Poe's material ourselves, along with a few interpretations of our favourite traditional blues covers. Songwriting is an important part of our sound… we feel passionate about being vulnerable through writing and try to put as much of ourselves into our music and lyrics as possible.

WHICH DO YOU PREFER – PLAYING LIVE OR BEING IN A STUDIO? WHY?

Both have their own beautiful energies and challenges. Being in the studio is like solving a musical puzzle and there's a lot of joy and satisfaction when you step back after months of work to see the whole picture. But then there's truly nothing better than playing in front of an enthusiastic crowd of people who are singing the lyrics back to you! That's definitely a high that's hard to beat!

HOW DO YOU FIND THE RIGHT MUSIC PRODUCER FOR A RECORD?

Our last two albums have been self-produced, and we have found the experience so gratifying and freeing. Since we are sisters, we can move together very quickly in the studio – there's so much of our communication that's nonverbal – and our last two albums, *Peach* and *Venom & Faith*, have been our proudest, most authentic (and most well-received!) albums.

ARE AUDIENCES DIFFERENT AROUND THE WORLD?

We're really lucky to have gotten the opportunity to tour around the world a multitude of times (for over a decade!) and it's striking to note how similar we all are the world round. Though audiences differ in small ways, whether we're in Norway or Japan or Kentucky, we're all at a show for the same reason – a great love of music. It's a unifying feeling. Music brings us together in a really beautiful way.

HOW DO YOU PROMOTE YOUR IMAGE/YOUR BRAND?

Our *Tip o' the Hat* video series has been an incredibly fun outlet for our musical energies on social media. Having grown up in such a music-loving household means that we have a huge mental catalogue of classic hits rolling around in the back of our heads – especially from the 60s and 70s. We pick out songs that we love and then do our best to respectfully nip/tuck them into the Larkin Poe style. Also, some of the videos have gone viral, which has brought a bunch of new fans into the mix. Being able to keep in direct contact with our fans – be it on Facebook, YouTube or Instagram – feels like a gift.

Brighton, United Kingdom

IS IT IMPORTANT TO UNDERSTAND THE BUSINESS SIDE OF THE INDUSTRY?

I would say it's a necessary evil, except it isn't an evil. It can be very empowering to hold the reins of one's destiny. We're an independent band, which definitely means we're very involved with every business decision that's made. We feel this also makes us stronger and lets the fans know they're getting a very authentic representation of who we are.

Chicago Blues Festival

CONNIE LUSH

Connie Lush grew up in Liverpool and was singing in choirs from the age of five years. Her mother was into pop music and used to send Connie to the record shop each week to buy the latest hits. Aged sixteen, she met musician Terry Harris while watching a gig at the Cavern Club. Later, he encouraged her to sing with his band. They married and have been working together ever since.

Lush made her debut at the Great British R & B Festival at Colne singing covers of Bonnie Raitt numbers. Other influences include John Lee Hooker, Ray Charles and Lucinda Williams. She is also a songwriter, writing many of the songs in her repertoire including her favourite number 'Dog' about her relationship with her father.

In the 90s she went to the USA to record at Cotton Row studios in Memphis and sang in clubs in Beale Street. In 1998, Lush and her band supported B.B. King on his UK tour, kicking off at the Royal Albert Hall. She was voted Best UK Female vocalist by readers of *Blues In Britain* magazine five times, earning her a place in the Gallery of the Greats. She was also nominated in the Best Female Vocalist category of the British Blues Awards (2012). Connie has performed all over Europe in clubs and festivals, and was honoured in the French Blues Trophies Awards as European Singer of the Year (2002).

WHO WERE/ARE YOUR INFLUENCES?

Ray Charles, Muddy Waters, John Lee Hooker, Bonnie Raitt, Otis Taylor, Lucinda Williams, Foy Vance.

HOW WOULD YOU DESCRIBE YOUR APPROACH?

Instantaneous, go with the flow.

DO YOU WRITE OR COMPOSE YOUR OWN MATERIAL?

Yes, I write the lyrics and tune.

HOW DO YOU START MAKING MUSIC? WHAT IS YOUR PROCESS?

I always start with the title, and that gives me all the clues.

WHICH DO YOU PREFER – PLAYING LIVE OR BEING IN A STUDIO? WHY?

Live, always! Suppose I am a performer, yes I am! Studio is a necessity but not a joy for me.

HOW DO YOU FIND THE RIGHT MUSIC PRODUCER FOR A RECORD?

Always been within the band. Too many bad experiences using outsiders.

ARE AUDIENCES DIFFERENT AROUND THE WORLD?

No, just the language, so it can be difficult, but I like a challenge.

DO YOU HAVE A FAVOURITE VENUE? WHY?

It's hard to choose, but I'd say the 606 Jazz Club, a basement venue in Chelsea run by musicians for musicians… it's home, played there for the last twenty years or more. And I love being close to the audience.

WHAT WERE THE HIGHLIGHTS OF YOUR CAREER?

Playing Southern Ireland for around eight years – we were regulars on mainstream TV as well as festivals and gigs… the people, the humour and beauty of the country.

I am proud to say I have won five times "The best female UK Vocalist" and am now in the gallery of the greats. I have also twice won "The European Blues Vocalist of the year" in which there were no separate male or female awards… so I beat the guys! And of course not to mention the thrill of playing the great Glastonbury! Heaven it was!

Last but not least is my love affair with France, which lasted over twelve years, touring and loving the wine! I was lucky to be working there when the great blues artists of old were flocking there. I especially loved watching the women who were in their late sixties and seventies, sitting in the wings on a chair waiting for the call from the band leader, and when it came they jumped up with such energy and took the stage straight as a die and held it for a couple of hours – then back to the wings. I learnt a lot.

WHAT WERE THE CHALLENGES?

Keeping my voice! The biggest challenge ever, just getting enough sleep and avoiding gin!

IS THERE ONE SONG THAT IS CLOSEST TO YOUR HEART?

Yes, 'Roll Um Easy' by Little Feat. First song I ever recorded and have just recorded again for my new album *Blue on Blue*.

IS THERE ONE ARTIST WHO HAS TRULY INSPIRED YOU?

Ray Charles, no question.

606 Club, London

HOW DO YOU PROMOTE YOUR IMAGE/YOUR BRAND?

Sensibly… I leave it to other people. Not my thing.

HOW DO YOU DEAL WITH OBSTACLES SUCH AS AGEISM, SEXISM AND RACISM?

I ignore them.

IS IT IMPORTANT TO UNDERSTAND THE BUSINESS SIDE OF THE INDUSTRY?

Yes, but it still baffles me. You have to know what you are good at… and with me it's not business.

ARE AWARDS HELPFUL?

They make you feel good, but at the same time can make other people feel bad… am out on this one.

WHERE DO YOU SEE YOUR MUSIC GOING NEXT?

Singing please… just keep changing.

Lucerne Blues Festival, Switzerland

ANNIE MACK

Annie Mack is a blues singer from Rochester, Minnesota. She has performed at many top festivals and venues, including the John Coltrane Jazz Festival in High Point, North Carolina, the Lancaster Roots and Blues Festival in Lancaster, Pennsylvania, the Thunder Bay Music Festival in Ontario, Canada, the Minnesota State Fair, the Twin Cities Jazz Festival, the Bayfront Blues Festival in Duluth, Minnesota, Buddy Guy's in Chicago, Illinois, the Blues City Deli in St Louis, Missouri, and the Arts Garage in Del-Ray Beach, Florida. Annie is a regular performer around Minnesota, appearing frequently at venues such as the Aster Café, Bunkers Bar and Grill, Vieux Carré and the Dakota Jazz Club. Her EP *Tell It Like It Is* was released in 2018.

HOW DID YOU START IN MUSIC?

After my mother passed away back in 2006, I initially just started writing things down that were inside of me. A way to get some healing and really just process what my mother's death meant to me. It was not a simple relationship. I had a lot of things to address. I don't have a music background or education, so I honestly thought I was just gonna write poetry, etc. I never would have guessed I was writing songs. At the time I had no idea.

WHO WERE/ARE YOUR INFLUENCES?

Taj Mahal, Bobby Bland, Ruthie Foster, Nina Simone.

WHY CHOOSE THE BLUES?

It chose me. It conveyed my emotions honestly: the hurt, pain, sorrow and joy – the understanding that I had made it over or through some shit.

HOW WOULD YOU DESCRIBE YOUR APPROACH?

Pretty organic. My calling/job is to tell the story. To relate and to bring some hope and compassion.

DO YOU WRITE OR COMPOSE YOUR OWN MATERIAL?

Yes, I write and come up with the music for my songs, unless I'm collaborating.

WHICH DO YOU PREFER – PLAYING LIVE OR BEING IN A STUDIO? WHY?

I really love it all. They each serve a purpose in helping you tighten up as an artist and pushing you to really show who you are. They are different dimensions.

HOW DO YOU FIND THE RIGHT MUSIC PRODUCER FOR A RECORD?

Depends on what you're looking for artistically. The sound you want, the style, etc. Chemistry is important, and also who is going to challenge you and help bring out things you didn't know you were even capable of.

DO YOU HAVE A FAVOURITE VENUE? WHY?

I really appreciate Buddy Guy's. They provided a place for me to grow and really step into being a performer when venues and festivals in my own backyard wouldn't give me the time of day.

DESCRIBE YOUR JOURNEY AS AN ARTIST/MUSICIAN/SINGER.

A tough, fulfilling, beautiful one.

IS THERE ONE SONG THAT IS CLOSEST TO YOUR HEART?

I wrote a song called 'Closer'. It's reflective and vulnerable. 'I'll Take Care of You' by Bobby "Blue" Bland is a favourite.

IS THERE ONE ARTIST WHO HAS TRULY INSPIRED YOU?

Taj Mahal – he serves the music and is not afraid to really embrace what his creative space desires.

HOW DO YOU PROMOTE YOUR IMAGE/YOUR BRAND?

Oh goodness, gotta think about that one.

HOW DO YOU DEAL WITH OBSTACLES SUCH AS AGEISM, SEXISM AND RACISM?

With as much truth, fierceness and class as possible. Being a black woman that performs blues and other American music, the opportunities for me are not the same as a white woman doing the same music. The box I'm supposed to fit in is pretty damn small. I work hard and let that speak for itself. I also speak up, show up and unapologetically take up my space.

IS IT IMPORTANT TO UNDERSTAND THE BUSINESS SIDE OF THE INDUSTRY?

Yes. Absolutely. You have to.

ARE AWARDS HELPFUL?

Absolutely. Does it define who you are as an artist? No. Is it nice to be recognized by your peers and people in the music industry? Of course. Looks great on the resumé!

WHERE DO YOU SEE YOUR MUSIC GOING NEXT?

I want to create my opus. Collaborate with artists I respect. An album of original roots music.

Chicago Blues Festival

LIZ MANDEVILLE

Liz Mandeville grew up in an arty family in Wisconsin and arrived in Chicago in the early 80s to study theatre before turning towards music as a career. Bassist Aron Burton became her musical mentor and she made her recording debut on his Earwig release *Aron Burton Live* before recording four popular albums of her own, including *Red Top* (2008). Influenced by the sassy songs of Louis Jordan and Big Maybelle, she trained as a singer and developed her songwriting skills. She has been a prolific songwriter for three decades, winning Best Songwriter USA for 'He Left It in His Other Pants' (2005).

In 2013, Mandeville was inducted into the Chicago Blues Hall of Fame as a Master Artist, for her lifelong devotion to the blues. She is known for her witty use of double entendre on chart-topping tracks such as 'Scratch the Kitty' (2010). Her on-stage humour, high-octane performances and swinging guitar playing have made her a favourite on the Chicago blues circuit, where she has been artist-in-residence at Kingston Mines and other top clubs. She is a regular too at the Chicago Blues Festival and a member of Chicago Women in the Blues, appearing on the compilation album *Red Hot Mamas* (1997).

Mandeville created her own Blue Kitty Label in 2012, releasing records such as *Heart o' Chicago* (2014) to both popular and critical acclaim. She has led her own band since the 80s, now known as the Blue Points. Among her other awards and distinctions: she was nominated for Blues Songwriter of the Year (2008) by the American Roots Music Association and was named semi-finalist in the International Songwriting Competition (2006) for her composition 'Juice Head Man'.

HOW DID YOU START IN MUSIC?

I wanted to be an actress, but I was painfully shy and fearful. I hated auditioning and feared rejection. Because I was a good mimic and I could sing, I started sitting in with some guys I'd met in Chicago blues bars. It always took me a few drinks before I'd have the nerve to stand up in front of a crowd, but people seemed to like what I did. Then I discovered you could get paid for singing, and that was that.

WHEN DID YOU START SINGING OR PLAYING AN INSTRUMENT?

I've been singing all my life. I was a sickly child and spent a lot of time out of school, so my dad gave me a transistor radio to keep me company. I learned all the songs on the AM hit parade, copied all the parts. My mom and dad both had lots of records, and I learned all the songs, my mom's Broadway show tunes and my dad's country and folk music. My brother and I would pretend that we were a radio station – he was the announcer and I was the music, shouting the songs out the attic window to the neighbourhood! When I was thirteen, my parents had moved us to a new town. Starting high school I didn't know anybody, so I looked around the school to figure out who I might be friends with. I wasn't good at sports and had no team spirit, but there was a clique of kids that played folk music. One of the girls helped me buy my first guitar, and I started playing at jams and coffee houses with her.

WHO WERE/ARE YOUR INFLUENCES?

My earliest influences were very diverse. I saw Tina Turner on a TV show and decided I wanted to be like her. Much later, when I started singing professionally, I would buy every Ike and Tina record I could find! I studied her every word, every inflection and every dance move! We never missed *American Bandstand* or *Hullabaloo* or *Soul Train*; although I was really little, I studied all that stuff.

My mom loved Mahalia Jackson and the Reverend James Cleveland; church was a very big part of our lives, but the music there wasn't as inspiring as those records. I got a lot of my soul licks from Aretha Franklin, who came right out of her daddy's church.

My dad was into Hank Williams, Johnny Cash and Chet Atkins. He played ukulele and he could really sing. When my dad was young, he'd run away from home and went out west to play "bull fiddle" in a Western swing band by night and cow hand all day. He never stopped loving those western ballads.

As a singer, my biggest influence after Tina is Big Maybelle. Her choice of material, her tone and delivery are perfect. I have spent hours listening to her and copping her licks. A lot of my humorous songs are written with her in mind – she was saucy! Oh! I almost forgot Bobby Bland! I have worn-out tapes, records, oh my God!! Bobby Bland in the 50s and 60s was as smooth as silk and twice as sexy. And my girl Etta James. I wish I'd had her brass.

As a guitarist, my first influence was Mississippi John Hurt. I've been playing some of his tunes since forever! I also love the first position on the guitar and frequently play those Jimmy Reed lumps in E or A on those low strings. I love rhythm. Magic Sam, Albert Collins, T-Bone Walker, Johnny Guitar Watson, Lightnin' Hopkins, those are my biggest thrillers! Lately, I've been listening a lot to Debbie Davies, she's great! But I also love horns and piano players, so I've copped some of their licks to add to my vocal repertoire, and I love to take piano lines or melody lines and put them in my guitar parts. I can't get enough of Herb Alpert and Sergio Mendes.

WHY CHOOSE THE BLUES?

I had a pretty messed-up childhood: my mom was an undiagnosed, untreated, violent manic depressive. She terrorized our whole family, tried to kill me on a couple of occasions; there were regular bouts of serious madness followed by an uneasy peace when the bad times weren't mentioned. My dad tried to balance the craziness with love and compassion, but he'd come home from Korea with a serious case of PTSD, and he couldn't do much about my mother's rage. It was so stressful that I left home at seventeen. I was left pretty shell-shocked by the experience, felt like an outcast, like damaged goods. When I heard Tom Petty's song 'Refugee' I thought he'd written it for me. In the blues I found redemption. I discovered other people like me, who accepted me without question, just on my talent. I had a way to express the things I was feeling and fit in somewhere.

HOW WOULD YOU DESCRIBE YOUR APPROACH?

I'm a classic blues woman in the sense that I like to get dressed up in fancy threads and jewellery, tell bawdy stories and sing emotional songs about life. I'm a totally modern woman in that I like to be boss. I run my own label, lead my own band, write my own material, do my own taxes, drive my own van, own my own equipment and call my own shots. I care deeply about the people I work with and demand excellence of myself in all I do.

HOW DO YOU START MAKING MUSIC? WHAT IS YOUR PROCESS?

I start with an idea, the chorus or hook for a song. Then I flesh it out with my guitar. If I sit down with the intention to write, it comes like magic – or rather I've been working at songwriting for so many years that I've learned to get out of the way of the flow. I get a lot of ideas while driving or while in the shower – don't ask me why! I try to write down the idea ASAP so it doesn't get away. Sometimes the songs come in threes, meaning I get a humorous song, a shuffle and a more complex song. I'm a voracious reader; some songs come from a book I've read or a news story I heard. It's important, as a writer, to feed your inner muse. To do this I like to visit art museums, spend time walking and doing solo travel. I used to go to a Monday-night writers' group. These days I find meditation and yoga are important parts of my process. I've learned that when I feel good physically my mind and spirit work more in tandem and the flow is better.

WHICH DO YOU PREFER – PLAYING LIVE OR BEING IN A STUDIO? WHY?

I love them both! My fire side loves the live feedback, the "in the moment" aspect of live performance, the energy of creating on the fly. While my Earth Mama side loves the building of the recording from writing the tune, selecting the musicians, cutting the rhythm tracks, adding the solos or horns or singers to editing and mixing! I have worked with the same engineer, Jim Godsey, since the 90s. We are so in sync that our work is really fun. We are always creating something, exploring sounds. Whenever I make some money I go into the studio!

DESCRIBE YOUR JOURNEY AS AN ARTIST/MUSICIAN/SINGER.

That is a *book*! I met the bass player Aron Burton when I first hit town. He was playing at the Kingston Mines with Lavelle White, his brother Larry and Robert Plunkett, and I was knocking around trying to find myself. I went up to him and asked him how I could do what he did. He said, "Weeeeell, first you gotta learn three songs and what key you sang them in. Then you go out to the jams and sang." So I did that, met some people and started singing a little bit. A year or so later I ran into him again and I said, "I did what you told me, now what?" and he said, "Weeeeell, you got to get you a little demo tape together with three songs on it and go out and book you some gigs." So I did that. I put a little band together and I started going out and booking them wherever they'd hire me. We called the band the Supernaturals, after a gospel show I heard on the radio. We did covers of everything from James Brown to Jimmy Reed. This went on for seven years. I booked us all over the Midwest and, with the help of my friend Steve Arvey, all over Canada too. I did this until somebody told me it would make a whole lot more sense if I had a record out. So I took every dime I had in the world and took the band into this studio and recorded a seven-song demo of my original songs. I booked a tour to tighten the songs up and booked a showcase at Buddy Guy's to shop us to the biggest labels of the time. At that exact time, the guitarist, who was also my significant other, was offered his dream job: playing with the Legendary Blues Band. So he quit, and when he left all the other guys left too. I was up a creek with a lot to learn! I got some hired guns and went out and do the tour, but I couldn't seem to get these guys to learn my original songs. When it came time for the showcase, we got up and played cover tunes, and that was that. Those record labels wrote me off as a cover-band singer.

I decided to get off the road and go to Columbia College in Chicago, a music-and-arts school where I could learn to be a musician, not just an entertainer. I had no way of knowing how much earning that degree would do for my self-esteem. It took me five years, because I was still singing in the bars at night to pay for my classes during the day. I also worked as a shot girl at Excalibur, Chicago's premier dance club.

Another chance meeting with Aron Burton also proved pivotal to me at that time. I was sitting in at Rosa's Lounge one night, and Aron heard me and offered to have me sing on his show at the Chicago Blues Festival. At that time Aron Burton had the most diverse band in Chicago – male, female, black, white, Latino, Native American, Aron didn't care. If you had talent, he'd give you a chance. So that performance led to me working weekly with him at the Peacock's Nest in the NBC Tower and at Blue Chicago. Once again I thought I was off to the races. Our band was getting better, more high-profile gigs, and Aron cut a deal with Michael Frank's Earwig Music Company to make a live recording at Buddy Guy's.

The year was 1996. I had my debut recording, two songs on *Aron Burton Live* at *Buddy Guy's*, the same year I graduated with honours from Columbia College. Talent scouts had cast me in a movie role that seemed tailor-made for me, and Michael Frank had offered me my own record deal after he'd spent several hours listening to me play some of my original songs. Off. To. The. Races. Well, the movie fell through the night before production was to start, when, after a couple bottles of wine, the director and producer got into a serious near fist fight. When Aron heard that Michael had offered me a record contract, he had some issues with making my record, even though he had been mentoring me for years! In my mind it just made me a more legit part of his revue and would help us get more dates, but he saw it differently. It was an incredible band. We recorded seven tunes. I also licensed the seven tracks I'd recorded for the ill-fated label shopping fiasco from my previous band, so the record had fourteen songs.

Aron reluctantly performed on my record and then suddenly moved to Europe. So my solo debut, *Look at Me*, was released in 1996 and signalled the end of my mentorship with Aron. This time I wasn't going to let one person derail me. My first move was to rename the band the Blue Points. The name stuck, and I've had several memorable incarnations of Blue Points! I had to figure out what to do without Aron as bassist and band leader. I turned to my friend, guitarist George Baze, for advice. George had survived the devastating van crash that had killed other members of Junior Wells's band, and he was hosting the weekly jam at Buddy Guy's. He said, "Go talk to Willie Kent. Kent will know what to do." So, that's how I ended up working with Willie Kent and the Gents! Willie agreed to do all the gigs I'd booked for Aron's band with a blending of our two bands.

We kept our Tuesdays at Blue Chicago, with George taking over as co-band leader, along with Allen Batts and either Kenny Smith on drums or, sometimes, his dad, Willie "Big Eyes Smith", if Kenny (who was about sixteen years old at the time) had a big day at school to prepare for. Because Willie Kent had his own nights at Blue Chicago, we used Orlando Wright on bass. This band rolled along until dear George succumbed to bone cancer. It was the first time someone I played with and really cared about died, and it was devastating to all of us who knew him.

I made two more records for Earwig under my married name, Liz Mandville Greeson. They were all my original songs, and Michael Frank gave me tons of artistic freedom to explore and learn about the process. *Ready to Cheat* came out in 2000 with Bill McFarland and the Chicago Fire Horns, Bruce Thompson and the Black Roses gospel trio, and a host of other great musicians. For our 2005 release, *Back in Love Again*, I had put together another incarnation of the Blue Points. This was Twist Turner on drums, Dave Kay on bass and Mike Gibb on guitar. We toured all over the world on that record, with some memorable dates in Germany After about six years, the band imploded when individual personalities collided after too much time in the van together.

By 2007 I'd regrouped with a new version of the Blue Points. This time featuring Janet Cramer on drums, Andre Howard on bass, Luke Pytel on guitar and Rodney Brown on sax. We had a weekly house gig at the Kingston Mines playing opposite John Primer, and my old friend Willie Kent was across the street at the B.L.U.E.S. on Halsted. These were heady times, the economy was rocking and we were playing regular tours to the East Coast and Canada, and south to Florida. I hooked up with a Dutch blues band and did two tours in Holland and Belgium, and came back to play the Chicago Blues Festival.

I'd had enough of carting around my ex-husband's name and decided it was time to rebrand myself. I became Liz Mandeville, the woman with the Devil in her name. Michael Frank and I made a deal to release *Red Top* in 2008. The record featured the stellar sax of the wonderful Eddie Shaw, onetime sax man for the Howlin' Wolf. I felt like I had an awesome band and a great record, and once again we were off to the races.

Little did I know that the world economy was about to slide into the crapper and the music business was about to change forever. Clubs were closing and festivals were folding. Clubs that survived were paying the same for a solo or duo act as for a band, so I went into the woodshed with my guitar and reinvented myself as a solo/duo singer/guitarist. I put a duo together with slide guitarist Donna Herula, who'd made a name for herself with her tribute to Robert Nighthawk. She and I won the Windy City Blues Challenge in 2011 and went to Memphis to compete in the International Blues Challenge, where we made it to the semifinals. We had a wild two-year ride making several trips to Helena, Arkansas, and Clarksdale, Mississippi.

About the same time I'd gone out to Rosa's Lounge to see Debbie Davies play, and Willie "Big Eyes" Smith was there with Bob Stroger and other members of his band Joined at the Hip. I bought them a round of drinks and asked Willie, "So when are you and I going to make a record?" He said, "You want to make a record with me?" I said, "Hell yeah, I been wanting to make a record with you since we played together back in the day. I pitched the idea to Michael Frank, but he nixed it."

So I called Jim Godsey the next day and booked time for a session. It was me on guitar and vocals, Willie on drums, harp and background vocals and Darryl Wright on bass and background vocals. We went into the studio and in two days we'd recorded five songs! Willie had a full touring schedule for the summer, what with his record being a big hit, so we planned to go back in and record five more in September when things cooled off for him. But I saw him in Memphis in May and he wasn't feeling well, said his bones ached. Then I saw him in June at the Chicago Blues Festival and he was in a wheelchair. By September he was dead. I was so depressed I couldn't even go to his funeral. But I knew I had to finish that record. I'd been so inspired by my trips to Clarksdale that I decided to make the record a comment on the music that had come north from the Hill Country where Willie Smith came from. That meant field hollers, Delta blues, jug-band music, culminating in the electric Chicago sound of Chess records. The record came out in 2012 and launched my label, Blue Kitty Music.

For the next project I wanted to pay tribute to the artists who'd formed my Chicago musical consciousness. The songs echoed the styles of Tyrone Davis, Cicero Blake and Floyd McDaniel, all artists whose shows I'd seen and records I'd played time and again. The record, *Heart o' Chicago*, was a smash! I was booked for tours all over the Midwest all summer, but a karmic bill had fallen due and I was in for trouble again!

In July, I was out walking my dog and tripped and broke a bone in my foot. The doctors put me in a boot and told me to rest for the next three months, but I had people I was responsible for and bills to pay, so I got people to help me (I'd broken my driving foot) and kept working. Two weeks later I got the flu. I figured, well, it's a virus, so what are the doctors going to do? So I kept working… for the next four months. By October I'd been coughing and had a headache and fever for months, so I lay down in my bed and had a near-death experience! I finally called the doctor, and she said I had pneumonia. She gave me two courses of antibiotics before my fever broke and ordered me to three weeks of complete bed rest. While I was resting, I watched these documentaries on Netflix: *GMO OMG* and *Farm Inc.* I became so incensed at the things I learned in them I became a complete vegetarian! My body was wiped out and my voice was completely trashed, but I'd woken up from my near-death experience with a new sense of purpose, and I was determined to rebuild my strength and come back to health. I'd been casually practising yoga since 2001 at the Sivananda centre near my home, so I decided to go to their ashram in the Bahamas and take a certification in sound healing. I came home renewed and started practising daily. I went in the studio and started working on a new project.

I'd actually started recording the tracks that became the *Stars Motel* in 2013. People were booked to play in Chicago and the clubs weren't offering rooms. A guy who'd released a record on Earwig at the same time I'd released *Red Top* had called asking for recommendations for a place to stay. I offered that he could stay in my basement rehearsal studio with one catch: while here we had to co-write and record three songs. By the time 2016 had rolled around I had tracks with him, Miami guitarist Rachelle Coba (I'd met her in Clarksdale) and Italian guitarist Dario Lombardo, who'd played with Phil Guy back in the day. Minoru Maruyama, who'd been playing with me for several years at that point, rounded out the disc with two songs that we co-wrote and by the fall of 2016 we had the project finished. We did a series of record release parties around the Midwest, culminating with a blow-out party at Buddy Guy's.

After the hubbub died down and everyone had gone home, I was back to playing club dates, maybe feeling a little post-release depression. After a gig the night before Thanksgiving out in the 'burbs, I packed up my van and was driving home, thinking bitter thoughts about myself and my career. Like, why am I still doing this? And who do I think I am to dress up like a bombshell, tell my jokes, sing my songs and expect people to care? Well, God was listening. God was like, "This is what you think? That you wasted your life and nobody would care? Well, let me show you!" And at that moment I ran headlong into a car that was parked in my lane on the highway.

A state trooper saw the whole thing. He was investigating another accident, so he was there immediately. Andy Sutton, who was playing drums that night, fortunately was driving his own car and wasn't injured. I kicked into band-leader mode. I got out my phone and started making calls. I was so busy worrying about taking care of business I didn't give a thought to myself! My husband wanted to take me to the hospital, but I was adamant that I was fine – just give me two ice bags, I told him. I couldn't sleep. I had my ice bags, one on my heart and one on the giant lump on my forehead. I think I posted something on Facebook, or maybe Andy did. Then I got the first phone call. My friend Betz called in her gentle way suggesting that I might want to go get checked out. About an hour later, my friend Kristjian called from Miami, telling me a little more forcefully that I needed to go to the hospital. An hour after that my friend David called and barked at me in no uncertain terms, "Liz, get your ass to the hospital!!" Carl took me to Northwestern ER, where they admitted me immediately, took my blood pressure, pumped me full of morphine, hooked me up to wires and tubes and started running tests. Carl snapped a photo of me lying there on that gurney with my two black eyes and all those wires coming out of me, and I had him post it to my Facebook page with the message "I'm grateful to be alive this Thanksgiving". Then I went into a morphine dream where I felt like I was swimming beneath the ocean. Later Andy called Carl to tell him that I was blowing up on Facebook with thousands of people posting prayers and get well wishes.

The doctors said I had a frontal-lobe concussion and that I'd bruised my heart and lungs. They said it was a miracle that I hadn't broken my ribs. They gave me oxycodone and told me to go home and that I wouldn't work for two years! No screens for four months, or until they cleared me. So I listened to the radio. WDCB, the local public radio station played jazz and roots music 24/7, and I discovered I loved jazz! For the first time in years I had time to write Christmas cards. I read books, *lots* of books. It hurt to breathe. Coughing was unbearable, so my husband erected a shield of protection around me. No visitors, no outings besides doctor visits. My balance was whack, my hands were numb and any time I heard a loud noise I freaked out, but I was alive, so I could get better.

The first thing I did was stop taking the oxycodone. I had my husband take me to an acupuncturist his buddy from work had suggested, Dr Young. He put needles all over my body and gave me Chinese herbs to dispel the pooled blood in my chest and help my body heal. After the first month he told me I should walk. My husband had scheduled knee-replacement surgery before I'd had this accident, and it couldn't be moved. He had the surgery and they told him he had to walk too. So in January I took him out for a walk, lost my balance, fell and sprained both my ankles! Dr Young gave me acupuncture and I had the easiest recovery from any sprain in my life!

Little by little I was making my way back to health. My friend Betz had started a GoFundMe campaign for me, and I was overwhelmed and filled with gratitude for the love and concern that was shown me by people as far away as South Africa and people from my distant past who rallied to help me pay my bills and get better.

After three months, Dr Young told me to go back to yoga. I was scared, but he told me just take it easy on my ribs, and that stretching gently would help the healing process. In March of 2017, just four months after the accident, I did a one-hour gig. I still couldn't play the guitar, but I sang for an hour for the senior citizens at Little Brothers of the Poor.

By 2018 I was healed and the amazing things that happened in my career still fill me with joy and wonder. The Dynocasters, the German band that Aron Burton played with after he left Chicago in the 1990s, contacted me and invited me over to play with them. I was invited to sing in Paris and had a wonderful time with Big Dez at La Heuchette. I was invited to sing on the European Blues Cruise, and to do a tour in central France. Dario Lombardo brought me back to Italy to do the Gilgamesh Blues Fest and a tour.

In March of 2019 I went back to the Sivananda ashram and did a total immersion residency, graduating from their yoga teacher training programme. Since then I've been teaching yoga several times a week. I also offer sound healing with crystal singing bowl meditation and mantra. I'm going back to do advanced teacher training in January of 2020.

Thanks to my forced screen fast and the music on WDCB, I'm finally using that Columbia College training, singing jazz in duo and trio and band formats. My band, the Blue Points, has had yet another incarnation. This time it's Minoru Maruyama on guitar, Andre Howard on bass, Andy Sutton on drums and Johnny Alto on sax. Jim Godsey and I have been having fun in the studio too. I have enough back recordings from the past three years for nearly four albums. We're working on a project, *Blues from the Stars Motel*, scheduled for release November 2019. With tracks co-written with Big Dez from Paris, Dario, Peter Struijk from Netherlands and Boston-based fiddler Ilana Katz Katz. They run the gamut from swing to slow blues. A second release is planned for May of 2020 with work from Minoru Maruyama and others. With a working title of *Get Away*, this album is a soul and R & B recording. I'm pretty excited about this new work and have really enjoyed having my body back in full working order.

HOW DO YOU PROMOTE YOUR IMAGE/YOUR BRAND?

I have a website, www.lizmandeville.com. I'm on Facebook, (I have Liz Mandeville, Liz Mandeville & the Blue Points, Liz Mandeville Jazz and Liz Mandeville's Om Shanti Vibe for my Yoga Activities.) I do Twitter as @LittleRedTop and Instagram, and I finally started working on a website for the record label. I hope to have it finished soon: www.bluekittymusic.net.

HOW DO YOU DEAL WITH OBSTACLES SUCH AS AGEISM, SEXISM AND RACISM?

I just do what I do. Not everyone will understand or appreciate what I do, but I just try to express myself in as truthful a manner as I can.

IS IT IMPORTANT TO UNDERSTAND THE BUSINESS SIDE OF THE INDUSTRY?

The business is constantly evolving. It's important to understand how to protect your work, how to promote it and how to get paid. I'm always trying to educate myself and get better, but really there are only so many hours in the day!

ARE AWARDS HELPFUL?

I'll let you know if I get any, haha. I felt very honoured to be inducted into the Chicago Blues Hall of Fame in 2013. And I was flattered to win the USA and International Songwriting Contests, but it didn't really change anything. I still have to work very hard.

WHERE DO YOU SEE YOUR MUSIC GOING NEXT?

To the *moon*, Alice. To the moon.

LISA MANN

Lisa Mann is a contemporary blues singer-songwriter, bass player and recording artist with many different influences, including classic blues, blues rock, R & B, soul and even country. She has her own record label and has released several full-length CDs, many of which have landed on the Living Blues charts and have been heard on radio throughout the world. She is also a working musician and enjoys doing projects and performances in collaboration with other artists. She has toured the United States with her own band, and also plays with a band occasionally in the United Kingdom led by guitar guru Dudley Ross. She has also travelled the European continent with Blues Music Award nominees Karen Lovely and Ben Rice.

HOW DID YOU START IN MUSIC?

I was born in Charleston, West Virginia, but I consider Portland, Oregon, my home town. I had a difficult early childhood, and my parents divorced when I was eight years of age. I shuffled back and forth between them for a while. I loved to sing at a very early age, but started getting interested in bass guitar when I was nine years old. I would learn how to play bass lines on my mother's acoustic guitar. When I was eleven, and living in West Virginia with my father, I saw a copy of Paul McCartney's violin-shaped bass at a pawn shop. I put ten dollars down on layaway for it, and saved my lunch money and allowance to buy it over the course of the next year. The shop was kind enough to let me visit the bass during this time, so I learned how to play it in the shop.

Bass lines always stood out to me, in songs on the radio, music in movies, anywhere I heard them. Once I got that bass home, I could not put it down. The first song I learned all the way through was Deep Purple's 'Space Truckin''. I learned everything by ear, playing along with records or the radio, or even with the music in TV shows and commercials.

Having moved back to Oregon to live with my mother, I upgraded to a G&L Precision-style bass. At fifteen, I joined my first band, a crossover punk/metal outfit called Dead Conspiracy. We received $13 at our first show at the Satyricon in Portland, and we had to find someone who had four quarters' change so we could split that money between the four of us.

I played in a few heavy metal bands that never really went anywhere, then at nineteen I started playing Top 40 songs in nightclubs, so I could play and sing for a living. That's when I started playing six-string bass. At first it was mostly pop, funk and alternative music; however, when I moved to Seattle in the 1990s it was mostly classic and hard rock.

When I moved back to Portland, I discovered a very lively blues scene. I connected with soul singer Linda Hornbuckle (rest in peace), smokin' guitarist Sonny Hess, as well as the late great harmonica god Paul DeLay, among others. Soon I was working full time in the blues scene, and fell in love with the blues. In 2006 I started writing and recording my own music, and started fronting my own band.

WHEN DID YOU START SINGING OR PLAYING AN INSTRUMENT?

I started singing along to the radio as well as my mother's records at a very young age. I loved Barbara Streisand, Judy Garland and even Yma Sumac. I loved her rock records too, like Cream, Led Zeppelin and Deep Purple. I learned to play 'Smoke on the Water' on Mom's acoustic guitar around age nine or ten.

WHO WERE/ARE YOUR INFLUENCES?

Those English blues-based rock bands were my first influences… Jack Bruce of Cream, Roger Glover of Deep Purple, John Paul Jones of Led Zep and Geezer Butler of Black Sabbath. Later I really got into heavy metal – that's when bassist Steve Harris and singer Bruce Dickinson of Iron Maiden became massive influences, as well as singer Ronnie James Dio with Jimmy Bain, and Ozzy Osbourne and his incredible bassist Bob Daisley. I've been inspired by bass players of every genre – Geddy Lee, James Jamerson, Johnny B. Gayden, Leon Wilkeson, Bob Babbitt, Duck Dunn and the great local bass players in my area like the late Phil Haxton. Vocal influences also run the gamut, from rock singers like Bruce Dickinson, Paul Rogers, Ronnie James Dio and Pat Benatar to soul singers like Gladys Knight, Sam Cooke, Chaka Khan and Linda Hornbuckle, and to blues singers like Little Milton Campbell, Etta James, Johnny Guitar Watson and Koko Taylor.

HOW WOULD YOU DESCRIBE YOUR APPROACH?

I'm the band leader, so I am blessed to be able to mostly do whatever I want! So it's everything but the kitchen sink for me, so long as something sounds good and adds to the song. I prefer to work with musicians who also care more about the song than they do about showing off.

DO YOU WRITE OR COMPOSE YOUR OWN MATERIAL?

The majority of the music I record is original, although I work in a few covers of artists that inspire me, or songs written by friends that have meaning to me. Most of my songs are about real life experiences, my own or fictionalized, that people can relate to.

HOW DO YOU START MAKING MUSIC? WHAT IS YOUR PROCESS?

I hear a chorus or verse in my head, then I let the rest of the song tell me how it's supposed to go. If I try to "write" a song, it won't be any good. I let the songs write themselves. I put aside time to engage with them – they want to be born.

WHICH DO YOU PREFER – PLAYING LIVE OR BEING IN A STUDIO? WHY?

I can't say I prefer either, as I do so love both. I can't imagine one without the other.

HOW DO YOU FIND THE RIGHT MUSIC PRODUCER FOR A RECORD?

I look in the mirror! Although the engineer always has excellent suggestions and usually gets a production credit. The fact that I'm a musician and not a singer only makes it possible for me to self-produce, as I'm able to explain what it is I'm hearing and guide the musicians in the studio.

ARE AUDIENCES DIFFERENT AROUND THE WORLD?

I haven't done too much international touring, but I have been to the UK, Germany, the Netherlands and Switzerland. Audiences are a bit more subdued in the UK and Europe – Americans are a loud and rowdy bunch, I suppose. It can be a little startling at first, as you wonder if they're enjoying the music or not. But the fact is they're listening intently, and I appreciate that.

DO YOU HAVE A FAVOURITE VENUE? WHY?

Sadly, my favourite venue just closed its doors – Highway 99 in Seattle. Co-owner Ed Maloney is a great guy, he and his business partner Steve put a lot of love into that place. It was a combination juke joint and listening room, with people sitting intently in the front rows paying rapt attention, while another group of people packed the dance floor on the side. And the staff! Truly welcoming and wonderful people. So sad to see the club go, but the entire area where the club was located is being redone. I hope everyone there finds a happy work situation in the future.

DESCRIBE YOUR JOURNEY AS AN ARTIST/MUSICIAN/SINGER.

I never wanted to have a real job, so as soon as I was able, I began working in clubs as a Top 40 musician. I learned so much through those years, as you have to play for different audiences and need to know lots of tunes from many different eras and styles. Top 40 club musicians are too often looked down upon, but I have respect for the hard work they do entertaining people who themselves have put in a long day's work and need to go out and have fun. I was also in and out of many different kinds of bands working freelance – country bands, rock bands, disco bands, metal bands, a reggae band and even an Irish band!

WHAT WERE THE HIGHLIGHTS?

The highlight of any kind of gig I've done is bringing joy to an audience. Especially since becoming a singer-songwriter – when someone comes up to me and tells me that one of my songs has gotten them through some tough times, it fills me with gratitude for this crazy musical life. I also very much appreciate the opportunities to travel.

Artists like Karen Lovely, Diane Blue and Dudley Ross have collaborated with me and provided me with some unforgettable travelling adventures.

WHAT WERE THE CHALLENGES?

The main challenge has always been making money! Especially in America – there is little public support for the arts, and frankly public support of just about anything is culturally frowned upon. People tend not to go out as much, and find entertainment at home. And nowadays with streaming on the internet, folks just aren't buying CDs and downloads as much as they used to.

IS THERE ONE SONG THAT IS CLOSEST TO YOUR HEART?

I wrote a song called 'Doin' OK': it's about being grateful for the very simple things in life, like having a roof over your head and food to eat, even when everything else seems to be crashing down around you. I don't know if it's closest to my heart, but it is straight *from* the heart.

IS THERE ONE ARTIST WHO HAS TRULY INSPIRED YOU?

It's impossible to narrow it down to one artist. I'm inspired by everything I hear. My husband Allen Markel is an amazing bass player; he inspires me all the time. Artists that persevere through tough times also inspire me, like my guitar-playing best buddy Sonny Hess, soul goddess LaRhonda Steele, the late blues *chanteuse* Candye Kane and heavy metal singer Bruce Dickinson. They all had cancer during their busy music careers, but just kept on going. I remember watching my friend Sonny sitting on a stool on stage, skinny as a rail and her bald head hanging low, but she still had her guitar in her hand and was determined not to miss a gig. I think she only missed one show during her whole chemo and surgery ordeal. Now that's inspiring!

HOW DO THEY FIND PEOPLE TO COLLABORATE WITH?

People usually find me! When you live in a musical town like Portland, you can get right in the middle of things. If someone needs a bassist or singer that can do what I do, someone will pass them my number. Same for me, if I need an engineer or musician for a project I'm working on, I'll always be able to find someone through the grapevine. For those folks out there who are having a hard time, just get yourself into a scene, go to live events and mingle and get to know people. Pretty soon you will make those connections, and friendships as well.

HOW DO YOU PROMOTE YOUR IMAGE/YOUR BRAND?

I've spent a lot of dough on print advertising. Many print magazines are designed for that certain set of eyeballs you're aiming to reach. I also try to reach folks on social media, as well as on radio. As for my "brand", I guess I'm just a woman who likes to play the blues, to paraphrase B.B. King. But someone once told me they named a playlist "Tough Girl Blues" on their phone and added me to it. So I adopted that as my motto!

ARE THERE PRESSURES ON WOMEN TO LOOK A CERTAIN WAY?

Yes, and it's bothered me more in the past than it has lately. I have little in the boobie department, and big boobies do help you get noticed in the music business. But it would be hard to play the bass with them! So I guess it's all good.

HOW DO YOU DEAL WITH OBSTACLES SUCH AS AGEISM, SEXISM AND RACISM?

I mostly press forward as if they weren't obstacles at all. Age, luckily, isn't as big an issue in the blues scene as it is in other genres. But sexism is sadly alive and well, especially in radio playlists and festival bookings. But instead of complaining so much about the "sausage fests", I try to congratulate those bookers and DJs who naturally mix in female artists.

IS IT IMPORTANT TO UNDERSTAND THE BUSINESS SIDE OF THE INDUSTRY?

This is vitally important, and even I can't say I truly understand it. But it is so important for musical artists to have at least a general grasp of the business, especially in legal matters. Those issues will always crop up, whether you're signing a contract for a gig, licensing a song to record or renting a venue and promoting your own show. Joining your local musicians' union can be very helpful, as they have legal assistance available as well as educational opportunities.

ARE AWARDS HELPFUL?

I've got a mantel full of awards and I am grateful for them all. They typically come from a general audience, a membership base, or a board of some kind. In any case, it means someone appreciates what you do, and that adds to a warm sense of accomplishment! For the artist, it's something positive to promote on your website or in advertising. For the musical societies, awards are a great way to expand their base. Oftentimes only members can vote for the nominees, so it behooves those nominees to ask their fan base to join up. Those that do join up just to vote for you are often happily surprised by the benefits of joining – being introduced to new artists, invited to fun events, getting discounts, etc. Sometimes an award can tie you in with an important cause. I won the Sean Costello Rising Star Award from *Blues Blast Magazine* a few years ago, and I feel it's important to tell people about the Sean Costello Fund for Bipolar Research. It's an important resource for people out there who are suffering the way Sean did.

WHERE DO YOU SEE YOUR MUSIC GOING NEXT?

I'm full of surprises! I even surprise myself sometimes…

Chicago Blues Festival

KATE MOSS

Kate Moss has enjoyed playing guitar since her teens, but it wasn't until she met Buddy Guy at the age of 21 that she realized what genre of music commanded her focus: the blues. Exploring Buddy's music and that of his contemporaries, she fell in love with the sound and the heartfelt, improvisational nature of the blues. Over the years, she has shared the stage with not only Buddy on several occasions, but other top performers, like her husband Nick Moss, Jimmy Vivino, Benny Turner, Tommy Castro, Jimmy Johnson, Walter Trout, Eddie Shaw, Curtis Salgado, Ana Popovic, Smokin' Joe Kubek, Lurrie Bell, and Mud Morganfield, among many others. In 2012 Kate was part of an all-star outfit, The Healers, which also included members Jimmy Hall (of Wet Willie), Reese Wynans (of SRV's Double Trouble and now Joe Bonamassa's band), Samantha Fish, and Danielle and Kris Schnebelen (of Trampled Under Foot). The Healers released a critically acclaimed DVD/CD *Live at Knuckleheads*, with net proceeds from sales benefitting Blue Star Connection. Today Kate performs weekly with the Smiley Tillmon Band in and around Chicago, and hits the road from time to time for special events and festivals.

HOW DID YOU START IN MUSIC?

As a kid, my older brother had hipped me to some great bands – Stevie Wonder, Earth Wind & Fire, the Beatles, the Stones… my course was set.

WHEN DID YOU START SINGING OR PLAYING AN INSTRUMENT?

When I was just a youngster – and it was with a tennis racquet. It's true – I used to pretend I was playing guitar like Chrissy Hynde of the Pretenders… except I didn't have a Gibson, so I used a Spalding instead. I then took guitar lessons as a kid, but would lose interest in all of the "method" books of old folk songs… I must've started and quit two or three times. It wasn't until I found the blues that it stuck, and I stuck with it.

WHO WERE/ARE YOUR INFLUENCES?

Initially, Clapton. But as I read and read and absorbed everything "EC", it became very clear to me that he was influenced by so many others, and there was an article in one of the guitar magazines around 1992 where Clapton was going on and on about a certain guitarist named Buddy Guy. Obviously, I was going to take Eric's advice and search him out. With that, I mean buy his music, read up on him, see him live maybe… never in a million years would I imagine *meeting* him at a gas station in the south suburbs of Chicago, but that's exactly what happened.

I was on my way to pick up some business cards I had designed for myself as junior in the Visual Communications Department (Graphic Design) at the School of the Art Institute of Chicago, and had to get some gas before making the trip. As I pulled into the Shell station on Vollmer Road, I spotted a red Ferrari, definitely a bit out of place for our modest neighbourhood and surrounding area. As I looked more closely, I saw that the gentleman pumping his own gas was that guy in the guitar magazines I had been reading about! I pulled up to a pump, continuing to check to see if it was really him, as he was getting back into his car to head out of the parking lot. Luckily, he had to pass my car to do so, and as he did, I enthusiastically yelled, "Buddy!" I can't tell you how out of character that was for me to do – I'm not exactly the extrovert who would readily blurt out someone's name. It must've been meant to be, because he stopped his car, rolled down his window a bit more and said, "Hi!" He seemed a bit surprised that I knew who he was – remember this was just after *Damn Right, I Got the Blues* came out, signalling the resurgence of popularity for him. *Feels Like Rain* was in the can and soon to be released, and – as it would happen – the photo shoot for that record was very close to that gas station in Matteson, Illinois, where we met. We exchanged pleasantries, I think I told him I played guitar (almost a complete fabrication), and after a few minutes he suggested I check out his new club Legends some time. (The venue was in its infancy then, just three or four years old at the time after opening in 1989.) For months and years after that day, Legends was my second home.

WHY CHOOSE THE BLUES?

I realize it doesn't affect everyone, but the blues just spoke to me as soon as I heard it. I suppose it was a gradual initiation from listening to rock and the Clapton discography backwards: his solo stuff, Derek and the Dominoes, Cream, John Mayall & The Bluesbreakers, the Yardbirds. That stuff is all Blues… so that's how I got there… and then after discovering Buddy Guy, Otis Rush, Freddie King, Magic Sam and so many others, that's where I stayed.

HOW WOULD YOU DESCRIBE YOUR APPROACH?

My approach is to try the best I can to play the right parts. I don't think anyone should play a cover blues song note for note (although to be honest that's how I learn patterns and stylistic nuances sometimes), but one should know where it comes from. All of the originators had such signature licks – each and every one of them… from Lonnie Johnson to Elmore James to Earl Hooker to Albert Collins. Scrolling through my blues collection is like a masterclass every time I sit down to listen and learn something. Once I become familiar with patterns and parts, I can stretch out on my own a bit and improvise more, but I try to keep the song or groove grounded in the place from which it came.

Lincoln Park Festival, Chicago

DO YOU WRITE OR COMPOSE YOUR OWN MATERIAL?

I don't really. Once in a while I'll stumble upon a cool groove, but I never remember it later, nor do I write it down or record it. Definitely on my bucket list. I should note that in addition to playing guitar in the Smiley Tillmon Band a couple of times a week (as well as one-off gigs here and there with Nick Moss Band, Benny Turner and others), I work a full-time graphic design job in downtown Chicago and design freelance as well (mostly music-related packaging and such). Also, Nick and I have a fifteen-year-old daughter Sadie, who of course is a priority – so I unfortunately don't have a ton of extra time to stretch out musically as much as I would like. Perhaps in the coming years...

WHICH DO YOU PREFER – PLAYING LIVE OR BEING IN A STUDIO? WHY?

I prefer live, only because it's more natural to me, more organic (and less pressure!). Plus, you can feed off the energy of a crowd, large or small. There's definitely some magic in that.

DO YOU HAVE A FAVOURITE VENUE? WHY?

Well, Buddy Guy's Legends still feels like home to me. He and his staff have been so hospitable since 1992. (Wow I can't believe it's been that long!) Any time I perform there (these days with the Smiley Tillmon Band), it's just a good time – great crowds from all over the world and a warm vibe.

IS THERE ONE ARTIST WHO HAS TRULY INSPIRED YOU?

To be honest, my husband Nick really inspires me. Nick started playing blues bass at age eighteen (with Jimmy Dawkins!) and has been in the business for thirty-two years now. His own band and brand just keeps getting better and better, and his guitar-playing just blows my mind. I'm extremely proud of all the hard work he has put in to carrying on this Chicago blues, as he first learned it from the masters like Dawkins, Buddy Scott, Jimmy Rogers, Willie "Big Eyes" Smith and so many more. Of course these icons and others also inspire me to learn more and more, as they created so much amazing and original music. I love to absorb it and learn what I can.

HOW DO YOU PROMOTE YOUR IMAGE/YOUR BRAND?

Mostly social networking. I pass out cards at gigs and have T-shirts in lieu of recorded material these days. I have finally got a good portion of my website done, so that can work on its own as a promotional tool – e-store, social hub and all.

HOW DO YOU DEAL WITH OBSTACLES SUCH AS AGEISM, SEXISM AND RACISM?

Well since I'm forty-eight now, we'll see how I deal with ageism soon enough! As far as sexism, I've always been "one of the guys" since grade school, forever the tomboy

House of Blues, Chicago (pictured with Samantha Fish)

– and I don't really experience sexism too much, because I don't care to let it bother me. I don't believe I've felt discrimination because of it, so it really hasn't been an issue. If anything, it's pretty obvious that being a woman who plays guitar is very much an advantage, due to the fact that we're the minority there and tend to stand out from the crowd.

IS IT IMPORTANT TO UNDERSTAND THE BUSINESS SIDE OF THE INDUSTRY?

Absolutely. I'm not saying I *do* understand it, but every musician should take a business course. I wish I had taken business courses as a graphic design student. Basically, if there is any chance you'll work for yourself (as musicians and artists do), you need to know how to handle your business.

ARE AWARDS HELPFUL?

I think they're a bit of a validation – to let you know that you're doing something right and that people are listening, but I don't know the true measurement of how helpful they actually are. My husband Nick Moss has been nominated for something like twenty-five Blues Music Awards since 2003 and just won his first BMA in 2019. It's great to be recognized by your peers (who get you the nomination), but it's the fan base that will get you the award, and that's another hurdle altogether.

WHERE DO YOU SEE YOUR MUSIC GOING NEXT?

I intend to continue to work on my guitar-playing, keep doing weekly gigs, and hopefully record something soon – I just need a little focus and a lot of direction.

TERRIE ODABI

This is an edited version of an interview by Heikki Suosalo, which appeared in *Soul Express* in 2018.

An almost ominous cloud of mystery was hovering in the air from the first chanting bars of *Wade in the Water*, and the mysterious but fascinating "voodoo" feel remained intact till the wailing end of the song. The singer was Terrie Odabi, and this performance took place on Friday evening, July 20th in 2018, at the Porretta Soul Festival in Italy. Terrie: "It's an old Negro spiritual. It goes back to slavery. It was a code song to help lead slaves, who were running to freedom. It's just a song that I always thought was very beautiful. I like to be connected with the past, and I wanted to pay tribute to where the music comes from."

Backed by the excellent Anthony Paule Soul Orchestra, next in the concert the tempo was picked up for the jazzy 'Live My Life' and for the funky 'Man-Sized Job', written and first cut by Denise LaSalle in 1972. The deepest and the most thrilling part of Terrie's thirty-five-minute stint came next, when she delivered her version of O.V. Wright's mid-1960s gem, 'You're Gonna Make Me Cry'. 'Gentrification Blues' is an upbeat blues number with a social message and below in this article Terrie tells more about the history of the song. The arousing 'Don't Play that Song' closed her set on Friday, but two nights later she returned for a duet with Wee Willie Walker called 'Lovey Dovey', a cover of Ike and Tina Turner's 'Funkier than a Mosquito's Tweeter' and a rerun of 'Wade in the Water'.

Terrie Juanita Wright was born in Albany, Georgia, on April 7th 1963. "My father was in the military. I don't remember Albany, because we just moved soon after I was born, I guess, to California. I was still a baby. I remember living in California and Turkey." From the age of four until she turned six Terrie was living in Turkey. "I do remember Turkey. At the time it was a stark contrast from the United States. I remember the smells, a different language and I remember the curse words (laughing) – because the taxi cab drivers always cursed – and the babysitters, Turkish women, who were very nice to us."

"I moved to Oakland when my father retired from the military." At that point Terrie was ten years old, and she's been living in the Bay area ever since; more precisely in East Oakland, next to San Francisco. She has one thirty-three-year-old daughter, who, however, is not involved in music. "My very first idol was Aretha Franklin, and early on I really loved Natalie Cole and Chaka Khan. In my twenties I started really loving jazz and singing jazz – so Sarah Vaughan and Ella Fitzgerald – and later I became a fan of Dianne Reeves."

"I did not grow up singing in church. In my high-school choir at East Oakland's Fremont High School a lot of the people were very heavy into church, and so I started singing gospel with them – we also visited Walter Hawkins' church – but I did not actually sing in church." Terrie took her first singing lessons from one of the top tenors those days, Mr John Patton Jr (1930–2005), an authority on spirituals, black art songs and classic music – "and jazz, a lot of jazz".

"I started in a local theatre in Oakland, where I performed. Actually, Larry Batiste was one of the music directors, and he told me that I should start singing and performing professionally, and probably at seventeen or eighteen I was sneaking into clubs – sneaking because I was supposed to be 21 – and sometimes I would sing background, but sometimes I would sing by myself and I would do jazz.

"My first group was Nitelife in the early 1990s. There were six of us. Joseph Rasheed was the leader of the band and Joyce Harris was the other lead singer. We did R & B covers, and the group existed for about five or six years.

"In 1993 I was hired to sing on D'CuCKOO's CD called *Umoja* – just chanting and wailing – and they liked me and kept asking me to do performances with them… until I was a part of the band. *Umoja* is the first CD my voice is on."

This so-called multimedia ensemble was formed in the mid-1980s, and the number of members ranged from three to ten ladies, including Tina "Bean" Blaine. *Umoja* on RGB Records was their second album, and the group disbanded in 1998. Their music is described as a mixture of African choral and Asian harmony, even techno-tribal, interactive funk. "It was world music. They were ladies who were very intelligent and very smart. They designed instruments that looked like marimbas and drums, but they were digital. Before I was with the band, they performed with the Grateful Dead, and so we had a big following. I was with D'CuCKOO for quite awhile."

"Right after D'CuCKOO broke up, RhythMixx was formed. It was an acoustic version of D'CuCKOO. We played together in RhythMixx with Carolyn Brandy."

For the next ten years, starting from 2005, Terrie sang neo-soul. "I was a solo artist and I worked with a lot of musicians. I was the band leader, so I hired musicians for the gigs."

Besides music, Terrie's main interest is to work with disabled students, mostly in Castlemont and Skyline high schools in Oakland. "I've been doing this since 1991, and it's always been a full-time job. I started off as a paraprofessional and have been working as an employment specialist since 1999. I work with students who have disabilities in high school and young adults. I help them create goals of what they want to do in life and, if possible, I help them get job experience or direct them to education like college."

In January 2014 and 2015 Terrie entered International Blues Challenge (IBC) in Memphis, and made it to the semifinals. "When I competed for the IBC, a gentleman by the name of Angelo Rossi saw me. He had a recording studio and he asked me if I would be interested in coming to record in his studio. I wanted to record in a studio but I could not afford it, but he helped me to create the CD. Through Angelo I met Kid Andersen. After the first guitar player quit, he went and got Kid."

As a result of this meeting, in January 2014 in The Cave Recording Studio they recorded Terrie's first solo CD, a six-track EP called *Evolution of the Blues*. The only outside song is Elmore James's slow and mournful 'The Sky Is Crying'. The other five songs were newly written with IBC in mind. "I like the song that Kid and I did together, 'I'll Feed You Real Good', and I think my next favourite would be 'The Sky Is Crying'. I love 'Daddy-O' because I wrote it about my father who had passed away in 2011."

Terrie's first full-length CD called *My Blue Soul* was released in April 2016. Produced by Kid Andersen, engineered and mixed by Kid and Angelo Rossi and recorded at his Cave Studios, besides Kid on guitar, organ and bass, among other eleven musicians you can spot such names as Derrick "D'Mar" Martin on drums, Kirk Crumpler on bass, Ken Cook on keys and Terry Hiatt on guitar. Add to that still a three-piece horn section and three backing vocalists.

Terrie wrote or co-wrote eleven songs out of the thirteen on display, and they range from such jazzy numbers as the swinging 'Live My Life' and the slow 'He Wouldn't Let Go' to blues and rhythm & blues by way of the slow 'When You Love Me' and 'Life Is so Good' and a live scorcher named 'Born to Die'. If your preference is soul music, look no further than the mid-tempo 'How Dare You', the inspirational 'Hold up the Light' and the deep and impressive 'Will You Still Love Me'. "I think the CD presents my influences. I'm not one-dimensional. All of those influences play a wide role in who I am as an artist."

The two outside songs are 'Wade in the Water' – arranged by Terrie herself – and a cover of Big Mama Thornton's 60s slow blues called 'Ball and Chain'. The opening song on the set is the mid-tempo 'Gentrification Blues'. "The CD was pretty much finished. I was going to the studio to just listen to the different takes with Kid. Oakland is culturally very diverse. There's a place called Lake Merritt, and there used to be drumming on the lake. Someone, who had recently moved there, did not like the drumming and called the police on the drummers. Then there's a church that had been in Oakland for sixty-seven years, and people who recently moved there started calling the police on the church and they were fined for making too much noise. It was something they've been doing for a very, very long time, which is worshipping. So this really upset me and I wrote 'Gentrification Blues', and Kid said, 'OK, let's do it.'"

Besides Anthony Paule and his orchestra backing Terrie up on festivals, she has her own six-piece band. "I don't tour a lot. I do a lot of concerts in the area that I live in, but as far as touring in Europe… maybe once or twice a year." Terrie is scheduled to perform at the Blues Heaven Festival in Denmark in early November this year, and hopefully soon after that we are treated to a new CD. "Kid and I have been talking about doing something else. I would like to do an acoustic project with him, but we still have to talk."

Brooks Blues Bar, London

DOÑA OXFORD

Doña Oxford was born in New York City, and by age seven she was already performing publicly and started formal classical training. At seventeen, she applied and was accepted to study drama at New York University's prestigious Tisch School of the Arts. While in college, she began working as a waitress at the Lone Star Café, a legendary New York City get-together of the blues and roots music elite. Soon she was sitting in at open-mic nights. At one of these jam sessions Doña became close friends with veteran guitarist Arthur Neilson, and the Oxford Blues band was formed as a result, gigging regularly and eventually releasing a self-produced and critically well-received debut CD. As well as leading the band, Oxford continued to work as a sideman, as her reputation as an outstanding keyboardist and vocalist grew. She has performed with such legendary performers as Keith Richards, Buddy Guy, Son Seals, Lonnie Brooks, Sam Lay, Jimmy Vivino, Kenny Neal, Shirley Dixon, Jimmy Johnson, Willie "Big Eyes" Smith and her idol, former Chuck Berry sideman, Johnnie Johnson. She has toured in Europe, Japan, Canada and the United States. In addition to playing keyboards all around the world, she is also an accomplished drummer, graphic artist and auto mechanic.

HOW DID YOU START IN MUSIC?

I fell into it. I was going on acting auditions in New York City and came across a blues jam one Saturday afternoon. I went in and got up to sing; they leader liked me and invited me back. Eventually I told him I played a little keyboard, and before you knew it I was the house keyboardist for the most prominent blues jam in New York.

WHEN DID YOU START SINGING OR PLAYING AN INSTRUMENT?

I was six years old. A teacher came into the first-grade classroom and asked which one of us were taking piano lessons. It sounded like fun, but I didn't know that our parents had to enrol us and pay for the lessons, haha! So I started taking lessons unbeknownst to my mom, and a month later the teacher called my mom to ask for payment and was shocked to find out that I didn't own a piano. Apparently I was practicing on the multicoloured toy piano that I got when I was three. The teacher said I had a natural ear and recommended I get a real piano and continue the lessons. After much resistance, my mom got me a piano and lessons!

WHO WERE/ARE YOUR INFLUENCES?

For the keyboards, Johnnie Johnson (Chuck Berry's pianist), and for the vocals, Gladys Knight and Koko Taylor

WHY CHOOSE THE BLUES?

When I was seventeen, I was the first female rapper signed to a major label in the 80s, but I quit because the industry was treating my like a piece of meat. They wanted to sue me – it was a mess. I had a nervous breakdown – I had the blues! And the only music that soothed my soul was the blues.

HOW WOULD YOU DESCRIBE YOUR APPROACH?

I was playing for legendary Chicago bassist Willie Kent, who called out a familiar song title that was not in his regular repertoire. I asked him what key he wanted to start the song in. His reply was: "It doesn't matter what key you play the song in – I will find a way to tell the story!" That comment changed the way I looked at music for ever: it's a story, through your voice, your guitar, your drums, whatever... STORY is everything!

HOW DO YOU START MAKING MUSIC? WHAT IS YOUR PROCESS?

I have a story I want to tell, and the words just sort of come to me. The music follows the cadence of the lyrical content.

WHICH DO YOU PREFER – PLAYING LIVE OR BEING IN A STUDIO? WHY?

Playing live is my favourite: there's nothing better than the rush of thousands of people dancing and smiling and singing with you!

HOW DO YOU FIND THE RIGHT MUSIC PRODUCER FOR A RECORD?

Ha! I have yet to find one! Usually you wind up doing it yourself out of necessity.

ARE AUDIENCES DIFFERENT AROUND THE WORLD?

Yes! The British are polite. The Germans are rowdy and raucous. The Norwegians are total partiers. The Belgians listen to and hang on every note and don't make a noise until the song is over. To the Americans we are more like the background music of their experience.

DO YOU HAVE A FAVOURITE VENUE? WHY?

Not really. There are so many great venues, and there are a *lot* of shitty ones too. Festivals are usually the best. Typically better technically, and large crowds always make a performance fun!

DESCRIBE YOUR JOURNEY AS AN ARTIST/MUSICIAN/SINGER.

It's been about thirty years. I started out playing at the jam sessions in New York City. That lead to local gigs, which lead to me creating my own band and touring the

606 Club, London

North-East for years. In that time, I played with blues and rock legends such as Keith Richards, Bob Weir, Honeyboy Edwards, Hubert Sumlin and Levon Helm. I then did a three-year stint with Shemekia Copeland, and in 2001 I moved to Chicago and played with Buddy Guy, Lonnie Brooks, Son Seals, Jimmy and Syl Johnson and countless other local blues legends. I always had my own band and would gig locally. In 2005 I moved to Los Angeles, where I continued playing with celebrities and legends such as Albert Lee, the cast of Spinal Tap, Steve Lukather and many others. I've been touring with my own band in Europe since 2014 and continue to play music locally with my own band. In LA, I started playing on movie scores and lots of session work, as well as writing jingles and songs for other artists.

WHAT WERE THE HIGHLIGHTS?

Meeting, befriending and playing regularly with my idol and mentor, Johnnie Johnson, who was Chuck Berry's pianist for thirty years. The night I played with Keith Richards is particularly memorable because, in a very complimentary way, he called me a bitch! And the most recent highlight was being hired by Van Morrison to do a recording session with Roger Daltrey and Ginger Baker.

WHAT WERE THE CHALLENGES?

Life on the road is very hard. It's physically back-breaking. Bad food. Cheap Hotels. Low budgets. And driving for hours in a small van with five smelly guys!

IS THERE ONE SONG THAT IS CLOSEST TO YOUR HEART?

For a long time I used to open every show with 'Tanqueray', a song written by Johnnie Johnson and Keith Richards. It was my favourite song of Johnnie's.

IS THERE ONE ARTIST WHO HAS TRULY INSPIRED YOU?

As I mentioned before, Johnnie Johnson, long-time pianist for Chuck Berry, has been my biggest inspiration. His timing is impeccable and he *is* the father of the rock-and-roll piano. He, along with Chuck Berry, created that rock-and-roll sound and groove.

HOW DO YOU FIND PEOPLE TO COLLABORATE WITH?

I don't do much collaborating, but I get hired by a lot of people for my specific skill of boogie-woogie and traditional rock and roll.

HOW DO YOU PROMOTE YOUR IMAGE/YOUR BRAND?

I suck at it! Hahaha. I think most true artists dread the promotion and booking part of the business. We just want to play and make music. But when we have to do it, we

Bull's Head, Barnes, London

use the traditional social media methods: building fanbases on Facebook, Twitter and Instagram, posting music videos on Youtube as often as possible, etc.

ARE THERE PRESSURES ON WOMEN TO LOOK A CERTAIN WAY?

YES! Men can dress as grubby as they want, but women definitely have to show up presenting their best! It's a shame that this stereotype still exists.

HOW DO YOU DEAL WITH OBSTACLES SUCH AS AGEISM, SEXISM AND RACISM?

Not very well! I've worked hard to prove myself as a legit player. There's that fine line when you're the only woman in the band and you have to skate between being "one of the boys" by telling dirty jokes and allowing "locker-room talk" and also maintaining your femininity. It's very difficult. I've had many male band leaders rub my ass at the end of the night while paying me and offering me a future gig. It's hard to smack someone's hand away when they are offering you a job. As women, we have to play coy. Tease with "look but don't touch" and then play our asses off and play better than the guys, in order to keep getting hired and proving our worth as musicians. It's terrible!

IS IT IMPORTANT TO UNDERSTAND THE BUSINESS SIDE OF THE INDUSTRY?

Yes!! Very important. So many musicians get taken advantage of by managers, agents, record labels. But even if you read every book on the subject, unfortunately you have to experience it all for yourself.

ARE AWARDS HELPFUL?

Yes and no. Yes, it gives you a higher profile, but in the end, it's your ability to draw a crowd that gets you booked. And in order to draw the crowd nightly, you have to bring the talent nightly and rock the house!!

WHERE DO YOU SEE YOUR MUSIC GOING NEXT?

I've recently taken a break from touring, as it's been physically brutal. So this year I'm all about sitting still and writing new music, working on a new album and creating a new show. Beyond that I'm not sure where I'm going. Just happy to be home for a while.

Ealing Blues Festival, London

KAT PEARSON

Kat Pearson was born in East Long Beach, California, where her family lived until she was seven years old. They moved to the South Bay area of Los Angeles, where the young entertainer sang in the school choir, played guitar, bass and drums and formed bands for local talent shows. In her early twenties, she visited London and returned year after year, eventually making it her home. Soon Kat was gigging with her band Jeff in venues like the King's Head, the Dublin Castle and the Water Rats. Whilst taking some time out in Spain, she rediscovered the blues, a genre of music that was closer to her roots than she had ever imagined. Upon returning to London, she founded Kat & Co., a band with a contemporary sound of blues, which gained rave reviews. In late 2018 the Kat Pearson project was created to deliver the traditional side of the Blues seen and sung from a female perspective.

HOW DID YOU START IN MUSIC?

I dreamt I was on stage singing in front of a few hundred people, and the audience went mad with appreciation of my performance. I awoke with a new song and a feeling that this is what I wanted to do for the rest of my life.

WHEN DID YOU START SINGING OR PLAYING AN INSTRUMENT?

I've always "dabbled" in music, in the beginning at home with my brothers. Music is the tapestry of my family – everyone sings, and a few of us play an instrument to some degree.

WHO WERE/ARE YOUR INFLUENCES?

Shirley Caesar, Etta James, Carol King, Tina Turner, Big Mama Thornton, Janis Joplin, Sister Rosetta Tharpe, Annie Lennox, Grace Jones, Chrissie Hynde, Nina Simone… and not just because of their vocals, but because of their voice and tone in the world!

WHY CHOOSE THE BLUES?

Blues was always played in my home as a child. But I didn't know how much that style of music was ingrained into my DNA until I was asked to come on stage and sing the blues for the first time with this band. I sang about a difficult situation I was going through… and felt so at home with the style that I formed the band Kat & Co.

HOW WOULD YOU DESCRIBE YOUR APPROACH?

In two ways. Kat & Co. approach the blues in an urban and contemporary way. And my approach as Kat Pearson is more in line with the traditional way of expressing the blues.

DO YOU WRITE OR COMPOSE YOUR OWN MATERIAL?

Yes, most of my material is original. I also collaborate with other writers like Francesco Accurso, John Fiddler and John Bell.

HOW DO YOU START MAKING MUSIC? WHAT IS YOUR PROCESS?

It varies. Sometimes lyrics pop into my head in a dream, or when I am collaborating with other fluid musicians. Sometimes I can hear lyrics in their instrument, and this allows me to build the skeleton of a song then build and shape the message by adding or subtracting elements.

WHICH DO YOU PREFER – PLAYING LIVE OR BEING IN A STUDIO? WHY?

I love playing live because of the emotional effect it has on me and the audience. Sometimes I feel as if I'm floating a foot off the floor in a performance. And there are times when the audience is just dancing away and times when people approach you after the show with tears, smiles and hugs! It's so *organic*! In the studio it's a much more clinical process, it's precise, technical and repetitive, but after the album/single is completed, you can go back and listen to it for a lifetime.

HOW DO YOU FIND THE RIGHT MUSIC PRODUCER FOR A RECORD?

I've been very blessed to meet my current producer Francesco Accurso, through an audition process when I was looking for a guitarist. I've worked with many producers and I don't always choose the right one – it's experience mixed with trial and error.

ARE AUDIENCES DIFFERENT AROUND THE WORLD?

I've performed in Australia, USA and Europe, and to be honest I don't think so. We are all there for the same reason, which is to be awash with music!

DO YOU HAVE A FAVOURITE VENUE? WHY?

No. Any venue can be my favourite when filled with people.

DESCRIBE YOUR JOURNEY AS AN ARTIST/MUSICIAN/SINGER.

As an artist, my journey is daily, idealistic, with music being as necessary as sleep, food and water. If I were to name only one particular high point, as there were many, it was when I was doing a support performance to Yothu Yindi at the Grand in Clapham, and for the first time in my performance life I felt elevated, connected and present. I had a strong sense of "I am where I am supposed to be".

WHAT WERE THE CHALLENGES?

Keeping a healthy voice.

IS THERE ONE SONG THAT IS CLOSEST TO YOUR HEART?

'Low Down' by Kat & Co.

IS THERE ONE ARTIST WHO HAS TRULY INSPIRED YOU?

Not an artist but a past relationship inspired that song.

HOW DO YOU FIND PEOPLE TO COLLABORATE WITH?

It happens in various guises, no two situations are the same.

HOW DO YOU PROMOTE YOUR IMAGE/YOUR BRAND?

Live performances, magazines, radio, social media.

ARE THERE PRESSURES ON WOMEN TO LOOK A CERTAIN WAY?

If she is the lead singer, I think there is a "responsibility" to feel and look your best without pressure but with love of what you do.

HOW DO YOU DEAL WITH OBSTACLES SUCH AS AGEISM, SEXISM AND RACISM?

Just sing the blues and keep your intentions and message clear.

IS IT IMPORTANT TO UNDERSTAND THE BUSINESS SIDE OF THE INDUSTRY?

Yes, it is important, because along with the artistry of what you do, you are also running a business.

ARE AWARDS HELPFUL?

Awards bring a wider exposure to an audience that you may not have been exposed to without the recognition.

WHERE DO YOU SEE YOUR MUSIC GOING NEXT?

In two directions… we are pushing the Kat Pearson side of the project to a more traditional style of blues. Whilst the Kat & Co. project runs into a more modern stadium sound.

Blues Heaven Festival, Frederikshavn, Denmark

KAT RIGGINS

Kat Riggins was born in Miami, Florida, in 1980, and grew up in a very musical family. She sang in church and at local events with her sister and cousins, and at the age of 23 she started working as a singer of jazz and blues standards in Sunny Isles Beach, Florida. She became a figurehead in the Blues Revival movement, and has toured in the USA, Asia and Europe. She has released one EP, *Seoul Music* (2012), and three albums, *Lily Rose* (2014), *Blues Revival* (2016) and *In the Boys' Club* (2018).

HOW DID YOU START IN MUSIC?

My start in music came about pretty organically. My mom and dad kept music playing in my house almost always! We listened to everything from soul, gospel and R & B to rock 'n' roll, country and hip-hop! There were no real borders when it came to music in my house. Also, on my dad's side of the family there were a lot of beautiful voices (including my dad's). Before his stroke he had a voice like Sam Cooke! My paternal cousins and I used to record demos in an empty swimming pool for acoustics. We didn't sound half bad either! On my mom's side, we used to jam with my cousins in the basement of my great-aunt in Philadelphia. So music was a big part of my upbringing.

Any chance I got to be on stage as a child, I took! I performed in school musicals and church pageants, and even joined a youth-produced theatre troupe when I was a teenager.

WHO WERE/ARE YOUR INFLUENCES?

I have to say that my greatest influences were the women in music with voices that I heard my own in. Women like Koko Taylor, Tina Turner, Betty Wright, Gladys Knight, Etta James, Janis Joplin, Denise LaSalle and Tracy Chapman helped me to have confidence in my voice where I didn't before. Not only that… each of these women displayed a kind of strength that I admired. Each in their own way, they were/are iconic.

WHY CHOOSE THE BLUES?

I always say that I did not choose the blues. The blues chose me! I have always loved all genres of music, but none of them welcomed my voice the way the blues does. That's why I think it meant so much for me to hear the voices of the women that I mentioned before. I have always known that I am meant to be on stage. The problem was my confidence in my gritty, low, husky, dirty voice. I remember being teased as a child about "sounding like a man". That kinda thing sticks with you when you know that all you wanna do is sing! Add to that that the women in music at the time were Whitney Houston, Mariah Carey,

Janet Jackson, etc. I loved their music, but I couldn't sing along to those songs and sound like them. The blues and my daddy told me that my voice was special and perfect just as it was. The blues showed me strong frontwomen who commanded the stage without a gaggle of background dancers and without all the smoke and mirrors! The blues opened its arms to me, and I happily fell into its embrace!

HOW WOULD YOU DESCRIBE YOUR APPROACH?

I guess I would describe my approach as genuine and honest, because that's what the blues is. I feel like as long as I come at this thing from a place of truth, then what I do will be appreciated… or at least that's the goal.

DO YOU WRITE OR COMPOSE YOUR OWN MATERIAL?

I do write my own material. The composition is usually done by a musician that I'm working with at the time.

HOW DO YOU START MAKING MUSIC? WHAT IS YOUR PROCESS?

Usually it starts with one line. It can be something I read or something someone said… or anything that makes me say "hmmm". From there it becomes conceptual. What does that line mean to me? What memory does it spark? What action does it provoke? What does it make me feel? What do I want to say? Then I hear the line melodically and I repeat that to myself over the course of a few hours, days or even weeks. It depends on the emotions involved. The line grows from there into a chorus/hook… then verses are born and it tells me if the featured instrument is guitar, harmonica, organ, etc.

I talk myself through everything and record it all on my voice recorder and in my journal. This way, if I have to let it rest and come back to it after some time, I haven't lost the whole groove. Once the song is complete in lyrics, melody and form, I take it to a musician that I trust to help me develop the musical story behind it. From there I take it to the rest of the band to learn and then finally to the studio to lay it all down!

WHICH DO YOU PREFER – PLAYING LIVE OR BEING IN A STUDIO? WHY?

I prefer playing *live* of course! Don't get me wrong. I love being in the studio, because it means that I am about to share my new music with the world. It's exciting to record and release something that has been gestating in me for however long. It's always fulfilling. However, the live audiences are my power source! I draw energy from them to keep myself going and I *love* the surge that I get when I'm with them! When I am on stage and I can see the people that I do this for… when they dance along… when they sing my songs… it is the best feeling ever! The live show allows me to vent to my fans and let them vent to me, and in that 60 to 90 minutes, or whatever the time frame is, we are there for *each other*!

HOW DO YOU FIND THE RIGHT MUSIC PRODUCER FOR A RECORD?

Well, in the three albums that I have released, the producers have been referred to me by people that I trust. My *Lily Rose* album started off production in South Korea when I was on tour with a Top 40 cover band. That producer referred me to a friend of his in Miami to help finish the project when our Asia tour wrapped. I guess I lucked out, because we meshed from the first moment!

Both *Blues Revival* and *In the Boys' Club* were produced by the same person. I met him through my USA agent who executive-produced *Blues Revival*. I stuck with him for *In the Boys' Club*, because he understood my crazy! That's very important to me. I need someone in the studio who can translate what's in my head and make it make sense in reality. He also didn't let me slide when I was off key or off tempo or even off the mood of the song! His ear is impeccable and he demanded my best performance in the booth. I *love* that!!!

Photograph: Walter Vanheuckelom

ARE AUDIENCES DIFFERENT AROUND THE WORLD?

Audiences *are* different around the world. Their customs are different, as are their social norms. So the way they behave at a live show is different one part of the world to the next. Not to say that any one is better than another… They're just different. My goal when I'm on stage is to make sure that they feel comfortable enough to let go of their inhibitions and just have a good time. When you're at a blues revival, you are free to dance like no one is watching and sing along like it's just you and your closest friends… because in that moment, it is!

DO YOU HAVE A FAVOURITE VENUE? WHY?

I honestly don't have a favorite venue. I get to perform in some really cool places! I have played juke joints, pubs, clubs, festivals and theatres. They all have something special about them that I appreciate. I love the realness and intimacy of the juke joints, clubs and pubs. I really dig playing festivals, because it's like looking out on to a never-ending sea of people! When *that* many people are singing along to *my* music, it's like a fantasy come true! The theatres are gorgeous, usually historical and kinda posh. I get a kick out of encouraging my audience to misbehave a little bit in places like that. No matter the venue, we are there to have a good time in the name of keeping the blues alive and thriving! That is what the #BluesRevivalMovement is about!

DESCRIBE YOUR JOURNEY AS AN ARTIST/MUSICIAN/SINGER.

My professional career started in a small lounge in Sunny Isles Beach, Florida. I sang jazz and blues standards with the accompaniment of only a piano player. I kept my job as a bartender in order to put food on the table and keep the bills paid. From there I went on to sing with the house band on open jam night at a little nightclub in Miami Beach that I tended bar at on weekends. I pretty much kept my beak wet in music with cover gigs here and there, while bartending kept me fed.

The shift came when I took a job managing a bar in New Orleans. I began to frequent the open jams in and around the French Quarter, and I was truly inspired by the musical personality of the city! While I was living there I saw an online ad that I had seen years before, seeking singers and musicians to perform in luxury hotel nightclubs in Southeast Asia and the Middle East. Long story short, *this* time I went for it and I landed the gig and sang with a Top 40 cover band throughout five countries within a year and a half. It was the experience of a lifetime and it was exactly the kick in the butt that I needed to make me realize that I *could* do this full time!

So, when I got back to the States I moved back home to South Florida and took a job in a nightclub in Wilton Manors while putting a plan in place to commit to music full time. I started singing with a really cool thirteen-piece old-school soul, blues and doo-wop band, which put me in front of the live music loving audience in

South Florida. Somewhere along that timeline I saw the remake of the movie *Sparkle* and thought to myself, "I should just put on my own show!" After a few months behind the bar, I worked up the nerve to submit my resignation *and* my pitch to the club owner to put on my first concert at his club. His response was, "Do you mean to tell me that you have the audacity to quit on me and ask me if you can put on a show in my club?" "That's the gist of it!" I said. He said, "Of course I'm gonna say yes, but you've got some nerve!" I hired a band, chose our music (all covers at the time), produced and promoted the concert all on my own dime and time. It wasn't easy, but it was worth it! That live-music-loving audience came out in full force to support me! I caught the eye of the man who is now my USA agent. Although at the time he wasn't interested in representing me, he still introduced me to what would be my Blues Revival band. I spent my days online and on the phone soliciting gigs and promoting my band so that I could spend my nights on stage. Again, it wasn't easy, but it was worth it! We attracted the attention of a Dutch entrepreneur who *loves* the blues, while playing at B.B. King's nightclub in West Palm Beach. He immediately hired us to play at his festival in Curaçao and his nightclub in Amsterdam! He encouraged me to put out a CD, advised me on the structure and direction I should consider and even allowed me to record demos from his studio in Miami Beach. A few months later I was ready to record an original project, and that's when my agent became my agent and funded the project!

Blues Revival was released to rave reviews and incredible radio traction. We began booking more and more gigs and playing to larger audiences. Now that I didn't have to worry about doing my own booking any more, I could focus on developing my stage show and making new music! That Dutch entrepreneur, whom I affectionately call my fairy godfather, introduced me to my agent in Europe in order to increase my fan base in that part of the world. With the successful release of my last album, *In the Boys' Club*, my reach has grown! Now my team has grown as well. It went from just me to include two agents and even someone who acts as a liaison between my fans and I… Not to mention my two kick-butt Blues Revival bands!

I'm still an indie artist, so I rely largely on crowdfunding and what I earn from gigging and merch sales in order to record and release new music, go on tour and just keep the business afloat. The biggest takeaway is that now I enjoy a full-time career in music, and the journey has been the best part!

WHAT WERE THE HIGHLIGHTS?

There are too many highlights to mention here! Among them are the fact that I get to travel the world doing what I love and what I am meant to do! I get to share my love of music and particularly blues music with thousands and thousands of people. I've made so many friends that I wouldn't have made if I weren't doing this. I have been able to influence, motivate, strengthen and heal people that I don't even know with my music.

That is my constant prayer! So to me, my career in music (though still in its humble beginnings) is one of the highlights of my whole life!

WHAT WERE THE CHALLENGES?

Though the highlights outweigh the challenges, there were a lot of those too. Being a female front person and bandleader who doesn't play an instrument was a huge one! It took a lot of proving myself in order to get to a point where I am respected as "the boss" and taken seriously as a musician. I guess it's hard for some people to recognize the voice as an instrument too. Hell, I'm still "paying dues", and I've been at this for over a decade.

The biggest challenge of all, however, is being away from my loved ones so often and for so long! I know that they support me and are proud of me. It doesn't make it any less difficult when I miss out on all of the special stuff, though. That's why it is so important to me that I make a success of the gifts that God has given me. I need for all of this sacrifice and hard work to not be in vain. In the end I wanna *know* that my love for my family and my commitment to our future wasn't overshadowed by my love for the blues, but on the contrary, it was illuminated and nourished by it.

IS THERE ONE SONG THAT IS CLOSEST TO YOUR HEART?

There are so *many* songs that are close to my heart! If I have to choose only one, it has to be 'Change Is Gonna Come' by Sam Cooke. He was one of my late mother's favourite singers, and this song was like an anthem in our house. My dad used to sing along to it and sound just as beautiful as Sam did! As I got older and began to understand the meaning behind the song, it became more than just a pretty song that sparked fond memories for me. It became a source of hope for me too. That's powerful! Today, the song is still very relevant and still stirs up all sorts of emotions inside of me. I hope that one day someone is describing a song that *I've* written in such a way!

Photograph: Joseph A. Rosen

IS THERE ONE ARTIST WHO HAS TRULY INSPIRED YOU?

All of the artists that I mentioned above have inspired me greatly in one way or another. Everyone knows that Koko Taylor and Tina Turner are like my spirit creatures.

I'm also inspired by artists who are currently rocking the charts!

I am comforted and encourages by Ruthie Foster's music.

Buddy Guy is, of course, a deity!

Bonnie Raitt's voice is distinctive and legendary, but more than that, her activism is inspiring!

Eric Gales is *electric*! He and his band are so gratifying to watch!

I *love* Jonny Lang's voice and guitar-playing, but his lyricism is what moves me most about him. I recently got to see him *live* for the first time, and it was like the music and vocals were coming directly from heaven down to and through his body and out of his fingers to the guitar and out of his throat to the microphone! He's other-worldly!

I am also inspired by Nikki Hill's energy on stage. Her band is killer and she is such a joy to watch, let alone listen to.

I love the way Marquise Knox is fearless and unapologetic in his performances! He's raw and *real* and a force to be reckoned with!

Annika Chambers-DesLauriers caresses her audience with her voice, and while she is most definitely unabashedly sexy, she doesn't rest on that. She makes it plain to see that she's not only a brick house… she is a powerhouse!

I wish that I could choose just one, but there are so many! I find new inspirations every moment!

HOW DO YOU PROMOTE YOUR IMAGE/YOUR BRAND?

When I first started it was all about email, phone calls and in-person appearances. Now with the emergence of the social-media monster, it's easier to get in front of more people in more places all at once! So while my agents still utilize emails and phone calls, I take full advantage of Facebook and Instagram. I'm not as present on Twitter or Snapchat as maybe I should be, but I'm still learning these systems and figuring out what works. My fans help a lot when they post videos of my live shows to YouTube and pics and stuff to Facebook and Instagram. I really appreciate that!

The best promotional vehicle, in my opinion, is still a *live* show! When folks get to experience a Blues Revival for themselves, it means more than any video clip they could come across online. I aim to connect with each spirit in my live audiences. My hope is that when people feel that for themselves, they know my love first hand. Hopefully that prompts them to tell more and more people about the #BluesRevivalMovement!

HOW DO YOU DEAL WITH OBSTACLES SUCH AS AGEISM, SEXISM AND RACISM?

I deal with that stuff the only way that I know how. I keep doing what I'm here to do! I give all of myself on stage and in my music and hopefully those limited minds change. If they don't... well they just don't. I *know* that I'm right where I belong. The people that matter appreciate me regardless of any of those superficial concepts. For that, I am grateful!

IS IT IMPORTANT TO UNDERSTAND THE BUSINESS SIDE OF THE INDUSTRY?

It is essential to understand the business side of the industry! If it is your goal to make a living doing this... if you are hoping to do more than just use it as an outlet or expression of your love and passion... if you mean to feed yourself and your family... well then, love is not enough, by a long shot! This industry, like any other, is swarming with people who will exploit you if you don't know any better. Your only protection against them is *to know better*!

ARE AWARDS HELPFUL?

In my opinion, awards absolutely help. I'd love to say that the accolades mean nothing and that I do this for myself, but that just isn't true. What I do is appreciated by a great many people. I am thankful for that appreciation. If I am being totally honest though, an award or two under my belt would earn me the recognition and respect that I don't currently have from some of the more sought-after venues/bookers on the circuit. Like I said, I'm still paying these dues. If they don't see a couple of awards next to your name, some bookers don't want to take a chance on your name at all. Although it's frustrating, I understand where they're coming from logistically. The problem is that *some* awards don't even consider artists whose names they haven't seen on the programmes of said venues/bookers. It's kind of a Catch-22!

That's why I always say that this business ain't for the faint of heart. If you are easily discouraged, this ain't for you. You gotta be willing to push through the barricades to get where you need to be. When it comes to the blues in particular, you have to really love it. Anything less won't do! My love for this is what fuels my desire to do my part in making sure that it has a bright future. That means that I can't get comfortable with where I am now. I have to strive for more. If a few awards can help with that, then I'll keep busting my butt to deserve them!

WHERE DO YOU SEE YOUR MUSIC GOING NEXT?

I would love to expand into more of Europe! I have developed an incredible following in the Benelux countries, and I have made so many wonderful friends there. I've branched out into France, Sweden, Norway and Denmark. My hope is to grow my audiences in Spain, Italy, Switzerland and the UK! I'd also like to get back to East Asia, this time performing my own music!

I am hopeful that I will be more visible and relevant at home in the USA as well. Maybe my dream of sharing a stage with Buddy Guy, Ruthie Foster, Bonnie Raitt, Eric Gales and Jonny Lang will come true one day soon!

I'll ride this wave as far as it'll take me… then I'll catch the next one and ride it even further!

CHICK RODGERS

Chick Rodgers was born in Memphis, Tennessee. She grew up singing in church with her father, and in the 1980s she sang for the group Clockwise, before moving to Chicago in 1989, where she gained a name for herself on the blues circuit. She performed as a support act for Koko Taylor, has toured in Europe and Japan and has appeared at major international blues festivals.

This is an edited version of an interview by Terry Mullins, which appeared in *Blues Blast Magazine* **on 16th October 2015.**

Chick Rodgers is one of the most soulful singers around, and she has the remarkable ability to transfer emotion from her voice straight to the heart of her audience.

Her version of 'Somewhere over the Rainbow' is guaranteed to induce chill bumps just a few seconds into the venerable tune. When she lists off the singers that she admired as a young woman trying to find her own voice, that power is fully understood.

"Aretha Franklin, of course. And from the gospel side, Shirley Caesar. Also, there's Diana Ross, and as far as male singers, it's always been Stevie Wonder and Sam Cooke for me," she said. "I just open my mouth and it comes out. It's like a blend of all my influences."

Rodgers has busily been sharing her amazing gift with music lovers everywhere in 2015, from right in her own backyard to way, way across the high seas.

"It's been a great year. I did the Chicago Blues Festival again this year and I was also in Italy and got my first chance to go the Canary Islands in Spain," she said. "I've worked more this year than I've worked in a long time. God is good all the time, but He's really been good this year."

In addition to hopping all over the globe, Rodgers has also begun work on a new recording project.

"We've not gotten too far into it yet – it's still in the first stages," she said. "We're working on getting all the songs together."

There's long been an old saying along the lines of "you are what you eat". That's probably true for all of us, but for Rodgers, you could probably tweak that phrase into something like "you're named for what you eat".

"I love fried chicken. In high school, from 10th to 11th grade, everyday – Monday through Friday – I was at Church's Chicken for lunch," she said. "Everybody just started calling me 'Chick' Rodgers because of that. That's how it happened and it stuck."

The daughter of a minister, Rodger's first real exposure to music – and to performing in front of a live audience – came via the church.

"Absolutely it did. And my father was a quartet singer. Me being the oldest, sometimes he had to take me to his shows with him," she said. "I just admired how he moved people, and how the women would be shouting in the church. That made me want to sing. As a family, me and my brothers and sisters used to sing as a little group. My mom and dad used to put us on the Easter programme and have us sing."

That path of singing and performing went from the church to high school for Rodgers.

"I did a lot of singing in high school for assemblies, then I went to west Tennessee for vocal competitions," she said. "That was when I realized that this is what I want to do. My very first trip to Germany was my first professional show. I didn't want to have no kids, I didn't want to get married, I wanted to be able to go and sing at any moment."

Although she's called Chicago home for several years now, Rodgers's formative years were spent down south in Memphis.

"I used to work on Beale Street at this place called the Club Royale. There was this guy from Chicago that came to Memphis twice a year because he had a farm in Mississippi. On his way back to Chicago from Mississippi, he would stop in Memphis to hear me. He did that for five years," Rodgers said. "One time, he asked me if I would come up (to Chicago) for either his fortieth or fiftieth birthday and sing at it. I said that I would. The club I sang in there was the Sandpiper, and they received me so well that they asked me to stay another week."

That one week quickly turned into a whole lot more and Rodgers has been a fixture on the Windy City scene ever since. Once she hit Chicago, her boundaries really started expanding at a rapid rate.

"Chicago has so many different opportunities. I got into theatre and started doing plays… there was just so much to do," she said. "I really do think that Chicago was just where I was supposed to be."

When Rodgers hits the stage, fireworks are bound to go off. She's part ministry, part night club and one limitless bundle of energy on the bandstand. It's usually not long before she has her audience eating out of the palm of her hand. This is even more remarkable when Rodgers reveals a part of her personality that many may have missed.

"I used to sing all the time, but I was shy. When I got ready to audition for the USO tour of Germany (on her first professional gig), this guy (involved in the tour) came up to me and said, 'Chick, you have a beautiful voice, but you need to get off that microphone stand and engage your crowd.' He told me what to do, and ever since I saw that it worked, that's what I've been doing," she said. "He told me to make sure to find someone in the crowd to sing to and to take that mic off the stand and move around the stage. I mean, it didn't happen overnight – it took years of experience for me to get where I am. It's something I've had to work at."

The incident that really set the wheels in motion for Rodgers to become one of the brightest stars on the soul scene took place back in the late 1980s in Memphis. It was there that she went from being a face in the crowd to the talk of the town, overnight.

Rodgers was in the back row at a Patti LaBelle concert when the star of the show innocently asked if there was anybody in the audience that could sing.

"I was way, way in the back and was with my godsister and her husband. When she asked if anyone could sing, three guys went up there. She was like, 'No, no. I need some real singers,'" explained Rodgers. "So my godbrother picked me up and literally put me up on the stage. He pushed me, so I had no other choice… I had to do what I do or fall out."

Rodgers didn't "fall out"; instead, she delivered a rendition of LaBelle's 'Lady Marmalade' that left everyone in attendance – including LaBelle herself – speechless.

"I took the mic and she looked at me like, 'You can sing? You're too little.' I opened my mouth and sang, and then I got nervous and tried to give her the mic back, and she was like, 'No! Hell No. You go ahead and finish this !#*! song!' So I did," Rodgers said. "That's how that happened. I was not going to go up there, because, like I said, I was shy. If my godbrother had not picked me up and put me up there, I just would have sat quietly in the back. It hit the newspapers the next day with an article about what happened."

One of the things that has sat Rodgers apart from other talented vocalists is her refusal to get pigeonholed into one style or one form of music. Sure, she can belt out the blues with the best of them, but when you get down to brass tacks, she really doesn't consider herself to be a "blues singer".

"I didn't want to be considered strictly a blues singer, because I love and can sing so many other different styles. I just didn't like the idea about singing about how pitiful my life has been," she said. "I didn't want to sing that kind of blues. I wanted to sing soul music. So I was able to mix different styles and still be able to work on the blues circuit."

It was when she first hit Chicago and started trying to find a steady gig that Rodgers learned that her mix of styles was welcomed with open arms by the movers and shakers on the scene, although a few other artists didn't share that same thought process.

"It was when I first went and auditioned at the Kingston Mines for a job when I first got here. My first songs at the audition were 'Dr Feelgood' and Gladys Knight's 'Midnight Train to Georgia'. He (the club owner) heard those songs and hired me on the spot," she said. "I got a lot of mouth about that from some of the other female blues singers who said, 'She ain't singing no blues… that's soul music. How is she going to get a job in a blues club singing that stuff?' Well, I told them up front I'm not a blues singer per se. I can sing the blues if that's what the job calls for, but I can do so much more than that too. Just don't look for me to do a whole set of the straight Delta blues… no way. I don't sing like that."

According to Rodgers, the message contained within the song is what matters most at the end of the day.

"Blues has a message too, but soul music is just powerful… I mean, I really can't explain it. But let me say this – what comes from the heart reaches the heart. And if you sing soul music, it has to come from the heart. That's the way I relate the power of soul music," she said. "I sing from the heart and in order to get it over, it has to have a message. Nobody wants to hear about people being depressed. People want to hear songs that are uplifting and talk about love. People want to hear inspirational music. That's what I sing."

Chicago Blues Festival

JACKIE SCOTT

Jackie Scott was born in Virginia and spent twenty years singing gospel in church. Inspired by seeing Buddy Guy and B.B. King live, she turned to the blues and moved to Chicago to learn her craft, with the help of Nellie Travis and Eddie Shaw. With her band The Housewreckers, she has performed all across the US, as well as Japan, France and Brazil, and has opened up for and performed with the likes of B.B. King, Taj Mahal, Magic Slim & The Teardrops, Eddie Shaw & The Wolfgang, Ronnie Baker Brooks, Keb Mo and Lyle Lovett. She won the Baltimore Blues Society's Battle of the Bands and was a finalist in the annual International Blues Challenge held in Memphis, Tennessee, and when not performing she mentors young singers at the Fernando Jones Blues Camp held in Chicago. Jackie Scott and the Housewreckers have released two albums, *How Much Woman Can You Stand* (2009) and *Going to the Westside* (2011).

HOW DID YOU START IN MUSIC?

My musical journey, like many, started in church. It wasn't long before I discovered the common bond between blues and gospel.

WHEN DID YOU START SINGING OR PLAYING AN INSTRUMENT?

I've been singing all my life… just not out loud. There's not a day that goes by that I don't sing. My father was a mechanic and I used to listen to him sing while he worked on cars. I never got dolls or anything like that from him at Christmas… it was always something musical like a guitar or a keyboard, and I never mastered any of them, but I've always loved to sing.

WHO WERE/ARE YOUR INFLUENCES?

Believe it or not, it was gospel music that led me to blues, so from that approach it was many old-schoolers in gospel… Shirley Caesar, Mahalia Jackson, Rosetta Tharpe and such. From there it was anybody from Nina Simone, Sarah Vaughan, Aretha Franklin and the likes. When it came to blues… Big Mama Thornton, and of course Koko Taylor, Etta James, Big Maybelle, Joe Williams, Esther Phillips and many more.

WHY CHOOSE THE BLUES?

I didn't choose the blues, it chose me. Blues is the only music that could move me like gospel, so I think I naturally gravitated to it.

HOW WOULD YOU DESCRIBE YOUR APPROACH?

To me gospel and blues are first cousins, so my approach comes from a gospel-like ear. I can't listen to blues without hearing gospel and vice-versa.

DO YOU WRITE OR COMPOSE YOUR OWN MATERIAL?

Yes, I do. It's one thing to hear a song that expresses how you feel, but it's quite another to tell your own story in your own way. That's what writing a song is all about… telling it and expressing the story in your own way.

HOW DO YOU START MAKING MUSIC? WHAT IS YOUR PROCESS?

For me it starts with a phrase or a powerful bass line. Eddie Shaw would be giving me advice about something, and I could hear a rhythm in the way he talked… thee highs and lows in his voice. He would say that he'd have to be in a certain frame of mind to write a good song. For me it can be a sound or one word that rings true for me. I keep my voice recorder with me, so whenever something catches my ear I try to record it. I may not think about it for weeks or months, and then something puts it all together.

WHICH DO YOU PREFER – PLAYING LIVE OR BEING IN A STUDIO? WHY?

I think most artists would say live, and I would agree. In the studio you have to mentally create an audience and a certain level of excitement about the music you're performing. With an audience the excitement and anticipation is kinda built in, and there's no substitution for that.

HOW DO YOU FIND THE RIGHT MUSIC PRODUCER FOR A RECORD?

I've only had one – me. Hopefully one day I'll have so much going on I'll need one. Maybe one day somebody will hear my voice and have a project waiting for me. The Bible says your gifts will make room for you, so I look forward to that happening.

ARE AUDIENCES DIFFERENT AROUND THE WORLD?

I really don't think so. I think people who love music just love music… maybe different genres of music, but the love of music is the cord that binds us all together.

DO YOU HAVE A FAVOURITE VENUE? WHY?

There's a place called The Taphouse in Hampton, Virginia, that was started by a guy named Peter Pittman, and Peter loved all kinds of music. There was something special about the place. It wasn't that big, but it just had this very special feel to it. I've always felt like the audience and I connected in that place. You could see their faces and interact with the audience in a close and personal way. I just loved performing there.

DESCRIBE YOUR JOURNEY AS AN ARTIST/MUSICIAN/SINGER.

My journey started like most, I would think. It's not the start or the end of my journey that I even think about. It's what has happened in between. I've had the opportunity to meet people that I've only read about and go to places where I didn't speak the language. Above all, I've made friends everywhere I've gone, and that is an important part of my journey. My picture is still being painted as an artist. You start out mimicking some of your favourites until you develop a style, if you want to call it that, of your own. That's where the artistry begins… the canvas is empty and, note by note, stroke by stroke, you start your painting. Along the way you start to develop as a musician, even if like me you don't play a physical instrument. Your ears become sharper to sounds, and you can for the first time hear your own voice. By the time you reach this level you no longer compare your voice to others… you can hear your own voice and respect it. I think when you get to this point you begin to develop and the journey truly begins.

WHAT WERE THE HIGHLIGHTS?

Over the years I've have the opportunity to meet, perform with and open up with some of the greats in blues, and they've all been highlights. Volunteering with Professor Fernando Jones at Columbia College (Chicago) for the Fernando Jones Blues Camp, held in Chicago annually, has definitely been a highlight. Working with the kids has been a blessing to blues and kids all over the country. Being able to encourage and teach the next generation of young people about blues is a gift that keeps on giving. Making the finals at the International Blues Challenge held in Memphis was also a highlight on my journey.

WHAT WERE THE CHALLENGES?

I've been so blessed beyond all expectations that nothing appears as a challenge. Knowing that my gifts will make room for me prevents anything from looking like a challenge.

IS THERE ONE SONG THAT IS CLOSEST TO YOUR HEART?

Yes… 'Don't Give Up'.

HOW DO YOU FIND PEOPLE TO COLLABORATE WITH?

I don't… I let them find me. I think looking for someone to collaborate with can be tricky… like dating (hahaha). You may find the person you think is best for a project, only to find out they're not what you thought. When someone approaches you about collaborating, most likely they've observed you, listened to your music, like your style, think they can put something in the pot to add to the flavour, and there you go. Again, not always true, but at least they know what the deal is, and together you build from there.

HOW DO YOU PROMOTE YOUR IMAGE/YOUR BRAND?

I promote mainly on social media, but the greatest way to promote your image or your brand is to consistently put on great shows… good news still travels fast!

ARE THERE PRESSURES ON WOMEN TO LOOK A CERTAIN WAY?

Maybe in other genres, but not blues or gospel in particular. Blues is everyday people's music. Blues goes beyond what you see, and the focus is on what you feel and how it makes you feel. For me the music is not constrained to what someone looks like. If that's the mindset of others, then it's your job as an entertainer to take them beyond, so they don't see with their eyes but see with their ears and heart.

HOW DO YOU DEAL WITH OBSTACLES SUCH AS AGEISM, SEXISM AND RACISM?

I don't deal with them. Those types of things are problems for others and not for me. If you choose to give those things energy and become a part of your thought process that's on you. I couldn't care less if you were green with purple stripes… treat me with the same respect I give you. I have a choice, and since I do they aren't obstacles to me. I can't change my age, my sex or my race. The fence you build to keep folks out is the same fence you build to block yourself in… have at it.

Blues Heaven Foundation, Chicago

IS IT IMPORTANT TO UNDERSTAND THE BUSINESS SIDE OF THE INDUSTRY?

Very much so! If you feel this is the profession for you, then you'd be very foolish not to understand every aspect of the business. After all, this is the way you will earn your living, take care of and raise your family... why wouldn't you? Music is very addictive. The bright lights, the cheers and accolades of audiences and fans provide for immediate satisfaction, but when is the next payday? How many streams of income can you position yourself to receive? Does the pay outweigh the sacrifices? If you don't know you need to know... your future depends on it.

ARE AWARDS HELPFUL?

It's nice to be acknowledged by peers and fans alike. I think awards are a testament to what others think about you and what you do, and that's wonderful. Truth be told, you're only as good as your last performance. With that in mind, you have to strive to be your best at all times. The awards end up on a shelf or on the wall, and while you appreciate them and they may look good on your resume, you still have to put the work in to maintain that "title". I guess the short answer is yes... it may help you earn a spot on a big show or two, but much more than that they are reminders that you have set the bar, not necessarily for others, but for yourself.

WHERE DO YOU SEE YOUR MUSIC GOING NEXT?

Hard to say, since I live in an area that doesn't have an established "blues scene". Clubs, venues and such in this area are sporadic when it comes to blues, and that can stifle your creative flow. I say that because it's something magical that happens with a live audience. The audience is there to see you, and even though you're there to entertain them an exchange between audience and entertainer takes place and an atmosphere of creativity develops. On more than one occasion in a live environment something just pops in my head and it's fuelled by the audience. My music will eventually go where the audience takes me and creates in me.

Bread and Roses, London

SISTER COOKIE

Lagos-born Londoner, singer-songwriter and self-taught pianist Sister Cookie grew up surrounded by all manner of solid sounds. Her youth saw her absorb the jazz, soul, highlife and juju LPs in her parents' collections and make further musical discoveries of her own throughout her teenage years and beyond. Eventually, she decided to have a go at performing herself, becoming a regular at London venues such as the Black Gardenia and the George Tavern.

In 2009 she became a mum and following a few years' hiatus to focus on family life, she returned to music at the end of 2012. To date, Sister Cookie has wowed audiences with her unique sound and charisma all across Europe and guested on records by bands including Jim Jones & The Righteous Mind, MFC Chicken and The Future Shape of Sound.

Sister Cookie now performs with her own band – a London-based quartet consisting of some of the capital's finest veteran musicians. They are currently working on her debut album – an assemblage of original material, all composed by Cookie herself. The record is nearing completion and is expected to be released this year.

SISTER COOKIE – IN HER OWN WORDS

I didn't choose music. It chose me. My earliest memories are of being around three years old, improvising little tunes on my keyboard and singing along to them. I now realize that I was one of those annoying kids who used to interrupt family gatherings with impromptu performances. In childhood, creating music and performing were the only things that really felt natural to me. My first love, however, was bittersweet. Though my parents did not fully *disapprove* of the affair – in fact, they quietly encouraged it – I was never allowed to forget that being a musician was not considered to be a valid career choice. As I got older, I consequently suppressed the urge and focused on other things (none of which, by the way, worked out), while still playing music as a hobby. I did sing in the church choir, probably between the ages of eleven and whenever I began to question religion – but I had a Catholic upbringing, which never sounds as authentically bluesy as raising hallelujah in one of the less repressed sects.

I performed a fair bit throughout school. Talent shows, school events, plays and the like. Because I had no formal training, I was never really included among the pupils who were seen as legitimate performing-arts talents – I was a self-taught pianist and singer. As such, I was tolerated, and no more. I was probably eighteen or nineteen when I first dared to take my talents on an excursion outside of my immediate locality and lay them bare in front of the great unwashed. I performed in London for the most part. Usually solo, though I also had three brief spells fronting bands, playing mostly rock 'n' roll and blues, and dolling myself up like an extra in *Cry-Baby* – getting "all painted up like trash" if you will. Headline bands on the same bill must have hated me, because I rarely got through a set without getting lipstick all over the microphone.

Like most kids, I went through lots of different musical phases – I'm talking everything from pop to psychobilly. I won't bore you with a chronological breakdown, but I changed my style a lot. The only true constant was my status as the weird kid. When I was about seventeen, I had a copy of the Clash's album *London Calling* and I was deeply in love with it. What struck me the most, though, was the wide variety of influences that wove their way through the songs – reggae, ska, rhythm and blues, rockabilly, rock 'n' roll… Long story short, at some point I discovered that 'Brand New Cadillac' was a cover (I'm not as young as I look, and back in my day the internet wasn't what it is now), sought out Vince Taylor's original recording and promptly fell in love with rock and roll – American and British. Soon afterwards, a boy I fancied introduced me to the music of the Cramps, and the search for a deeper understanding of their musical origins led me down the twisted path of rockabilly. It wasn't long, however, before I felt something missing. I had long been aware of the fact that it was people who looked like me who actually started this thing we now call rock 'n' roll, Now, I'd always loved the music of legends like Louis Jordan and Cab Calloway (my dad liked them), but I began to unearth so much more. People who had been largely written out of history at that point. Women. Women who sang about love and life with everything they had, unapologetically. Women who played their instruments (and here I include the voice) with just as much virtuosity as any of their more celebrated male counterparts, if not more so. I'm referring to such goddesses as LaVern Baker, Memphis Minnie, Sister Rosetta Tharpe, Willie Mae Thornton, and of course, the first to really make it all make sense for me – the Empress, Bessie Smith.

I'm afraid the story of how I first heard Bessie's music will disappoint you. One night, as I did most nights when I was eighteen, I was illegally downloading music on Limewire, when I came across a song entitled "'Tain't Nobody's Bizness'. I do love a word spelt phonetically for dramatic effect, so I gave it a listen. What happened next is indescribable. As the tinkling piano and the gramophone crackles caressed the rolling thunder of Bessie's voice, the light of the computer screen in the dark room seemed to grow larger and larger until I could see nothing but its glow, hear nothing but her voice and feel nothing but the words she sang. It was genuinely magical. I felt like she'd been there for me my whole life, although I was discovering her for the first time.

Bessie was the first to teach me to really feel The Pain. Later on, I discovered Billie Holiday, and then Edith Piaf, and then Hank Williams, who all taught me to feel The Pain in a song in different ways – but Bessie's blues really made me feel sadness in a manner that I had hitherto never explored. She opened up my avenues of expression, and many rickety old carriages, each laden with the burdens of my soul, made their way through

Paper Dress Vintage , London

those lonely streets. As a girl who had experienced bullying and other abuse I had never even been able to speak about, it was beyond therapeutic. When I began to research her and found out what she looked like and what she liked to do, and started to try to get close to understanding what kind of a woman she was, it almost felt like an awakening. At last, somebody I could *truly* relate to. I can remember buying a DVD compilation of early blues performances in the Covent Garden Fopp one day because it contained the short film *St Louis Blues* (featuring the only known footage of a Bessie Smith performance) and watching it over and over and over again. I still can't watch it without fighting tears.

By now I was making regular appearances at the Black Gardenia on Dean Street. For those who weren't there, the Black Gardenia was a bijou bohemian basement bar, back when Soho was still pretty boho. I cut my teeth playing the piano there, sometimes up to three nights a week, often three sets a night of mostly improvised tunes – fuelled by wine on the house (purchased at the Tesco Express directly opposite the bar's street-level entrance and sold on to punters at West End prices). I have many happy memories of playing there, allowing all other troubles I might have thought I had then to flow through my fingers and out of my throat. My sets covered a mix of styles at this time, from attempts at boogie-woogie and New Orleans R & B to bluesy covers of Hank Williams and Johnny Cash tunes (I really have a lot of love for country music, but that's another story for another time), but I really got going when I'd get down to a sorrowful blues standard or, more frequently, improvise lyrics relating to my feelings at any given moment over a basic twelve-bar progression.

Growing up in a world I've never quite belonged to, it's interesting that I found comfort in the music of the past. However, I don't think of myself as a throwback. True, discovering the blues and implementing the form into my music was key to my artistic development, but I'm adding my own moody twist to my inspirations as opposed to being a carbon copy. The songs I write are all about – or directly related to – my life. I don't want to be the kind of artist who makes music that they think other people think they should make.

I've had a lot of challenges to overcome, and I'm still overcoming them. On a personal level, I'm quite introverted and also deeply sensitive. I'm also hyper-critical of everything I do, and I have a tendency to be pessimistic. These are all qualities that make setbacks harder to deal with and negatively affect the need to self-promote (which is integral to the music business nowadays). I often find social media upsetting and overwhelming too. On a practical level, trying to balance the unsociable hours and frequent travelling commitments with being around for my family is also really hard. But when it all comes down to it, I'm happier doing this than I ever was working for other people in jobs I didn't enjoy and wasn't cut out for. I think my son is proud of me – I know he shows everyone at his school YouTube videos of me doing what I do. Having his support, as well as the support of my other half, makes the difficult stuff a bit easier to face.

The Hippodrome, London

My writing process is never the same. Sometimes I start with an emotion and a melody, then the words come later. Sometimes I write down how I'm feeling, forget about it, come across it later and add a melody I've had in my head for a while if it fits. I've written complete songs in twenty minutes – and I've taken weeks to finish a single verse.

I enjoy the creative process that comes with being in the studio. It took me a long time to find the right band, but now that I have, any day we spend recording or rehearsing is a lot of fun. We all get on really well and feed off each other. I also love encouraging the band to take risks and play things differently from how they initially thought they should – I find I get the best out of all of them this way, and that's what makes our sound so interesting. One of the advantages of being a self-taught musician is that one has to compensate for one's lack of technical know-how with imagination and *feel*, so if one gets it right one's end result will never be dull. I like seeing a track grow from the seeds of an idea I had in my head to a complete and complex composition that is as dependent on the contributions of all involved in its creation as it is on the little demo I recorded on my phone, alone with my piano.

That said, nothing can compete with the feeling of performing live. I can't even adequately explain what it does to you. The pre-show nerves and tension. Being in front of an audience night after night. Knowing the thread which connects you and this space full of strangers runs directly from your own soul – and theirs. And when they dig it as much as you do, that's almost too much. When they ride along with you from that moment the spotlight hits to the point when you finally exit the stage, all of us spent and dripping in sweat with our souls aglow, it's addictive. People say audiences are different around the world, but I don't think so. You have great gigs, and then you have the rest. It depends on so many factors, most of which you can't control. We play to so many different crowds as well, from dive bars to high-tone places and community events to hip festivals, that I think it's futile to compare audiences according to geographical location. I've been very lucky to have played in some amazing places. I love repurposed venues, like old cinemas, theatres and churches. I once did a gig in a beautiful old cinema (which was named after Georges Méliès) in Pau, France. In my early days I was fortunate enough to be booked for a night at Bush Hall in West London, doing a solo set on their gorgeous piano right before Bearlesque did their thing. That was wild! I've played in the stunning Kafé Antzokia (occupying the site of the former San Vincente theatre) in Bilbao. We played in the Union Chapel right here in London last year, and that was truly a special place to be in. I've sung at the 100 Club a few times now, and it always feels like a privilege to be onstage in the same room some of my heroes have played to across its seventy-plus-year history – particularly these days when the powers that be are flattening its contemporaries to make way for nothing at all, as in the cases of iconic venues such as the Astoria and The Mean Fiddler, the 12 Bar and our own dear Black Gardenia. I've played at some incredible festivals over the years – the Mark Lamarr God's Jukebox stage at Latitude Festival was particularly memorable. I think my favourite ever festival was Funtastic Dracula Carnival in Benidorm in 2013. One of the craziest parties I've ever been to, and we were the only rhythm-and-blues act on a bill that otherwise boasted top names in the world of garage and punk – it was the first time I'd ever actually performed in Spain, and the crowd was the kind of crowd you wish for every night. Beautiful memories.

You ask how I have combated ageism, sexism and racism. Like many others, I've often had to deal with all three. I'm much younger than most of the people I work with, and let's just say many people have taken issue with a girl half their age, with half their experience, giving them direction. There are a lot of boys in this game, and unfortunately many of them don't want the girls joining in. I struggled to take control for a while – after being out of action for five years I'd lost a lot of confidence. Gradually I came to realize that age and ability deserve respect, but that doesn't make you better than me. I write the songs, I handle all the business, and everything that happens is ultimately down to me. If I'm going to fail, I'd rather fail on my own terms. Racism is a different kettle of fish. People see a black girl making music with roots in the roots, and they begin to objectify you. They expect you to adhere to certain stereotypes – and when you don't, they get annoyed. Sometimes they don't think you're good enough because you won't fit into their boxes. They refuse to view what you're doing with an open mind. Then there are all the white people who run events, etc., who are completely sheltered and have obviously never had any contact with Real Live Blacks, and believe that while they profit from our artistic contributions (from the historic to the present day) they have licence to disrespect us through employing the use of racist imagery for their promo, under the labels of "vintage", "kitsch" and "quirky", refusing to spare a second thought for the offence they cause. I love calling them out though. It's been a long time since I was a regular on the UK vintage music circuit – I've spent the past few years trying to branch out, because the overall whiteness, and a lot of the narrow-minded thinking that goes with it, was depressing. It's not just limited to promoters and audiences – many fellow musicians, sadly, equate their partaking in (and benefiting from) a black art form with being anti-racist, and a few conversations with some people will tell you that isn't true. We play to a wider range of people these days and my world is all the better for it.

Music has always been a means of self-expression for me, but I feel it's even more than that. "Self-expression" is a term insufficient to describe how much I need to make music to survive. It doesn't begin to evoke how lost I felt when I gave up music entirely for a few years after my son was born. I never regretted the decision, and I love my son more than anything, but I feel like a better person now I have achievements and goals to focus on attaining for myself which are outside my roles as a mother and a spouse. I'm really looking forward to my debut album being released. It's been a very difficult journey that's seen lineup changes, labels initially showing interest then dropping out when they realized I wasn't conforming to their ideals, me single-handedly juggling

The Hippodrome, London

everything and financing everything myself, stops, starts, tears, frustration and anger – giving way to joy and a sense of achievement. I've written and arranged every single song for the record, all by myself. It's a document of the difficult times I've experienced, particularly over the last few years and as such – recording these songs has been cathartic. I don't easily open up about my problems, but I seem to have no problem singing about them. Every song is personal, from revisiting shitty past relationships to grieving the loss of a loved one. I have had incredible opportunities to work with some amazing acts in my short time and I have been honoured to guest on some great records. Now, though, it's time to shine my light. I can't wait for you all to hear it.

Kingston Mines, Chicago

PEACHES STATEN

Peaches Staten was born in Doddsville, Mississippi, and raised in Chicago on a steady diet of blues, soul, gospel and R & B fed to her by her mother, who was a member of the Whale's Inn Cicero Bunch Social Club, while her stepfather was the DJ. She began her professional career in a zydeco band and an Afro-Brazilian samba ensemble and has gone on to work with the best that the blues has to offer and grace stages all over the globe. Her latest CD, *Live at Legends*, was released to critical acclaim.

HOW DID YOU START IN MUSIC?

Started listening to blues as a child. My mom and her siblings were a group of gospel singers around Mississippi when they were teenagers. My dad played drums. Grew up listening to blues in the home as a young girl. My oldest brother turned me on to rock as a teenager. My stepdad was a blues Dj back in the 70s.

WHEN DID YOU START SINGING OR PLAYING AN INSTRUMENT?

I started singing in 1994, with Guy Lawrence and Chideco Zydeco (Tex-Mex, blues, zydeco and country). That's when I met Lurrie Bell who was the guitar player with the band. Guy Lawrence introduced me to the frottoir (washboard). While playing with Chideco Zydeco, I was introduced to a Brazilian band (Maluco Samba) in '96. I couldn't speak the language, but learned to sing it. Then blues came along while performing at Rosa's Blues Club. Gino Battaglia from Blue Chicago approached me and offered me a gig with Willie Kent. It is also where I met Bonnie Lee and Karen Carroll, who shaped me into the blues vocalist I am today.

WHO WERE/ARE YOUR INFLUENCES?

My other influences are Tina Turner and Koko Taylor. These two ladies inspired me to choose songs that had a taste of rock and make them my own.

WHY CHOOSE THE BLUES?

I didn't choose the blues, the blues chose me, and I'm so happy it did.

HOW WOULD YOU DESCRIBE YOUR APPROACH?

My approach is engaging my audience in my performance. I love making eye contact and approaching them offstage while performing. My frottoir allows me to incorporate a little Louisiana blues with my show. I often call someone from the audience on stage to play it.

DO YOU WRITE OR COMPOSE YOUR OWN MATERIAL?

Yes I do. It can be found on both my CDs: *Time Will Tell* (Slang Music) and *Live at Buddy Guy's Legends* (Swississippi Music). I am currently working on my new CD with all original material.

WHICH DO YOU PREFER – PLAYING LIVE OR BEING IN A STUDIO? WHY?

I enjoy playing both live and studio. Playing live gives me a connection with my audience and allows me to take it to a higher level. Being in a studio setting allows me to find my highs and lows and correct them before going live.

HOW DO YOU FIND THE RIGHT MUSIC PRODUCER FOR A RECORD?

It can be difficult finding the right music producer. The best of the best may not be right with what you're trying to accomplish. There has to be an open mind between artist and producer.

ARE AUDIENCES DIFFERENT AROUND THE WORLD?

Sometimes I feel there is an audience difference around the world. Outside of the US, music lovers tend to listen more closely to the lyrics. They enjoy a good story about the song you're doing and the CD sales are high.

European Blues Cruise

DO YOU HAVE A FAVOURITE VENUE? WHY?

I used to think I had a favourite venue until I started travelling the world. Now I can't choose.

DESCRIBE YOUR JOURNEY AS AN ARTIST/MUSICIAN/SINGER.

My journey as an artist started out at Rosa's in Chicago as a waitress, watching and listening to the many great musicians that came through and me meeting the zydeco band. I remember a Monday-night jam with Buddy Scott at Rosa's. I attempted to sing Billy Holiday's 'Good Morning Heart Ache'. After the set was over, he took me to the side and said, "Girl you can sing, you just need to learn your right key." He gave me the Key G. Called me back on stage, same song, different key. A star was born! He taught me that it's not about the song, it's the key you choose to sing it in.

IS THERE ONE SONG THAT IS CLOSEST TO YOUR HEART?

'Blood Is Thicker than Time' by Mavis Staples.

HOW DO YOU PROMOTE YOUR IMAGE/YOUR BRAND?

Going out to shows and sitting in if they call you up. It's all about the vibes you share on stage!

The Park West, Chicago

SUSAN TEDESCHI

Susan Tedeschi was born in 1970 in Boston, Massachusetts, and grew up in the Norwell suburb. She began singing in a local choir at a young age, and when she was thirteen she performed with local bands and honed her craft as a guitarist. She formed the Susan Tedeschi Band in 1993, which became a staple in Boston's blues scene. With this band she released the albums *Better Days* (1995), *Just Won't Burn* (1998), *Wait for Me* (2002), *Live from Austin TX* (2004), *Hope and Desire* (2005) and *Back to the River* (2008), before the group merged with her husband Derek Trucks's band to form the Tedeschi Trucks Band and released *Revelator* (2011), *Live: Everybody's Talkin'* (2012), *Made Up Mind* (2013), *Let Me Get By* (2016), *Live from the Fox Oakland* (2017) and *Signs* (2019), winning one Grammy Award and six Blues Music Awards in the process.

This is an edited version of an interview by Iain Patience, which appeared in *Blues Matters!* **in November 2019.**

Susan Tedeschi is that rare thing, a female blues-cum-rock-'n'-roll artist with a life-long history of music performance and involvement. Speaking to her on the eve of the Tedeschi Trucks Band's latest release, *Signs*, she is open, laid-back but positively focused on the coming year ahead, with gigs already booked for around nine-months ahead, and a twin-night London Palladium set already sold-out, a gig she is particularly looking forward to: "I'm just so excited to be playing the Palladium in London. And both nights are already sold out, I believe. It's great to have multiple nights in London. The band loves a theatre setting, one that's big enough to hold us but small enough to have a real connection with the audience," she confirms.

Of course, Tedeschi is part of a greater whole, with her husband Derek Trucks and a full-throat twelve-piece Tedeschi Trucks Band roaring and rolling alongside. When asked about the challenges touring with such an expansive outfit must inevitably bring, she is quick to confirm that it can be: "...tricky at times. But we all get on so well, we're good friends. It's essential to be like that. We're on the road together for most of the year, so there will always be moments, but overall it works real well. It's important to let everybody have their own time and moments with the band. In effect, we are a three-section band with a three-piece vocal section, the guitars, drums and bass, and a three-piece horn section. It all comes together and everybody does their part and must have the space too."

Often likened to either Janis Joplin or Bonnie Raitt, Tedeschi herself agrees that both are huge influences in her own musical evolution, while husband Derek brings

215

his own stamp and input to everything they do together. So, I suggest gently, does the husband and wife thing create tensions or friction when on the road so much?

"Yeah, of course. It's naturally difficult at times, but I really believe it works best for us both. It means we're together more than many others and we always manage to work out any differences! We have our good days and our bad days, but generally it feels better, much better when we're together more. When you're a band and apart, well sometimes that makes things just that much more difficult, it can put a strain on some relationships. We are happy together. Derek's mother comes in and helps with the kids when we're out on the road, and his brother lives just down the road, so he also helps out. Though we will be taking them both out with us later this year, during school vacation – one's a freshman and the other is now in high school – on tour in Japan and the USA."

Back in 2010 Derek Trucks and Susan Tedeschi merged their respective bands, and Tedeschi reckons that could have been a tricky transition and time, but as they had both been working together in the soul end of the business, with the Soul-Stew Revival, it was surprisingly and refreshingly easy as a process: "In reality, it was simple. I had been working with a five-piece band and Derek with either a three- or four-piece. When we merged, apart from us both, we only had to bring in three players from other bands. Then in around 2008 we added the horns. I love the horn section. Now we are a twelve-piece and have that full sound that means we can cross genres easily. I'm not just a blues player – we can pull in jazz, soul, rock, country, whatever we like. We all work together, writing, bringing bits of the puzzle together. I just think I'm blessed to be able to do this, to be making music and playing with these great people, this great band."

Tedeschi adds that the writing process is a prime example of this approach, where each band member can bring something to the table: "We get together and everybody will be writing something, so we jam around and pick up the pieces, see where it all leads us. On the new album, *Signs*, we came together and Tim had a bassline that we worked on. We had no words, but Derek put more on it and sent it to our old friend, Warren Haynes, who put the lyric together. At other times, I might have a song or Derek might have one we can use. This is our first release in three years, and Derek did the production work on it. He loves to be involved in everything. He writes, he plays and he produces. It's all great and he enjoys it all."

One other major benefit, which she confirms features as a result of this process, is that with such a large band, the creativity is remarkable: "We have such a lot to draw on and from. We have the creativity of twelve musicians and we have the diversity, that all comes into the recording. With some bands there can be a sort of 'samey' feel. I think we avoid that because we have so much there – we all come together but from different angles. The horn section does its own arrangements, for example, and Cofey, our keyboard genius, does the guitar arrangements for us. It just all works so well."

By diversity, Tedeschi goes on to explain how important this is personally to her: "We have true diversity – I don't just mean that we have men and women: we have different races, religions, a whole range of differences that just come together and give us quite an edge."

Turning again to the new album, Tedeschi is clearly particularly pleased to have a father and daughter pairing playing on the recording: "We have four string players from the local Jacksonville Orchestra on it. They were great. They just turned up, could sight read it all; and we even had this father/daughter pair which gives it a nice family element."

In the past, she says, the band has been tempted to maybe deliver a live album when they're sort of between projects, possibly while they're all still working on a batch of new songs, planning ahead for another release. Now, however, she feels that approach and attack may have had its day, believing that the way everybody pulls together, bringing their own takes, touches, inspiration and creativity and writing to the table, means this is no longer necessary. She prefers to work on the basis of less is more and quality over quantity.

Looking back over her long career, Tedeschi, who started out as a six-year-old, has worked countless musical genres but always comes back to soul and blues. Blues music is always at the heart of everything she does, as she says: "Blues music is always there, it just is. It is always soulful, that gospel-blues music is the cornerstone of it all, all the genres."

Over the years, Tedeschi has been either nominated or won numerous international music awards, including a Grammy back in 2012 for the Tedeschi Trucks album *Revelator*. In addition the Americana music awards and blues awards have also given recognition to a genuinely inspiring career and her dedication to the music she so clearly loves. With the latest offering, *Signs*, being a genuine tour-de-force in many ways, it would come as no surprise to find it as either a contender or winner in this year's awards circus. Tedeschi, laughs at the suggestion, but is also evidently pleased with the possibility: "Who knows, who can tell? We'll just wait and see what happens. I'm just so glad I get to play music like we do. To travel the world, doing what I love most. I don't get caught up in the awards thing, worrying about it. At the end of the day it's always good to have the acknowledgement of our peers, but at the end it's just us doing our job, working, producing great music (I hope) and it's all been great. It's a real blessing to do it."

Lucerne Blues Festival, Switzerland

IRMA THOMAS

Irma Thomas was born in Pontchoula, Louisiana, in 1941. As a teenager, she sang for a Baptist choir, auditioning for Specialty Records at the age of thirteen. She worked as a waitress at the Pimlico Club in New Orleans, where she would occasionally sing with the band fronted by Tommy Ridgley. The latter helped her land a record deal, and Thomas's first single, 'You Can Have My Husband (But Don't Mess with My Man)' reached No. 22 on the Billboard Chart in 1960. From then on, Thomas would have a successful career, often in collaboration with the producer and songwriter Allen Toussaint, with hits such as 'It's Raining' (1962), 'Ruler of My Heart' (1963), 'Wish Someone Would Care' (1964) and 'Good to Me' (1968). In 1980, she opened the Lion's Den Club with her husband Emile Jackson. In 1991 she received her first Grammy nomination for the album *Live! Simply the Best*, and after releasing only gospel music for a few years she returned to secular music with *The Story of My Life* (1997) and *Sing It* (1998). She had another Grammy nomination for *After the Rain* (2006), and her latest album is *Simply Grand* (2008). She performs regularly in New Orleans and internationally. In 2007 Thomas was inducted into the Louisiana Music Hall of Fame, and in 2018 she received the Lifetime Achievement Award for Performance at the Americana Music Honors & Awards.

WHEN DID YOU START SINGING OR PLAYING AN INSTRUMENT?

I don't play an instrument with any degree of proficiency.

WHO WERE/ARE YOUR INFLUENCES?

All of the early blues singers – my Dad had a lot of B.B. King, John Lee Hooker, Ruth Brown, Mahalia Jackson, Percy Mayfield in the house, and he would play them on his days off. Plus the local radio stations would play a lot of the music of that time.

WHY CHOOSE THE BLUES?

It was what I heard on the radio most. I could have gone gospel, but rhythm and blues was what I got fired for for singing on the job, so that is what I stuck with.

HOW WOULD YOU DESCRIBE YOUR APPROACH?

I sing what I like and feel I can tell the story if it makes sense.

HOW DO YOU START MAKING MUSIC? WHAT IS YOUR PROCESS?

If I have an idea and put it on a recorder as soon as it comes to me, it makes it to a recording studio. Haha!

WHICH DO YOU PREFER – PLAYING LIVE OR BEING IN A STUDIO? WHY?

I don't make a difference between the two. When I am recording I sing the work as if I am with a live audience.

HOW DO YOU FIND THE RIGHT MUSIC PRODUCER FOR A RECORD?

They always find me. I can work with anyone who understands my voice and my singing ability.

ARE AUDIENCES DIFFERENT AROUND THE WORLD?

No. Not really, because if they are your fans they will give you the respect and love no matter what country I am in.

DO YOU HAVE A FAVOURITE VENUE? WHY?

No, anywhere I get paid to give a show I put my best into that show, because I love what I do and I respect my fans no matter where they come to see me.

DESCRIBE YOUR JOURNEY AS AN ARTIST/MUSICIAN/SINGER.

I am blessed to still be doing what I do, and my journey is not over.

WHAT WERE THE HIGHLIGHTS?

I have received many honours in my lifetime and they all mean a lot to me. The Blues Hall of Fame, the Grammy, an Honorary Doctorate from Tulane University among the lot.

WHAT WERE THE CHALLENGES?

Early in my career it was being a mother and trying to work in the business. Now it's the travelling as a senior person, but I still love the work and what comes with it.

IS THERE ONE SONG THAT IS CLOSEST TO YOUR HEART?

My one major hit 'Wish Someone Would Care', which went to no. 17 on the Billboard charts back in 1964, before the British invasion.

IS THERE ONE ARTIST WHO HAS TRULY INSPIRED YOU?

Not really, because all of us who were doing quality music back then were all trying to make our music heard.

HOW DO YOU PROMOTE YOUR IMAGE/YOUR BRAND?

Just being myself and let my fans speak for me.

Chicago Blues Festival

HOW DO YOU DEAL WITH OBSTACLES SUCH AS AGEISM, SEXISM AND RACISM?

It's a problem for the person who has an issue – I just be myself.

IS IT IMPORTANT TO UNDERSTAND THE BUSINESS SIDE OF THE INDUSTRY?

Yes. I have a two-year degree in business, and it has helped me understand the ins and outs of the business side of the music industry. I now know how to negotiate my contracts to my benefit.

ARE AWARDS HELPFUL?

They can be: it all depends on your management and how you are promoted after you win them.

WHERE DO YOU SEE YOUR MUSIC GOING NEXT?

I have not given that much thought, because I am still going to sing songs that tell a good story and make sense to me.

Chicago Blues Festival

NELLIE "TIGER" TRAVIS

Nellie "Tiger" Travis was born in the early 1960s in Mound Bayou, Mississippi. She was brought up primarily by her grandmother, who was a minister, and in whose church she began to sing at age five. After considering becoming an actress, she moved to Los Angeles and sang in various Top 40 cover bands. In 1992 she moved to Chicago to look after her ailing mother, and ended up staying there and discovering the blues. She had her first performance at the Kingston Mines venue in 1995, and established herself on the circuit, under the mentorship of Koko Taylor. Travis has performed across the world, and has shared the stage with the likes of Buddy Guy, B.B. King, Koko Taylor, Gladys Knight and Ronnie Baker Brooks. She has recorded several albums, including *Wanna Be with You* (2005), *I'm a Woman* (2008), *I'm in Love with a Man I Can't Stand* (2009), *I'm Going Out Tonight* (2011) and her latest, *Mr Sexy Man* (2017).

HOW DID YOU START IN MUSIC?

I started in the music business in church at an early age, singing gospel. I had to be about five years old that I can remember.

WHO WERE/ARE YOUR INFLUENCES?

In gospel, Shirley Caesar and Inez Andrews, and in R & B, Gladys Knight, Tina Turner and Koko Taylor.

WHY CHOOSE THE BLUES?

I chose the blues, being that it was derived from gospel, it was a twist and a twang more, so it made blues natural to do.

HOW WOULD YOU DESCRIBE YOUR APPROACH?

My approach vocally is strong and raspy.

DO YOU WRITE OR COMPOSE YOUR OWN MATERIAL?

I write and compose some of my own material.

HOW DO YOU START MAKING MUSIC? WHAT IS YOUR PROCESS?

My process in how I make or record music is that I have the musicians to lay the music down for all the songs, then I go in and lay vocals. I basically write songs to the music.

WHICH DO YOU PREFER – PLAYING LIVE OR BEING IN A STUDIO? WHY?

I like playing live and being in the studio, but live to me is the only way to go: you get to be close and personal with your audience. You are not limited when you are live, you get to stretch out and let it rip.

HOW DO YOU FIND THE RIGHT MUSIC PRODUCER FOR A RECORD?

How do I find the right music producer? I haven't – they found me, haha!

ARE AUDIENCES DIFFERENT AROUND THE WORLD?

Yes, my audience is very different around the world: they somehow show a greater love and respect for the craft of blues than some in the culture of blues.

DO YOU HAVE A FAVOURITE VENUE? WHY?

No favourite venue in particular, but the larger the better.

DESCRIBE YOUR JOURNEY AS AN ARTIST/MUSICIAN/SINGER.

My journey as a musician/vocalist is sometimes disturbing, but rewarding. I tend to do a lot of shows where I am the only woman and all the others are men. I learned that some guys are worse than women when it comes to that stage. I earn my rewards by showing up and showing out. That means I give a great show and show much love to my audience.

IS THERE ONE SONG THAT IS CLOSEST TO YOUR HEART?

The two songs that are closest to my heart are a song that I wrote in honour of Koko Taylor after she passed away, 'Koko the Queen of the Blues', and 'I'd Rather Go Blind' by Etta James.

IS THERE ONE ARTIST WHO HAS TRULY INSPIRED YOU?

Koko Taylor was a true inspiration for me, she was very dear to me. I learned a lot from her when it comes to musicians, other females and jealousy. In December 1998, New Year's Eve, I was performing at Koko Taylor's Banquet Hall and my mother was videotaping me, when she suddenly dropped to the floor after having a massive heart attack and aneurysm. She passed away right in front of me. I spent a lot of time with Koko and received the love of a mother from her in many ways. She will always be my queen.

HOW DO YOU PROMOTE YOUR IMAGE/YOUR BRAND?

I promote my image verbally, and via social media, my website and my performances.

ARE THERE PRESSURES ON WOMEN TO LOOK A CERTAIN WAY?

There are no pressures for me to look a certain way. There were tales in blues gossip that women in blues were always big and fat. I beg to differ. I don't have the blues, I am here to give you the blues: that's why I dress nice and sing good.

HOW DO YOU DEAL WITH OBSTACLES SUCH AS AGEISM, SEXISM AND RACISM?

Well, I don't have an issue with age or sexism, because I'm pretty protective of myself and I am one to get a person straight on anything if they come at me the wrong way. Racism I *hate*. I grew up in Mississippi and was taught to love all colour and all kind. I am that way to this day: I love people but can't deal with no racist. I am verbal about it as well.

IS IT IMPORTANT TO UNDERSTAND THE BUSINESS SIDE OF THE INDUSTRY?

It is very important to understand the business side of the industry, but yet it can be very complicated.

ARE AWARDS HELPFUL?

Awards are supposed to be helpful, but I guess it depends on where your award comes from.

WHERE DO YOU SEE YOUR MUSIC GOING NEXT?

I see my music going mainstream, meaning worldwide. I'm halfway there now – I've got many more miles to travel.

Buddy Guy's Legends, Chicago

Chicago Blues Festival

TEENY TUCKER

Teeny Tucker was born in 1958 in Dayton, Ohio. Her father was the seminal blues artist Tommy Tucker, and she sang from an early age, but only made her professional live debut in 1996. She has recorded six studio albums: *Tommy's Girl* (2000), *First Class Woman* (2003), *Two Big Ms* (2008), *Keep the Blues Alive* (2010), *Voodoo to Do You* (2013) and *Put on Your Red Dress Baby* (2018). She has performed at many major festivals around the world, and has won Monterey Bay Blues Artist of the Year in 2010, as well as being nominated for the Koko Taylor Blues Music Award in 2012 and 2014, Blues Blast Artist of the Year in 2008, 2011 and 2013 and Living Blues magazine Artist of the Year in 2014. In 2014 she gave an acclaimed seminar at Penn State University on "Women in the Blues and How to Overcome Obstacles".

HOW DID YOU GET STARTED IN MUSIC? WHEN DID YOU START SINGING?

I was born into music. My father was Tommy Tucker, who wrote and sang the 1964 classic, 'Hi-Heel Sneakers', a song recorded by more than a dozen other artists, including the Rolling Stones, the Beatles, Janis Joplin, Stevie Wonder and Elvis Presley. The track was inducted into the 2017 Blues Hall of Fame by the Blues Foundation in Memphis, Tennessee. My father's side of the family are made up of singers and musicians, and I guess it all rubbed off on me. I started singing in the church gospel choir at a young age, around eight or nine years old. Once I got the bug for the blues the rest was history.

WHO WERE YOUR INFLUENCES?

At my youngest age it was the "Queen of Gospel" Mahalia Jackson. I first heard her on my only affordable Christmas gift, a radio, when I was around eight years old. I was inspired by Mahalia to record my first song when I was chosen to record at age fourteen with my church gospel choir, a song written by gospel-hymn songwriter Doris Akers. These experiences lead me to become a "daughter to the blues", which became the title of a song I wrote for my *Keep the Blues Alive* CD.

WHY CHOOSE THE BLUES?

In the mid to late 1970s my father toured Europe often. In 1996, his German promoter contacted me, trying to locate female blues singer Christine Kittrell, who had signed with Vee Jay Records back in the 1960s and was famous for her 'I'm a Woman' and 'Sittin' Here Drinkin''. He wanted to write a story about her in one of the notable European blues magazines. I located Christine, who was living on the north side of my hometown. We became friends until her death. The German promoter sent me a cassette tape – sounds ancient, I know – requesting that I learn five to ten of the blues songs from various female blues artists like Etta James, Koko Taylor, Nina Simone, Wynona Carr, Wanda Jackson and others, after which he would bring me to Europe to perform at a few of the blues festivals. I ambitiously learned all the songs on the tape, went to Europe to perform accompanied by a German blues band, and the rest is history. I ventured out from gospel music and caught the blues bug.

DESCRIBE YOUR APPROACH.

I loved poetry and drama since my elective classes in middle and high school. I guess I intuitively write my life events down and add rhythms and melodies to make songs about my experiences in life. It's therapeutic for me, but I quickly learned that blues music is a universal story, and when it's told we all share common life events, events that are sad or joyful, breakups, depressions, oppressions. I am a vocal musician. I do not play an instrument, but I've have been collaborating with my music arranger, Robert Hughes, over the past eleven years. We are able to conceptualize the story and intertwine it vocally and musically.

WHICH DO YOU PREFER – PLAYING LIVE OR BEING IN A STUDIO. WHY?

It is incredibly rewarding to sing live. Blues fans and blues purists are the most gracious people on earth. They understand the story, they relate to it, and their excitement gets me excited during a live performance. They're not judgemental, and more importantly they are supportive. Recording and creating music in the studio can be a little more confined because you're working with others, and the momentum can be puzzling. Overall, the studio is fun and can have some magical moments as well.

HOW DO YOU FIND THE RIGHT MUSIC PRODUCER FOR A RECORD?

Robert Hughes and I have produced our last four CD projects together. We are doing something different for our new project, which will include some interesting guests and unique material.

ARE AUDIENCES DIFFERENT AROUND THE WORLD?

Music is universal. It is the thread that unites people from all walks of life. We all love, we all hurt, we all lose and we all gain hope, and it is precisely music that lifts our spirits, pricks our souls and unites us. So no, music audiences around the world are universally the same.

Buddy Guy's Legends, Chicago

DO YOU HAVE A FAVOURITE VENUE?

I love entertaining, whether there's only two people in my living room or two hundred people in a small space or venue. So yeah, it can be a venue or a backyard. Blessings from music can be received and displayed anywhere.

DESCRIBE YOUR JOURNEY AS AN ARTIST?

I was born to a mother who loved the blues clubs, various blues artists and blues music. In the 1950s my mother lived in the segregated Midwest, in what they called the lower valley of Dayton, Ohio. The white girls would sneak from the lower valley and frequent the upper-valley blues clubs without letting their parents know. My mother was one of those white girls. She met my dad, the handsome black man on the piano singing the blues in the night club to a mixed audience that came together even during the civil rights movement, almost three years after Rosa Parks refused to move to the back of the bus. Wow, blues music integrated folks even before it became popular. My father and mother were mesmerized by each other, even though my father was married and already had three children. My brother – my dad's fourth child between him and his wife – and I were born twenty days apart. My mother hid my birth from my dad until I was eight months old. Eventually I was exposed to music, and the only child out of eight of my father's children who inherited the

229

bug. He unknowingly passed the torch to me. It wasn't until after his death that I became the full-time daughter to the blues. I could highlight my entire blues journey here, but thirty years is a huge bundle of leaves to wrap into this question. I've been baptized in the blues and now not only perform as a blues artist, but am an advocate and a blues ambassador, teaching "Women in Blues" workshops and "Blues in the Schools" and mentoring. I'm now a member of the Blues Foundation board of directors in Memphis, Tennessee. I've participated and contributed my time and talent to the annual B.B. King at the Mississippi Valley State University, serving as lead panellist and sharing knowledge of blues history. I was honoured with the 2017 Blues Historian Award from the Jus' Blues Foundation. I have performed with legends both living and deceased such as Koko Taylor, B.B. King, Etta James, James Cotton, Bo Diddley, Louisiana Red, Robert Lockwood Jr and living legends such as Keb' Mo', Kenny Neal, Bobby Rush and Sugar Pie DeSanto. I've been nominated for several Blues Music Awards and was the 2010 Monterey Bay Blues Artist of the Year. I recently released a CD titled *Put on Your Red Dress Baby* in honour of my dad's 2017 Blues Hall of Fame induction. My journey continues. What makes it so sweet between now and the end of my blues music journey is that performing blues has no age limit, so I will be doing the blues until the day comes when I'm six feet under.

WHAT WERE YOUR CHALLENGES?

Well, when I was coming up in the blues, women weren't recognized the way that they are now. There is the #MeToo movement now, and women all over the world are standing up and demanding equal treatment, equal respect and equal pay. Let's say there is an unspoken #MeToo blues movement as well! Women are showing up at national and international blues festivals, clubs, theatres, kicking butt and taking names. They are winning awards and topping at number one in the Blues Foundation International Blues Challenges in Memphis and all over. It's awesome to see the young blues women gain the notoriety that men have had for decades. Blues girls rock!

IS THERE ONE ARTIST WHO HAS INSPIRED YOU?

There are several past and present artists who have inspired me. The late Aretha Franklin, Etta James, Koko Taylor, Ruth Brown and Linda Hopkins have all inspired my journey with tenacity and fortitude; as well as the living female legends and mentors Mavis Staples and Bonnie Raitt. My female inspiration even go back to the twentieth-century women pioneers of the blues such as Big Mama Thornton, Big Maybelle, Sister Rosetta Tharpe and others. Robert and I produced a tribute CD to Big Mama Thornton and Big Maybelle titled *Two Big Ms*. Gil Anthony, blues disc jockey and huge fan and lover of the blues, told me that the 'Two Big Ms' tribute song is one of the best original tributes he's ever heard. Blues history and its pool of talent continues to inspire me every day.

ARE AWARDS HELPFUL?

I would positively say that awards of any sorts can be abundantly inspirational, but I would venture to say most artists do this for the same reasons as me. It's in our blood! We all possess a passion, a calling, an inner drive and talent to bless others with music. If and when we are awarded for doing so, that's just icing on the cake.

WHERE DO YOU SEE YOUR MUSIC GOING NEXT?

I'm working on a new CD project hoping and preparing it to be my best ever, and my blues musical journey is taking me in a direction that is near and dear to my heart: that is, sharing, teaching and advocating for the rich blues music history, trying to preserve its legacy and making sure blues is introduced to every young artist.

Kingston Mines, Chicago

NORA JEAN WALLACE

Nora Jean Wallace was born in Greenwood, Mississippi, the seventh child of a sharecropper, and grew up with her fifteen brothers and sisters on the Equen Plantation. Having picked up blues singing from her family, Nora Jean Wallace didn't make her steps as a professional singer until 1976 in Chicago – where she had moved to live with her aunt – and she sat in with Scottie and the Oasis. She joined the band for several years, before she got her big break when she was hired in 1985 by Jimmy Dawkins to join his band, toured Europe, Canada and the US and appeared on two albums, *Feel the Blues* and *Can't Shake These Blues*. After a ten-year hiatus, she returned to the scene in 2001 when she recorded vocals for her friend Billy Flynn's *Blues and Love* album. The following year she made a notable appearance at the Chicago Blues Festival, and in 2003 she released her debut album *Nora Jean Bruso Sings the Blues* under her married name, to critical acclaim. Her follow-up, *Going Back to Mississippi* (2004) was an even bigger success. She continues to perform and tour internationally and has been nominated for seven Blues Music Awards.

WHAT AGE DID YOU START SINGING THE BLUES?

I started singing the blues when I was about six years old. My oldest brother – his name is Joe Lee Wallace – used to tease me a lot about singing, because I lived in a blues family. My uncle was a blues singer and a guitar and a harmonica blower. My father was a singer and a drummer, and a sharecropper – used to drive tractors. We all used to get together, my brothers and I – I've got eleven brothers and four sisters – and do what the grown-ups did during the weekend. My grandmother used to run a juke joint, and my father and his brother and my aunties and cousins and all of us used to go down to Miss Mae's juke joint, and we used to stay there until early Sunday night. My father's band was playing there, and there just was a lot of blues. Howlin' Wolf, Muddy Waters, Big Mama Thornton, all that good stuff.

WHAT AGE DID YOU COME TO CHICAGO?

Well, I was nineteen years old when I moved to Chicago. I had my first child when I was seventeen, outta wedlock. So I was nineteen when I moved to Chicago.

AND DID YOU COME UP HERE TO SING IN CHICAGO? OR DID YOU COME HERE FOR A BETTER OPPORTUNITY FOR ANY KIND OF JOB?

I came for better opportunity. I never thought that I would have a singing career. I came up to Chicago, my baby and I. We stayed with my mother's sister, Rose. She was working at a factory called National Picture Frames. They used to make TV frames there. She was gonna try to get me on where she was working. She told me, "Just keep the house clean and cook your auntie dinner every now and then." And so, one evening, she came in and I was in the kitchen, cooking, and I was singing this song by Betty Wright, 'Tonight Is the Night'. I don't know how long she had been standing there, listening to me singing, but when I finished she just came in and said, "Damn, girl, you can sing!" And she said, "I got a friend named Scottie. He have a band called Scottie and the Oasis. I've gotta go down there this weekend. I want you to go down with me, to introduce you to Scottie."

So that Saturday we went down, and Scottie was sitting there, collecting money, you know, for people to come in. And so my auntie Rose said, "Hi, Scottie, this is my niece, Elnora. From Mississippi. Let her get up and sing with the band a while, Scottie, she got a voice!" And Scottie said, "Can you sing?" And I said, "I don't know – Auntie says I can!"

So the next set, they got me up, and I introduced myself and everything. And he said, "What can you sing?" "I can do 'Tonight Is the Night' by Betty Wright." And he said, "What key you do it in?" I didn't know nothing about no keys or nothing. "I dunno." And he said, "Well, just start the singing." So I just started singing, and they fell right in, and it was a success. And he asked me if I knew any more songs. "Yeah, I know 'Shame' by Evelyn 'Champagne' King." He said, "What key you do that in?" "I dunno!" He said, 'Just start singing.' So I started singing. So that was another good song.

After this show he asked me, "Where are you working?" I didn't know singing was work! I said, "Well my auntie's trying to get me on out there with her where she's working." And Auntie said, "Baby, he means is you singing with anybody?" I said no, so he told me, would I like to work with him and his band? And I said, "Yes!" And so he gave me his card, with the address and everything on, and told me to come over Wednesday for the rehearsal. And I went over there, and that was it, I started working with Scottie and his band. From 1978 until 1982. That's when he got killed.

KILLED?

Yeah. When he got killed, the band just went apart. And then I stayed at home with my girlfriends. "Hey, you know, Nora, they opened a club up down there on Lake St Louis? Let's go down there!" So me and her went down there.

WHAT CLUB WAS IT?

The club was Mr A's Blues club, in Chicago, on Lake St Louis. So we went down there – that's when I met Jimmy Dawkins. And he asked me, "You that girl who used to work with Scottie? What you doing now?" And I said, "Nothing." He said, "Do you have anything out on wax?" When they say wax, that meant did I have a 45 out, 'cause there were no CDs. He said, "You write a song, I'll record it for you."

I went home that same night and wrote that song. And I called my ex-drummer over. Eddie Lord came over and gave me a beat. We was up all night long doing that song. So, the next day, I called Jimmy. He said, "You got the song together?" I said, "Yeah, come over and listen to it!" He said, "Man, I ain't never seen nothing like this!" He came over and I had wrote 'Untrue Love, I'm Gonna Leave You Alone'. That was my first – and the song on the other side was 'All My Love'. And he came over, and the next week we went and recorded it. That was my first single.

SO WHICH OTHER BANDS DID YOU SING WITH BEFORE YOU WENT SOLO?

After Scottie and the Oasis, I was with Jimmy Dawkins and his band, all over the country. I went to Europe for the first time, for a whole month, with Jimmy and his band. I mean, he was my mentor. He took me places I never dreamed I would've went. He really taught me how to sing, how to control my voice. And a lot of people come to me and tell me I sing too hard. But Jimmy Dawkins told me, don't let nobody change the way I sing. And the way I sing, it get across to peoples, you know? And if I do anything else, it's a lie. My fans ain't gonna feel it, you know – I'm for real. What I do comes from heart, and I work hard, I work hard for my fans.

DID YOU GO SOLO AFTER THAT?

No, I went with Johnny Drummer. And then, after that, I got my own band in 2006. Other than that one, I was working with different musicians like Carl Weathersby, Bob Stroger. I did a couple of things with Kenny Smith, Willie Smith and Johnny B. Gates. Billy Flynn. James Willow. Willie King.

I NOTICE THAT ONE CD HAS A LOT OF HEAVY HITTERS ON IT THAT HAVE NOW PASSED ON TO BLUES HEAVEN. LIKE WILLIE KING.

When Jimmy Dawkins wasn't touring or nothing, I was working with Willie King and his band at the 1815 club. Eddie Shaw used to own it, and used to give me and my band gigs in there. I mean, my band was my husband's band then, but now I got my own band. My band was Jerry Welsh's band. Basically, Jerry was in charge. But back in 2006, I started getting my own band together.

DID YOU SELF-PRODUCE ALL YOUR CDS OR ARE THEY OUT ON A RECORD LABEL?

I did my first recording on a CD in 2002. That's the one with all the big hitters on it: *Nora Jean Bruso Sings the Blues*. And I got only two songs on there that are mine, and all the other ones are covers.

AND SO YOU STILL LOVE SINGING THE BLUES AND YOU'RE JUST GONNA KEEP ON GOING?

I'm gonna keep on singing the blues till I can't sing no more! Yeah! Yeah, I love it. I love my fans. I love to see them smile. I love the feeling that my voice gives them, through the grace of God, because He's the only one in control.

Photograph: Laura Carbone

DAWN TYLER WATSON

Born in England and raised in Ontario, Dawn Tyler Watson adopted Montreal as her home after earning her BFA in Jazz Studies and Theatre from Concordia University. An accomplished and dynamic performer, Watson's fiery stage presence has earned her national and international recognition. In 2017 along with her backing band the Ben Racine Band, Dawn took home the coveted first-place spot out of over 260 acts at the 33rd International Blues Challenge, in Memphis, Tennessee. She's also the recipient of three Canadian Maple Blues Awards and nine Quebec Lys Blues Awards. She's earned the Screaming Jay Hawkins Award for Best Live Performance, a Trophées France Blues for Female International Artist of the Year, and a Canadian Folk Music Award nomination for Best Vocalist. Playing festivals and concert halls across four continents, recording four albums, and appearing on numerous compilations, she has shared the stage with an array of premiere artists, including Oliver Jones, Jeff Healy, Koko Taylor, Susan Tedeschi and Cyndi Lauper. Between gigs Watson gives clinics and facilitates workshops in vocal expression and improvisation while honing her chops on Montreal's vibrant jazz scene. Her 2016 album *Jawbreaker!* was nominated for a Maple Blues Award for Recording and Producer of the Year. She released her fifth album, *Mad Love*, in 2019, again with the Ben Racine Band backing her.

HOW DID YOU START IN MUSIC?

I was fortunate. My parents sent my brother and me to a choir school at the age of ten, where I learned the violin and the basics of singing. Guess my folks figured I had some talent, as I knew every word to every song on the CJBK radio station and was constantly wailing some hit song on repeat around the house. I also sang in the children's choir at church, and later in the youth choir.

WHEN DID YOU START SINGING OR PLAYING AN INSTRUMENT?

My older brother hit high school three years before me and formed a rock band. He taught me how to play a few chords on the guitar, and I found that, with time and persistence, I was able to learn many of the songs in his "Top 100 hits of the 70s" book. I loved it, and my parents bought me my first acoustic for my thirteenth birthday!

WHO WERE/ARE YOUR INFLUENCES?

My earlier influences were very eclectic. Being a black kid in an almost all white neighbourhood, I was exposed mostly to the Top 40 tunes of the time. My folks played Dean Martin and Andy Williams, and watched shows like the *Lawrence Welk Show*. My brother was into Supertramp and Styx. And I was listening to Barbra Streisand, John Denver, Kenny Rogers and Anne Murray. I especially loved anything I could play on guitar. Soul music started to influence my sound a bit later. Tina Turner, Stevie Wonder, Gladys Knight and Aretha… then I got into jazz, Billie, Ella, Sarah. Now I'm still highly influenced by jazz, especially jazz/blues.

WHY CHOOSE THE BLUES?

I often say the blues chose me. I was approached by a small Montreal label to contribute to a blues compilation they were doing… instead of doing covers, I decided to write something… they loved both songs, and we even added a third, a Negro spiritual to close off the record. That very next summer I found myself on the blues stage at the Montreal International Jazz Festival in front of 8,000 screaming blues fans. I said to myself right then, "Well, I guess I'm a blues singer then."

HOW WOULD YOU DESCRIBE YOUR APPROACH?

My approach to making music is to be myself. My goal is to be 100% authentic to who I am, onstage as well as off. Some people have a stage persona – not me. I need to be real.

DO YOU WRITE OR COMPOSE YOUR OWN MATERIAL?

Yes!

HOW DO YOU START MAKING MUSIC? WHAT IS YOUR PROCESS?

Often it's a lyric or even a title that comes to me first. I often get ideas while driving, so I record them on my phone. I also have a box full of pieces of paper with little scribblings on them… half-finished songs, seedlings of songs or bits of poetry. I will sometimes take a few days off to retreat somewhere with the express purpose of writing. I wish I had it as a daily habit, as many songwriters do, but I'm not that disciplined!

WHICH DO YOU PREFER – PLAYING LIVE OR BEING IN A STUDIO? WHY?

Live, definitely! I love to feed off the energy in the room. Performing for me is a two-way street. I need to feel the people receiving what I am giving them. The studio is so much like putting every song under the microscope and trying to put it into perfect focus. It's meticulous work and exhausting. Though it's fun to have that much control over your music!

ARE AUDIENCES DIFFERENT AROUND THE WORLD?

People are people. Again, it's an energetic thing. Being an Anglophone in a French-speaking province, it helps to perform where I know my stage banter and lyrics are being understood 100%. But I've played in Brazil, Italy, Russia, Switzerland – it's always the same energy. People want to be moved, to be touched, to feel connection. Music transcends mere language.

DESCRIBE YOUR JOURNEY AS AN ARTIST/MUSICIAN/SINGER.

Fortunate. Life has been good to me. It has supported my music, I feel… I've been able to make a living doing what I love for many many years now. I work hard, but doors were opened for me. Opportunity kept knocking, and I just kept opening up to it.

HOW DO YOU PROMOTE YOUR IMAGE/YOUR BRAND?

My website (www.dawntylerwatson.com), Facebook, Instagram and Twitter…

HOW DO YOU DEAL WITH OBSTACLES SUCH AS AGEISM, SEXISM AND RACISM?

I try not to see them as obstacles. As far as sexism goes, have always surrounded myself with guys. Back when I was working in restaurants and bars, I was always comfortable working with men. That's not changed. I try to surround myself with likeminded people as well, so I don't see much of these things. As for ageism, I am lucky that the blues doesn't really discriminate when it comes to age. We all get older, if we're lucky!

IS IT IMPORTANT TO UNDERSTAND THE BUSINESS SIDE OF THE INDUSTRY?

Yes, but it's exhausting! And very daunting for me. Can't stand doing the admin part of my career. Yes, I have some help (thank God!), but I always feel that there's so much more I could/should be doing, and frankly I don't have the time.

ARE AWARDS HELPFUL?

Being nominated is, to me, the big honour. It's always nice to win, but many of the blues awards are people's choice, which often means whoever works their socials best. I feel that I am not very good at the shameless self-promotion that it seems to take to get the votes. Case in point: I was just nominated for a Blues Blast Music Award for Female Artist of the Year… I sent out many PMs and texts and posted a lot about it, blatantly asking people to vote and show their support. Hated every minute of it. But I'd love to win… it's an American award that would help with my profile south of the border. Winning the International Blues Challenge was huge for me… but it doesn't mean that I am better than anyone else. I just happened to be in luck that day that the judges liked me. When it's a panel of your peers and contemporaries I feel that honour is deeper than if it's a people's choice.

WHERE DO YOU SEE YOUR MUSIC GOING NEXT?

I just want to keep on doing what the Creator gave me life to do. I always say: I love my job. I get to make a living with the thing I love most to do in the world! Wow… how blessed am I!? I think that we are all here to share the gifts that we've been given for the betterment of the world. And though I know that may sound pretty fluffy, I believe we are all given gifts when we come to this plane of existence that are to be used to serve those around us so that the world can be a better place. What I choose to do with my life ripples out, affecting others, hopefully in a positive way. When I was running wild back in my youth, sometimes those ripples were very negative. I was hurting everyone around me because I was hurting myself. Drinking, drugging and all the darkness that comes along with that. Today, decades away from that, I try to spread ripples of love wherever I may pass.

INDEX